Household Archaeology at
the Bridge River Site (EeRl4), British Columbia

Household Archaeology at the Bridge River Site (EeRl4), British Columbia

Spatial Distributions of Features, Lithic Artifacts, and Faunal Remains on 15 Anthropogenic Floors from Housepit 54

Anna Marie Prentiss, Ethan Ryan, Ashley Hampton, Kathryn Bobolinski, Pei-Lin Yu, Matthew Schmader, *and* Alysha Edwards

The University of Utah Press
Salt Lake City

The Defiance House Man colophon is a registered trademark of The University of Utah Press. It is based on a four-foot-tall Ancient Puebloan pictograph (late PIII) near Glen Canyon, Utah.

LIBRARY OF CONGRESS CATALOGING-IN-PUBLICATION DATA
Names: Prentiss, Anna Marie, editor.
Title: Household archaeology at the Bridge River site (EeRl4), British
    Columbia : spatial distributions of features, lithic artifacts, and
    faunal remains on fifteen anthropogenic floors from housepit 54 /
    editor, Anna Marie Prentiss [and 6 others]
Description: Salt Lake City : University of Utah Press, [2022] | Includes
    bibliographical references and index.
Identifiers: LCCN 2021042884 (print) | LCCN 2021042885 (ebook) |
    ISBN 9781647690519 (cloth) | ISBN 9781647690526 (ebook)
Subjects: LCSH: Indians of North America—Dwellings—British
    Columbia—Bridge River. | Pit houses—British Columbia—Bridge River. |
    Excavations (Archaeology)—British Columbia—Bridge River. | Dwellings,
    Prehistoric—British Columbia—Bridge River. | Indians of North
    America—British Columbia—Bridge River—Social life and customs. |
    Indians of North America—British Columbia—Bridge River—Antiquities. |
    Bridge River (B.C.)—Antiquities.
Classification: LCC E78.B9 H67 2022 (print) | LCC E78.B9 (ebook) |
    DDC 971.1/31—dc23
LC record available at https://lccn.loc.gov/2021042884
LC ebook record available at https://lccn.loc.gov/2021042885

Errata and further information on this and other titles available online at UofUpress.com

Printed and bound in the United States of America.

Publisher's Note

Raw data used to create the maps and supplemental maps referenced in the book can be accessed at this book's homepage on the publisher's website, UofUpress.com.

Contents

Figures

Tables

Acknowledgments

The Bridge River Archaeological Project (BRAP) began in 2003 and continues today as a collaborative partnership between the University of Montana and Xwísten, the Bridge River Indian Band. Research in 2003 and 2004 focused on village-wide mapping, testing, and dating. Ultimately, we tested 67 housepits and radiocarbon-dated 55 house-specific occupation sequences. Field seasons in 2007–2009 focused on lithic raw material sources in the Bridge River Valley and inter-house relationships during Bridge River 2 (BR2) and Bridge River 3 (BR3) time periods. To accomplish this analysis, we sampled six housepits dated to BR2 and BR3 in the north and south areas of the site.

Insights drawn from this research concerned refinements to individual household histories and recognition of change over time in socio-economic and political relationships between house groups. Housepit 54 was first recognized in 2004 and sampled further in 2008. Excavations focused entirely on Housepit 54 during the 2012–2014 and 2016 field seasons. The decision to do a major excavation at this housepit was a mutual determination of all collaborators. Housepit 54 appeared to represent a remarkable opportunity to gain unprecedented insights into the long-term history of a single house. Further, it offered potentially unique insights into the last period of traditional pithouse use before the onslaught of the gold rush in AD 1858.

This book is one of a series of publications focused on the record from Housepit 54. In this case, we examine change and continuity in occupation patterns and social relationships drawing on spatial analysis of features, lithic artifacts, and faunal remains from the 15 deep floors. We develop inferences drawing on contemporary St'át'imc knowledge of traditional life in the pithouse villages, along with a wide array of local and regional ethnographic sources.

Susan James, Bradley Jack, Florence Jack, and Gerald Michel played significant roles in facilitating the Housepit 54 project. Many members of the Xwísten community participated in the 2012–2016 field seasons at Housepit 54. We thank all of the elders who visited and offered their thoughts on the project. Carl Alexander was particularly significant in that regard. For their long hours of hard work on the excavation, we thank in particular: Brenda Frank, Josh Jack, Kat Street, Everett Tom, and Ina Williams.

Many students and volunteers from the University of Montana, Hamilton College, University of Notre Dame, University of Michigan, Portland State University, Boise State University, University of Washington, and Simon Fraser University participated in the 2012–2016 field seasons. We thank all for their hard work. A number of students played essential roles in the lab operation. The University of Montana team included Kristen Barnett, Kathryn Bobolinski, Ashley Hampton, Haley O'Brien, Nathaniel Perhay, Ethan Ryan, Dougless Skinner, Emma Vance, Matthew Walsh, and a long list of additional lab volunteers.

The 2012–2016 field/lab project also included a set of funded and unfunded collaborators. These included Tom Foor (quantitative methods), Nathan Goodale (geochemistry), Natasha Lyons (paleoethnobotany), Vandy Bowyer (paleoecology), Dana Lepofsky (paleoethnobotany), Dongya Yang (ancient DNA), Meradeth Snow (ancient DNA), Camilla Speller (ancient DNA), Mike Richards (isotopes), Pei-Lin Yu (household archaeology, Plateau archaeology), and Matthew Schmader (household archaeology). We thank the Philip L. Wright

Zoological Museum at the University of Montana for access to comparative collections. Prentiss thanks the University of Montana for a sabbatical during the 2017–2018 academic year and the McDonald Institute for Archaeological Research at the University of Cambridge for a Visiting Scholar position that provided time and space for writing. We thank the staff at The University of Utah Press and especially Reba Rauch for encouraging us to develop this work and for their efforts in moving it through the publication process. We thank peer reviewers Amber Johnson and Chris Rodning for their excellent comments. Finally, we thank our families for their support. It has been an all-hands-on-deck project for the last eight years to complete the fieldwork, lab analyses, map development, writing, and editing that led to this book.

The 2012–2016 field seasons at Housepit 54 were generously supported by two grants from the National Endowment for the Humanities (Grants RZ-51287-11 and RZ-230366-1). Any views, findings, conclusions, or recommendations expressed in this book do not necessarily represent those of the National Endowment for the Humanities. The 2008 and 2009 field seasons at Bridge River that included initial excavations of Housepit 54 were funded by a grant from the National Science Foundation (Grant BCS-0713013).

Housepit Floor Formation Processes, Activity Areas, and Sociality

The Record from Housepit 54

Since 2003, the Bridge River Archaeological Project (BRAP) has sought to address research questions in the realms of demography, subsistence, technology, and sociality in the Middle Fraser (Mid-Fraser) of British Columbia (Figure 1.1). More specifically, the project has focused on expanding our understanding of relationships between subsistence economy (Prentiss et al. 2011, 2014), technological innovation and change (Prentiss et al. 2015), demographic trends (Prentiss et al. 2008, 2014; Prentiss et al. 2018c), intra- and inter-household social relations (Prentiss et al. 2008, 2012, 2014; Prentiss et al. 2018c; Prentiss et al. 2018a), and inter-village political developments. Socioeconomic and political change has typically been interpreted within an evolutionary-ecological framework recognizing that climate and associated resource variability impacts household economies and consequently social relationships (Prentiss 2017a; Prentiss et al. 2011, 2014; Prentiss and Kuijt 2012; Walsh 2017). A significant outcome of this work has been the development of an increasingly nuanced understanding of the long-term history of the St'át'imc people, the original residents of the Middle Fraser Canyon (Prentiss ed. 2017; Prentiss and Kuijt 2012; Walsh 2017).

In 2012, the BRAP initiated a multiyear major excavation of Housepit 54, a midsized housepit in the northern portion of the Bridge River village. The goal of the project was to develop a comprehensive understanding of household history with a particular focus on the long sequence of floors predating 1,000 years ago. An extensive Fur Trade period occupation was discovered during the earlier testing phase (Prentiss et al. 2008), which caps the older floors and provides an excellent frame of reference for interpreting the record of more ancient occupations (Prentiss 2017a). A single house study permits us to address in some depth the role of individual households in wider processes of change and stability within the Bridge River village and wider region. This book seeks to address fundamental questions about occupational variability on the Housepit 54 floors as a means of testing more general hypotheses about village- and regional phenomena. A byproduct of this process is gaining an in-depth understanding of variability in the nature of pithouse occupations in the Middle Fraser Canyon (henceforth Mid-Fraser). Housepit 54 offers a particularly significant advantage in this regard over other previously more well-known housepits in the Mid-Fraser. This is because the previously fully excavated houses in the region (Keatley Creek [Hayden 1997] and Bell [Stryd 1973]) generally included only one or two intact floors per house. As detailed below, Housepit 54 features 15 intact stratified anthropogenic floors predating 1,000 years ago.

A central issue in Mid-Fraser archaeology concerns the long-term stability of the large aggregate villages and how that affects our understanding of social and political relationships

Middle Fraser Canyon
British Columbia

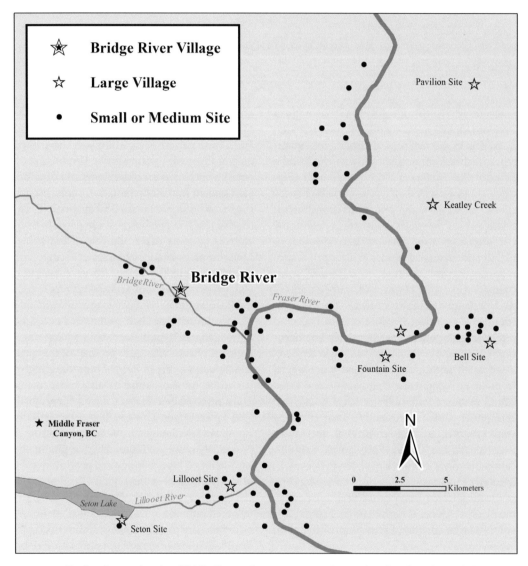

FIGURE 1.1. Regional map showing Middle Fraser Canyon area and associated archaeological sites.

between community members. Ethnography of the St'át'imc people (Kennedy and Bouchard 1998; Teit 1906) points to the late pre-Colonial to Fur Trade period presence of stable permanent villages organized around powerful clans whose influence could spread across multiple villages. Chiefly status could be inherited or earned and yet the designation of chief carried no coercive power (Teit 1906). Families and clan groups (Romanoff 1992a; Teit 1906) could control access to critical fishing, gathering, and hunting grounds. A consequence of this structure is that while the society was egalitarian from the standpoint of political power, individuals and groups displayed significant variation in wealth and community influence on scales that included families, lineage groups, and clans. Social relationships were negotiated inside and between long-lived houses within a complex array of large aggregate and satellite villages potentially resembling the "local groups" identified on the southern coast of British Columbia (McMillan and St. Claire 2012). This pattern of residential stability and complex sociality was underwritten by a subsistence strategy predicated around mass harvest and storage of salmon, geophytes (edible roots [Lyons and Ritchie 2017]), berries, ungulates, and a wide variety of other items of somewhat lesser importance (Alexander 1992, 2000; Lyons et al. 2017; Walsh 2017; Williams-Larson 2017).

The Mid-Fraser pattern contrasts with that of most traditional Plateau societies east and southeast of the Fraser River. Teit (1900, 1909, 1930) and later ethnographers (Ackerman 1994; Furniss 2004; Goldman 1941; Grossman 1965; Ray 1939; Wickwire 1991) recognize that typical Plateau societies were organized around autonomous villages with comparatively unstable occupation patterns due to flexible group membership, a lack of clans or phratries, variable inheritance systems, and the presence of often temporary elected chiefs with no coercive power. Furniss (2004) has argued that the annual movements of traditional Plateau groups were organized around a pattern of dispersal and aggregation as individual families sought to collect and disperse a variety of food and non-food goods. She further notes that interpersonal relations were underlain by a constant tension between the multifamily "bands" seeking to insure adequate resources for all and extended families with more self-interested goals. This relationship was ultimately responsible for the Plateau-wide ethic of egalitarianism.

The stark contrasts between the Mid-Fraser and the various other Plateau societies have led to a variety of speculations as to why that might be the case. Furniss (2004) simply reinterprets traditional St'át'imc sociopolitical relations in terms of her family-band model. However, influenced by Teit (1906, 1909), a number of scholars (Ackerman 1994; Grossman 1965; Ray 1939) suggest that the Mid-Fraser groups were different from those elsewhere on the Plateau likely due to late pre-Colonial and Colonial period borrowing of cultural concepts (lineages, clans, ranking, resource ownership) from nearby coastal groups. Harris (2012) suggests that this occurred as late as the Fur Trade period in British Columbia (ca. AD 1812–1858). Teit (1909) is quite specific in his argument that only the Canyon Division Secwepemc developed cultural trappings borrowed from coastal groups (he speculates that it came via the Carrier and Tsihlqot'in to the north and northwest) after ca. AD 1850. Teit does not offer such a specific argument for the historical origins of St'át'imc cultural traditions though he does vaguely speculate that the pattern may be Coast Salish in origin and that the Coast Salish owe their traditions to groups on the northern coast of British Columbia (Teit 1906:254). However, despite his significant influence on Plateau ethnographers and some archaeologists, Teit could not have been aware of the archaeological record of the Mid-Fraser and the potential to demonstrate a much more ancient and local origin for many aspects of the St'át'imc ethnographic pattern.

Resolution of this debate is important for understanding the development of the distinct St'át'imc patterns of cooperation and collective action within frameworks of differential wealth and influence held by individuals, families, and wider social groups (e.g., clans). If the standard Plateau model actually does describe the structure of past St'át'imc society, it means that archaeologically recognized patterns of inter- and intra-household wealth distinctions (Hayden and Spafford 1993; Hayden 1994, 1997, 1998; Prentiss et al. 2007, 2012; Prentiss et al. 2018c) and differences in inter-village and inter-regional interaction (Hayden et al. 1996; Prentiss et al. 2018b) do not reflect institutionalized wealth-based inequality and associated sociopolitical constructs (cf. Wiessner 2002) but rather instances where the extended family/band dialectic manifested as short-lived instances of competition and conflict that presumably would have been quickly resolved leading to a return to egalitarian conditions. In contrast, the Mid-Fraser ethnographic model implicates that possibility that under conditions of long-lived stable village life, institutionalized wealth-based inequality and supporting political structures could have developed in situ at some time in the more remote past and remained relatively intact in the memories of descendants interviewed by James Teit. Thus, within this scenario, traditional St'át'imc sociopolitical relations had developed as institutionalized cultural constructs held and maintained for a long time span.

Resolution of this debate is also important from the standpoint of expanding anthropological understanding of sociocultural complexity, particularly material wealth-based inequality. A growing number of studies have implicated several variables as important to the establishment of what Mattison and colleagues (2016) call persistent institutionalized inequality. Economic defensibility, or an emphasis on food resources derived from patches that can be readily controlled and defended, appears to be an underlying condition associated with inequality (Borgerhoff Mulder et al. 2009; Dyson-Hudson and Smith 1978). The salmon fishery in the Six Mile Rapids of the Middle Fraser Canyon certainly qualifies as a defensible high-density resource. The fact that the overwhelming majority of caught fish are preserved in highly defended and/or hidden storage receptacles (Alexander 2000) also supports this view (e.g., Bettinger

2015). For wealth differences to become institutionalized it is critical that they be transmitted between generations. Borgerhoff Mulder and colleagues (2009; see also Mattison et al. 2016) define three forms of transmissible wealth: material or capital assets; social/relational assets as reflected in, for example, networks of exchange partners; and somatic elements as might include knowledge and health-based factors. Mid-Fraser ethnography indicates that inheritance was important to maintenance of family wherewithal and social position. It is well known that rights to fishing rocks were passed down within families (Kew 1992; Romanoff 1992a), but we might also presume trade connections and other partnerships, along with elite knowledge, could be transmitted between generations (Hayden et al. 1996a; Hayden and Schulting 1997). Mattison and colleagues' (2016) final condition of inequality is population and resource pressure. Demography very likely plays a critical role in emergent inequality given the crucial relationship between population and access to defensible subsistence resources. As noted by Mattison and colleagues (2006), simple population pressure arguments (Keeley 1988) can be updated with more nuanced models as in the Mid-Fraser case where under a Malthusian demographic crisis households appear to have increased their control of subsistence access points and used that as leverage to attract recruits to their households who entered as subordinates (Prentiss et al. 2007, 2012, 2014, 2018a, 2018b, 2018c).

Given that the ethnographic record and the ecological context of the Mid-Fraser seem to meet all of the conditions that should be present for establishment of persistent institutionalized inequality, it would seem reasonable to predict that such a pattern (at least in its material wealth-based manifestation) would have developed here and persisted for some time. However, if Furniss's (2004) model best describes social and economic dynamics of traditional St'át'imc society, then perhaps until sometime during the Fur Trade period no settlement was ever stable enough for permanent resource defense, transmission, and related demographic factors to develop and play a role in the establishment of persistent inequality. In this case, the abundance of large housepits with their deep archaeological deposits in the Mid-Fraser is simply a byproduct of many visits by different groups leading to accumulation of materials.

Until now, no record of housepit occupation had been available to adequately test for relationships between occupational variation and social change. The lengthy floor sequence at Housepit 54 makes it possible to formally test alternative models of occupational stability and variability while examining indicators of intra-floor activity dynamics and where possible, social relations. More specifically, we examine stability from standpoints of floor-by-floor occupation and abandonment cycles, structure and organization of activity areas, and variation in positioning of wealth-related items. We accomplish this task by effectively repeating the same set of analyses (as appropriate) on a floor-by-floor basis. Thus, beyond the introductory and concluding chapters, the book consists of 15 chapters, each dedicated to a unique floor from Housepit 54. This structure also provides us with the opportunity to review basic stratigraphic and spatial data concerning the remarkable record from Housepit 54, as it will no doubt be of relevance and utility to a wide range of other future investigations.

In this chapter, we provide background on the Mid-Fraser with reference to life in traditional pithouses. We follow with a review of the Housepit 54 project emphasizing the establishment of the Housepit 54 chronology. Finally, we provide a detailed consideration of research goals that includes floor-specific hypotheses, test expectations, and research methods.

Background

The Housepit 54 project was designed to provide insight into the persistence of cultural traditions within a long-lived house. This task was accomplished by excavating the many anthropogenic floors and associated deposits with a focus on collecting data that would provide insight into the spatial organization of activities on each floor. In this section, we review ethnographically based expectations for variation in

the occupation and organization of space in Canadian Plateau pithouses. We follow with a review of the excavation procedures, stratigraphy, dating, and inferred house shapes given that Housepit 54 grew substantially over time likely from a small single family dwelling to a relatively large structure occupied by four or more families.

Winter Houses in the Middle Fraser Canyon

The following discussion is an abbreviated review of variation in St'át'imc annual cycles with a particular focus on life in winter pithouses. Information presented here derives from published ethnographic sources (e.g., Teit 1906). We also rely upon traditional knowledge conveyed by contemporary St'át'imc people (Table 1.1). More detailed reviews can be found in Alexander (1992, 2000) and Prentiss (2017a).

Traditional St'át'imc households followed an annual subsistence and mobility cycle centered on accumulation of food items and other goods in and around pithouses for winter use (Alexander 1992; Lyons et al. 2017; Prentiss and Kuijt 2012; Walsh 2017; Williams-Larsen 2017). In brief, springtime foraging was initiated in the vicinity of housepit villages but gradually expanded into both canyon bottoms and mountain valleys as groups pursued geophytes, larger game, and spring (Chinook) salmon. Mid to late summer activities focused on berry harvest and sockeye salmon fishing. By early fall late season (Coho) salmon fishing gave way to higher elevation hunting, fishing, and gathering with a particular focus on deer harvest. By late fall stored foods had been cached within houses and in exterior cache pits and platforms within and external to the village. Winter survival was dependent upon these stored items and whatever additional food could be procured during winter.

Alexander (2000) considered pithouse construction in depth, drawing ethnographic data from multiple sources (e.g., Hill-Tout 1905; Kennedy and Bouchard 1978; LaForet and York 1981; Teit 1900, 1906, 1909). Briefly, a depression was excavated to depths of one to two meters with sediment generally dumped around the

TABLE 1.1. Some Major Categories of Contemporary Traditional St'át'imc Knowledge regarding Landscapes, Pithouse Villages, and Tools.

Context	Specific Knowledge
Landscape	village locations; settlement patterns (including lookout sites); inter-village relationships that include territoriality, exchange, ritual (including marriage), and warfare; forest management; fishing, hunting, and gathering: places, procedures, and traditions; fisheries management; seasonal cycles; weather; place names
Pithouses and Villages	architectural traditions (entrances, floors, roofs); winter food storage; food sharing; winter activities (daily routine and ritual/ceremonial); occupational cycles (re-roofing and re-flooring); ash-related rituals (smudging to ritual burning of house roofs); coming of age traditions for men and women (including structures dedicated to such life events); social relationships within and between pithouses
Tools	traditional technologies for fishing (nets), hunting (bows and arrows, spears, traps), and gathering (baskets, digging sticks, and related technology); manufacture and use of select chipped stone tools (e.g., arrow points, knives, and scrapers); uses of stone abraders and fire-altered rock; hide working; gaming pieces; jewelry and exchange items

perimeter. Width varied with the size of the desired house. Ethnographies focused on circular depressions. However, from archaeological research, we know that houses could also be somewhat square to rectangular in form (Prentiss et al. 2005). Roofs were supported by thick posts cut from Douglas fir or yellow pine. The number of posts varied with house size and configuration. For larger round houses, four to five large posts near the floor center were established to support a series of beams that provided the foundation for additional crossing beams, woven mats or other vegetation, and earth insulation. Additional posts could also be established to aid in roof support around the margins of the floor. Smaller houses could have widely varying post configurations including small houses with superstructures resembling mat lodges and rectangular houses with linear distributions of central roof posts. The latter was far more common in coastal contexts but not unknown in interior Plateau contexts (e.g., Galm and Masten 1985).

Ethnographies suggested that house posts were secured with holes dug into house floors. However, Alexander (2000) noted that house posts could also be placed resting on the floor,

presumably held in place by the roof framework. This construction was likely the case on the Fur Trade period floor (Stratum II) in Housepit 54 (Prentiss 2017b). Alexander (2000) suggested that pithouses were occupied for about 20 years before roofs needed replacing due primarily to wood rot, but possibly also insect infestations or idiosyncratic events such as deaths (Kennedy and Bouchard 1978; Teit 1906). Roofs were replaced after dismantling or burning. Alexander (2000) pointed out that burning was not always a preferred option given that it could destroy still-useable parts of the house. Old roof materials were deposited around the periphery of the housepit forming a "doughnut" shaped ring or rim. In many archaeological contexts, it is evident that floors were removed with the old roof before reflooring and reroofing (Hayden 1997). However, in other contexts, old floors were capped with new floor material (clay loam at Bridge River, as observed in many Bridge River housepits including Housepit 54 (Prentiss et al. 2008).

Winter pithouses were typically occupied from late fall (late November to early December) to late winter or early spring (late February to March). Given the lengthy time, need to perform social obligations and prepare for springtime subsistence activities, winter household activities were highly diverse. We introduce several classes of activities that would be archaeologically visible to varying degrees including sleeping, storage, cooking, goods manufacture and maintenance, and social events. Given that housepits could be busy places and that number of occupants could be 20 or more (Hayden et al. 1996b), the organization of space was a significant concern. Thus, considerable planning was needed to design optimal sleeping spaces. Alexander (2000) summarized a number of possibilities including wooden benches around portions of the floor perimeter; bedding placed directly on house floors, and sleeping hammocks and cradles for young children (e.g., Nastich 1954; Teit 1900, 1909). If the roof cover extended over a portion of the rim above the actual floor, as is often visible on modern pithouse reconstructions in the Mid-Fraser and Thompson River areas, then these spaces might also have served as sleeping spaces.

St'át'imc households were highly dependent upon storage for winter survival and successful engagement in social obligations that could include sharing of food and other items (Alexander 2000; Kennedy and Bouchard 1978; Teit 1906). Different strategies for food storage were used depending upon expected time needed in storage and the nature of the item stored (Alexander 2000). Underground cache pits were excavated in resource procurement contexts, external to houses in villages, and within pithouses. They varied in size from about 1 to 2 m in width and depth. Generally, outdoor caches were used for long-term storage while internal pits were important for short-term storage needs. In order to reduce adverse effects of moisture, food cache pits were lined with sticks, grass, and/or birch bark. Food items (e.g., dried salmon or deer, dried berries, and dried roots) were wrapped or lined with birch bark and grasses. Grasses and needles were also employed to reduce exposure to mice (Alexander 2000). Archaeological research suggests that cache pits were often converted to refuse receptacles once their storage function ended. We could imagine that this shift

in usage would be most likely to have occurred immediately in advance of abandonment of a given floor.

Additional facilities for short-term food storage included racks, shelves, and roof rafters. A variety of baskets and bags containing food and nonfood items could be stored in these places (Alexander 2000; Teit 1906). Ethnographies also suggest that exterior platforms were sometimes constructed to hold dried fish, meat, and gear. Tools owned by individual families could be stored in a number of ways including under sleeping benches, on raised platforms within or external to houses, hanging in house rafters, or buried in cache pits (Alexander 2000; LaForet and York 1981).

Hearths of a variety of forms were used for cooking and heating in winter pithouses. During more recent times (late pre-Colonial, Fur Trade, and perhaps early Gold Rush) hearths were typically placed in the center of houses (Alexander 2000; Kennedy and Bouchard 1978; LaForet and York 1981; Teit 1900). We have direct evidence for this practice from the Fur Trade period floor in Housepit 54 and similar evidence from the late pre-Colonial period *S7istken* site[1] several kilometers up the Bridge River valley (Prentiss 2017b; Smith 2017). Alexander (2000) recognized that for larger houses with multiple families that individual families likely created their own cooking hearths. This practice seems to be a consistent pattern in older housepits in the Mid-Fraser region (Hayden 1997; Prentiss and Kuijt 2012). Hearths varied in form including nearly vertical sided roasting pits; shallow bowl forms for roasting food but perhaps most typically for heating boiling stones as cooking in winter houses commonly involved boiling (Alexander 2000); and ephemeral fire-reddened areas resulting from short heating events. The latter features could result from the use of short-lived fires for staying warm, brief cooking episodes, or even the effects of furniture burning during abandonment fires (Alexander 2000). Much larger roasting ovens were used external to houses for cooking plant materials, especially geophytes (Lepofsky and Peacock 2004), and meat and berries (Dietz 2005). As many as

75 of such features are visible on the surface of the Bridge River site, though some percentage of these could also be external cache pits.

During the long winter household members engaged in a wide range of activities. We focus here on a subset that theoretically could be identified archaeologically: food preparation, lithic tool production and maintenance, hide-working and sewing, heavy-duty tool applications (e.g., woodworking), kill/butchery operations, and ornaments manufacture. Ethnographies suggest that house floors were divided into distinct spaces often called "rooms" and designating particular functions, for example kitchens and store rooms (Teit 1900, 1909). This pattern was evident on the Fur Trade floor at Housepit 54 where cooking and storage debris concentrates in the southwest quarter, toolmaking debris is most abundant in the southeast, and empty spaces present around the central hearth, and northeast and northwest sectors. The latter have been interpreted as family/sleeping spaces (Barnett and Frank 2017; Prentiss 2017b; Williams-Larson et al. 2017). A similar pattern was identified by Smith (2017) on one late-dating floor at the S7istken site. However, an alternative approach to activity areas would be redundant domestic spaces associated with family-specific hearths. This pattern was recognized by Hayden at Keatley Creek (Hayden 1997; Hayden and Spafford 1993) and Smith (2014, 2017) on another floor at *S7istken*. In the latter scenario, the full range of domestic work would have been accomplished in much more constrained spaces reflecting family-specific household economies.

Alexander (2000) argued that early stages of large lithic tool production likely took place outside of pithouses while late stage resharpening and maintenance was most commonly practiced within houses. However, Prentiss (2000) documented evidence for widespread core-reduction within Housepit 7 at Keatley Creek, and French (2017) recognized extensive bipolar reduction during the fur trade occupation at Bridge River's Housepit 54. French also argued, supporting with data, that cores were

rarely transported and reduced in the Bridge River village as it was likely more cost beneficial to transport useable flakes and formed lithic tools (see Kuhn 1994 for economic logic behind this argument). Better ethnographic backing supports the argument that messy and spatially demanding activities (game and fish butchery, initial hide-defleshing and scraping, major woodworking, etc.) took place external to houses or within abandoned houses (Kennedy and Bouchard 1978; Teit 1909). While likely true to a substantial degree, house floor data often included evidence for animal butchery, hide-scraping, and woodworking (e.g., Prentiss 2017a, b; Spafford 2000).

A wide range of other activities undoubtedly took place within pithouses. These tasks included cooking as indicated by hearths, fire-racked rock (from using boiling stones), food-remains, and lithic tools used to help prepare foods (e.g., knives used to cut meat); later stage hide-working and clothing manufacture as might be reflected by a variety of tools including hide scrapers, piercers, awls, and needles; certain forms of wood/antler/bone working as associated with manufacture of weapons, handles, and architectural items and furniture; and finally manufacture of ornaments and ornamental items including stone, bone, and shell beads, pendants, and anthropomorphic or zoomorphic figurines. Spatial positioning of these activities could be affected by conceptions of gendered space such that one obvious implication is that women's activities involved with cooking, hide-working, wool-making, and weaving may have been prevalent in many indoor spaces (Teit 1900). However, typical men's activities, inclusive of weapons manufacture and some forms of wood/bone/antler working, may also have occurred indoors though perhaps spatially constrained to specific activity zones such as bench areas or external to the house on rooftops (Alexander 2000; Barnett and Frank 2017; Teit 1900; Williams-Larson et al. 2017). Activity spaces could also be constrained by practical contingencies (e.g., Binford 1978a, 1983; Schmader and Graham 2015) as for example, retaining open space at and around the base of the entry ladder for moving around the house floor, placement of hearths away from flammable materials, and taking some advantage of well-lit spaces for certain activities.

A diverse array of social activities was conducted in winter pithouses including routine socializing, smoking, game playing, child-rearing, and shared work (Alexander 2000; Barnett and Frank 2017). However, winter was also the season for large scale social events that, given adverse weather, were typically held within pithouses. Ethnographers have described monthly dances especially at the winter solstice (Teit 1906), marriage feasts (Nastich 1954), winter spirit or power dances (Teit 1906), and feasting events (Kennedy and Bouchard 1978; Teit 1900). Alexander (2000) noted that while potlatches could have been held (e.g., Teit 1900), some researchers have argued that these events only occurred in the Colonial period (Teit 1900, 1909). Identifying archaeological evidence for social activities can be challenging (but see Barnett and Frank 2017), though Northwest Coast archaeologists have had some success identifying likely spaces within houses as associated with social events involving large-scale cooking and food consumption (Coupland 2006; Samuels 2006). The latter studies serve as a useful frame of reference for recognizing similar signatures on Housepit 54 floors.

Activity space was also strongly constrained by maintenance of social relationships between those residing in the pithouse. Coupland and colleagues (2009) introduced concepts of communalism and collectivism in reference to traditional Northwest Coast houses. Communalism refers to the means by which a group of people beyond that of a nuclear family maintain cohesiveness and solidarity to engage in critical activities of production and consumption. This concept is best materialized in traditional North Coast houses, as floors were organized in residential (sleeping, storage, work areas) spaces for membership surrounding a single central hearth feature where food was prepared and shared by all members of the house. Commu-

nalist strategies in permanent houses are much like those of more residentially mobile egalitarian hunter-gatherers in that they promote feelings of group inclusiveness and thus encourage work toward the benefit of all (Coupland et al. 2009; see also Williams-Larson et al. 2017).

In contrast, collectivist strategies reflect a lowered interest in the well-being of the entire house membership and instead favor individual interests, resulting in what Blanton (1995:109) has called a "congruence of individual family interests." Collectivist households are well illustrated by Central and South Coast houses where family compartments are recognizable in the form of hearths and associated hearth-based activity areas evenly spaced down the center (Chinookan houses [Smith 2006]) or around the perimeter (Salish houses [Grier 2006]; Wakashan houses [Samuels 2006]) of the floor. Each of these spaces generally represents a family whose members may have routinely weighed up socioeconomic options to remain in this house or to move elsewhere. The wider house group nonetheless benefited from the collective actions of all despite the more self-centered motivations of the membership (Coupland et al. 2009).

Coupland and colleagues (2009) recognized that on the Northwest Coast, the strongest evidence for truly communal household organization occurs in contexts of the most rigid social hierarchies as associated with Haida, Tsimshian, and Tlingit groups where typically a rigid hereditarily structured distinction existed between title-holding and title-less members. They explained the dialectic between unequal social status and communal living as a strategy for reducing household tensions and thus enhancing performance and competitiveness. The reduced communalism reflected in more collectivist approaches is associated with groups with less rigid social rankings where options for social advancement can come with achievements and altered social alignments. In a social environment where options for socioeconomic and political advancement are more varied, it makes sense to have living spaces more independent and options for residents less constrained (Coupland et al. 2009; Williams-Larson et al. 2017).

Teit (1900, 1906) described two strategies for organizing interior house space on the western Canadian Plateau and adjacent Coast Range. One appears to be more communalist in Coupland and colleagues' (2009) terms, with a single central hearth and the remainder of the floor organized in activity zones inclusive of kitchens, storage, toolmaking, and sleeping. While Teit (1900) associated this pattern of organization with Thompson (Nlaka'pamux) groups, it was typically also a feature of St'át'imc house floors in both larger and smaller housepits. The latter pattern was recognized at Housepit 54 from the Fur Trade period floor (Williams-Larson et al. 2017), at the nearby S7istken site (Smith 2014, 2017), at late-dating small housepits at the Keatley Creek site (Hayden and Adams 2004), and in houses of multiple sizes at the Bell site (Stryd 1973). Teit (1906) also described a pattern of household organization more in line with a collectivist strategy as associated with the Lower Lillooet or Lil'wat people and very similar to Coupland and colleagues' (2009) depiction of other Coast Salish houses. This pattern of organization has also been frequently recognized in Mid-Fraser housepits. Housepits 3 and 7 at Keatley Creek have a series of ephemeral hearths often associated with cache pits and spaced relatively evenly around their perimeters (Hayden 1997). Geophysical investigations and test excavations revealed a similar pattern in many Bridge River site housepits (Prentiss et al. 2008, 2012). One floor at the S7istken site also featured this pattern (Smith 2014, 2017).

Social distinctions between communalistic and collectivist floor organization are not well understood. Hayden (1997; see also Hayden and Spafford 1993) recognized material wealth-based inequality on the Housepit 7 floor at Keatley Creek but not in nearby Housepit 3. Likewise, Smith (2014) did not recognize material wealth distinctions between hearth groups at S7istken. Possibly such distinctions may be present within some houses at Bridge River. The floors of Housepit 54 provide us with the opportunity to initiate research into this problem.

The Housepit 54 Project

The Housepit 54 excavation began in 2012 as the latest component of our ongoing collaborative partnership between the University of Montana and Xwísten, the Bridge River Indian Band (Figure 1.2). The broad goal of the project was to develop a detailed understanding of the history of a long-lived single house spanning the critical Bridge River 2 and 3 periods (Figure 1.3). In doing so, we assumed that close study of Housepit 54 would illuminate not only important aspects of traditional life in an ancient household context but also allow us to examine the contribution of an individual house to the major changes documented for the village in general during the periods of ca. 1,500–1,000 and 150 years ago. Excavations in 2012 focused exclusively on the Fur Trade period occupation, and those results are described in detail elsewhere (Prentiss 2017a). The 2013–2014 and 2016 field seasons focused on the floors pre-dating ca. 1,000 years ago.

The excavation relied upon the establishment of a grid system consisting of seven 4×4 m Blocks, four of which (A–D) became the primary focus of the Housepit 54 excavation (Figure 1.4). Each Block was subdivided into 16 1×1 m units, and each of these further subdivided into 50×50 cm quads. A system of 50 cm wide balks was used to maintain profiles spanning the house floor on a north–south and east–west basis. The balks also provided access to excavation blocks for the field teams. Excavators exposed, mapped, and collected samples from each cultural stratum using the following primary classifications: I=surface, II=floor, III=rim, IV=noncultural substrate, V=roof. Additional stratum designations were devised as needed. Given that there were multiple roof and floor strata, a letter system was added to the Roman numerals designating strata such that a multiple floor sequence would consist of II, IIa, IIb, IIc, and so on, as moving progressively deeper to IIo. A similarly structured roof sequence became somewhat complicated by use of sub-designations, given inconsistent presence of different roof strata between Blocks (V, Va1, Va, Vb1, Vb, Vb3, and Vc). Inclusive of a variety of generalized pits, postholes, cache pits, and

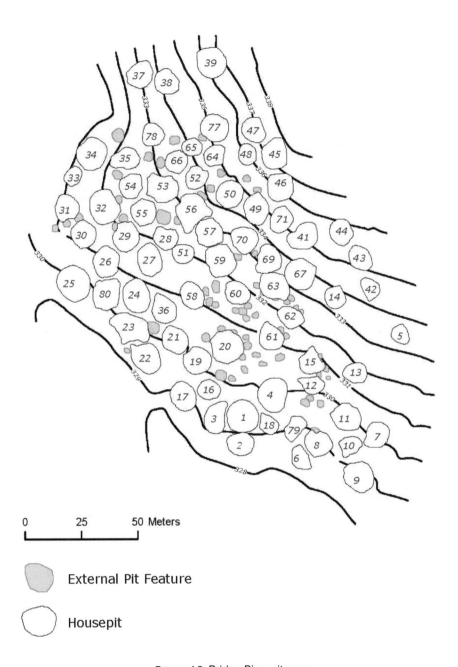

FIGURE 1.2. Bridge River site map.

hearths, features were tracked on a yearly basis by Block. Thus, a typical designation would read: Feature A1 (2013), reflecting Block (A), feature number in that block (1), and field season (2013). The year designation was not used for the 2016 season.

Excavation was conducted using trowels and often smaller implements (bamboo skewers, spoons, etc.). Where possible all artifacts and ecofacts from floors were point-provenienced and collected *in situ*. All fire-cracked rock (FCR) greater than 3 cm maximum diameter on floors was point-provenienced. If the latter items exceeded 5 cm in maximum diameter,

Bridge River Village Site (EeRl4)

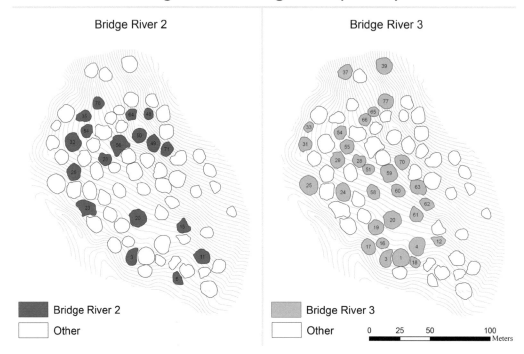

FIGURE 1.3. Bridge River site showing change in occupied housepits during the BR2 and BR3 periods.

they were also collected. Several kinds of sediment samples were collected from floors and features. For each excavation unit approximately two-liter samples for flotation were collected from the southwest and northeast quads and one .25-liter sample was collected from each southeast quad for geochemical study. Features were intensively sampled such that shallow hearths and postholes were typically collected in their entirety, while deeper features (various deeper hearths, deep postholes, and cache pits) were systematically sampled for collection of two-liter bags where possible. All other sediment was sieved through ⅛-inch mesh hardware cloth. Complete profiles were drawn of the west wall of Blocks A and C (Figure 1.5), north wall Blocks A and C (Figure 1.6), and east wall Blocks D and B (Figure 1.7).

A total of 17 anthropogenic floors and seven roof deposits were identified during the course of the Housepit 54 excavations. Of those deposits, 16 of the floor deposits dated to approximately 1,000 years ago and earlier, and 15 of

those were complete enough for spatial analysis in this book. One floor, designated IIa1, was largely removed by Fur Trade period occupants (floor Stratum II) such that only a section of floor in the northeast corner of Block D (with a dated hearth feature) and a portion of what appears to be a large cache pit in the western portion of Block D remains. Five roof deposits—Ia (roof Va), IIb (roof Vb1), IId (roof Vb), IIe (roof Vb3), and IIh (roof Vc)—predated 1,000 years ago and were associated with intact floors (Prentiss et al. 2020a).

Roofs were distinguished from floor deposits on several bases. First, floor deposits were generally higher in clay content (floors IIa-IId have less clay in estimated percentages than deeper floors) and virtually always have lower densities of larger (pebble and cobble) clasts. Second, floors contain frequent intact and fragile fish bones that are comparatively rare in roof deposits where they are more likely to be mechanically damaged. Third, floors are always capped by a somewhat greasy surface interface

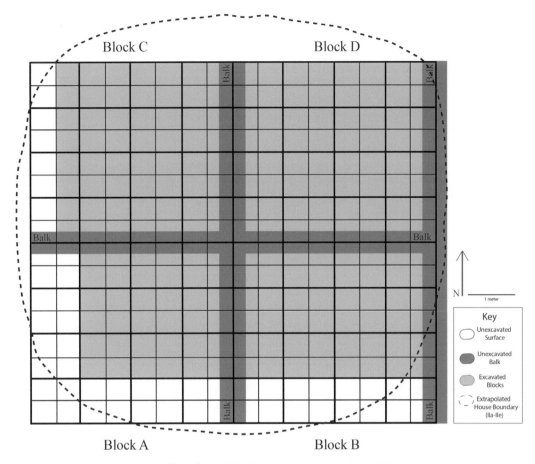

FIGURE 1.4. Plan view of the Housepit 54 excavation grid system.

containing artifacts and faunal remains lying horizontally. A micromorphology study in 2009–2010 by Paul Goldberg (2010) confirmed the field identifications of floor strata, though he was unable to reconstruct floor formation processes from a cultural standpoint due to within-strata bioturbation. Roofs, in contrast had fewer bones, but large numbers of stone artifacts and FCR, none of which was consistently positioned horizontally. Roofs also contained far higher quantities of charcoal in the form of staining, loose fragments, and portions of roof architecture including burned beams and small portions of woven mats. Only the Va roof covered the entirely of Housepit 54. The other roof deposits (Vb1 Blocks B and D; Vb Block A; Vb3 Block B; Vc Block A) varied in their coverage. Given inconsistent coverage but consistent evidence for burning, with the exception of Va, roofs appear

to have often been partially cleared before any burning took place. Then, for all earlier roofs (prior to Va), new floors were simply placed over the burned roof remnant, preserving the previous floor and that portion of its roof. Prentiss and colleagues (2020a) argued that the four roofs predating the IIa/Va occupation reflect rituals of house renewal, whereas the final roof (Va) marked the closing of the house.

Dating of the deep floors at Housepit 54 has been discussed in depth elsewhere (Prentiss et al 2018a). The floors of Housepit 54 were radiocarbon dated using the AMS technique, relying nearly entirely on charcoal from hearth features. A total of 30 dates were run at DirectAMS of which two were from the Fur Trade period floor and are considered elsewhere (Prentiss, ed. 2017). Two additional outlier dates were removed from consideration, dropping the total

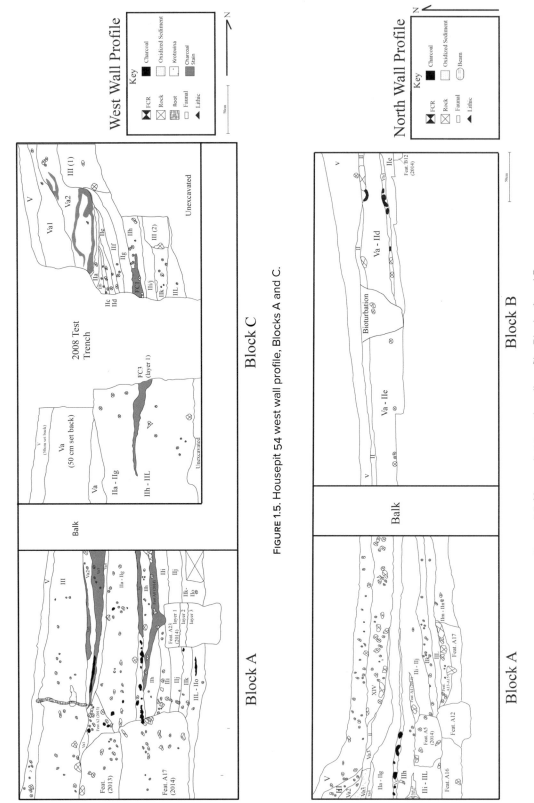

FIGURE 1.5. Housepit 54 west wall profile, Blocks A and C.

FIGURE 1.6. Housepit 54 north wall profile, Blocks A and B.

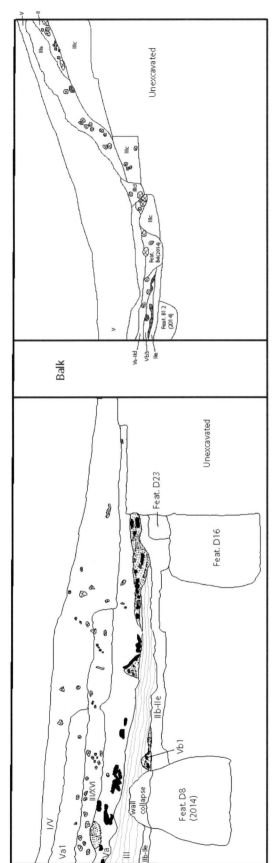

FIGURE 1.7. Housepit 54 east wall profile, Blocks B and D.

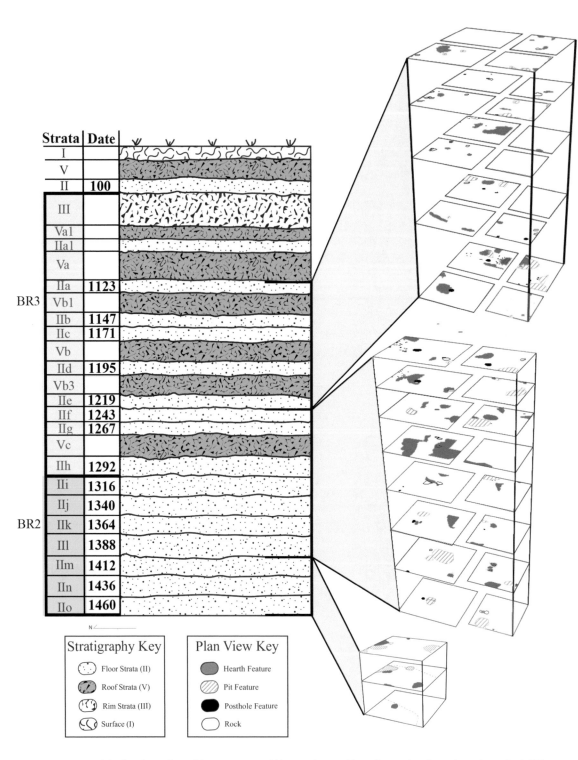

FIGURE 1.8. Idealized stratigraphic sequence of Housepit 54 with estimated radiocarbon dates (cal. BP) and associated floors. Dating draws from Bayesian analysis of radiocarbon dates (Prentiss et al. 2018a).

to 26 dates that were calibrated using OxCal 4.3 (Bronk Ramsay 2009) using the IntCal 13 curve to acquire the most probable results. Results, incorporating Bayesian modeling, suggested a tight range from 1461 to 1115 BP based upon mean scores for floors IIo to IIa (Figure 1.8). Thus, assuming an approximately 346-year range for all 15 floors, we project that each floor was likely occupied for about 24 years or about a generation. This estimate is relatively close to ethnographic predictions for the lifespan of a Mid-Fraser pithouse roof (Alexander 2000). We can also assign floors to the major Bridge River occupation periods: floors IIa–IIh fall within the BR3 period and floors IIi–IIo were occupied during BR2.

Rodning (2007) argues that in the case of Cherokee villages, the establishment of settlement permanence and stability can be assessed by examining rebuilding patterns of individual houses. He sees replication of previous construction patterns as markers of social continuity and attachment on the landscape. In the case of the Coweeta Creek site, evidence suggests the establishment of permanent towns developing from an earlier more dispersed settlement strategy as marked by the initiation of intensely reoccupied houses. The floor sequence at Housepit 54 permits us to offer similar reflections. The aggregated village at Bridge River was initiated by about 1800 cal BP (Prentiss et al. 2008), though socially meaningful arrangements of large and small houses only began to appear at some point during BR2 times. We know that both very large and much smaller houses were used from the earliest dates. However, to date we have not had the opportunity to assess continuity or lack thereof in the histories of particular houses.

The deep early floors at Housepit 54 (IIm–IIo) illustrate what we interpret to be small single-family dwellings reconstructed in a slightly offset manner (cf. Rodning 2007:473). House shapes were reconstructed on the basis of identified and extrapolated walls and also knowledge of space constraints. The very large Housepit 32 was likely in occupation at the same approximate time as floors IIm–IIo and would have significantly constrained expansion to the west. We know from excavations in Block A and the adjacent Blocks that the walls of the house did not extend beyond the east and north balks of Block A. Thus, we reconstruct the first three floors as reflecting smaller, probably somewhat square to rectangular houses with rounded corners.

The establishment of the IIl floor marked a major shift in the use of space. The house likely doubled in size, opening space for at least two families in a rectangular house form. We established the presence of the latter by assessing the likely east and west walls. The east wall apparently runs within the entire length of the north–south-central excavation balk. We recovered a portion of the west wall in our 2008 test trench, now identifiable as the western margin of Block C. Then, reoccupations consisted of, in Rodning's (2007) terms, effectively rebuilding in place from the IIl to the IIf floors. The house underwent a major expansion at the start of the IIe floor, and while we did not encounter the actual floor margin except in the southeast corner of Block B and northwest portion of Block C, the shape of the house's surface expression (combined with contact with rim sediments in the northwest corner of Block C) permits us to extrapolate an approximately oval shape to the final five floors (IIe–IIa) that were all rebuilt in place with space for at least four families.

In summary, the Housepit 54 floor sequence appears to reflect increasing dedication to this space and, if house size is a good indication, a growing number of occupants (Prentiss et al. 2018a). However, to fully investigate this process, we need to assess questions of occupational stability with reference to occupation-abandonment cycles, cultural frameworks for use of space, and wealth-related social dynamics between occupant groups.

Research Goals

The fundamental question driving the research presented in this book concerns whether occupations of Mid-Fraser pithouses were consistent and stable enough to generate long-term socioeconomic and political change. Data we have presented so far reinforces an argument that

Housepit 54 was a structure used in a recurrent manner with repeated reconstructions across several centuries. However, to investigate this problem, we need to explore the nature of occupations on each floor and to determine from the evidence whether they were consistent or variable. Variability can be measured a number of ways and we focus on stability of occupation/abandonment cycles, organization of activity areas, and evidence for changes in social relationships as tied to the accumulation of material wealth. Ultimately, this approach permits us to assess whether Housepit 54 might have been a simple domicile used by many groups for different reasons or if it might have represented the activities and investments of a single long-lived social group.

Household Archaeology

The question of persistent occupation of houses has significant ramifications for discussions in household archaeology. Essentially, we pose two alternative hypotheses: first, that despite repeated reconstruction in the same space, actual occupations were so variable in terms of activity types, expectations for return, and spatial logic on each floor, that it is impossible to conclude that a multigenerational group held the house and perhaps experienced a variety of social changes over the long term; second, that occupations of the many Housepit 54 floors were highly consistent in terms of conducted activities, expectations for return, and floor spatial logic, leading to the inevitable conclusion that a lineage-like multifamily group occupied the house across much or all of its life span (as measured from the IIo-IIa floors). In essence, we ask do the Housepit 54 data reflect the simple use of a domicile by many groups, perhaps in different seasons with different needs and expectations; or could Housepit 54 have been the core winter residence of a long-lived social group subject to transmission of traditions including the organization of living space on each floor.

Household archaeologists have invested considerable effort to address similar questions in many areas around the globe (e.g., Beck 2007a; Blanton 1994; Douglass and Gonlin 2012; Hendon 2010; Hofmann and Smyth 2013; Joyce and Gillespie 2000; Sobel et al. 2006; Steere 2017). A central concern within these discussions explores the nature of social units as independent family groups maintaining independent residential structures or cooperative social units organized above the scale of nuclear family maintaining a collective residence of some form. In an often cited and influential quote, Lévi-Strauss (1979:47) defined the *maison* or House as:

> a moral person, keeper of a domain composed altogether of material and immaterial property, which perpetuates itself by transmission of its name, of its fortune and of its titles in a real or fictive line held as legitimate on the sole condition that this continuity can express itself in the language of kinship or of alliance, and, most often, or both together [translation by Susan Gillespie 2007:33].

This term and its definition implicate both a social group and the space it maintains as its core property. Some important implications are that such a social group could reside entirely within a single structure (House) or membership in that structure might by spread more widely in a community such that not all members routinely reside in that core space. Likewise, it is also possible that some residents of the House in its physical sense were not actually members (Adams 2007; Chesson 2007; Gillespie 2007; Kahn 2007). Further complicating things is the fact that the physical manifestation of the House may not actually be a house but, for example, a religious or ritual building (Beck 2007b) or complex of tombs (Fleisher and LaViolette 2007). Often, however, it is indeed an actual house, though that house may periodically need replacing or could even be moved (Ames 2006; Marshall 2000). Inherent within Lévi-Strauss's conceptualization of the House is the ability of such an entity to gain (or lose) property, which can be accomplished in a myriad of ways that may include establishment of alliances for exchange with other such groups, to wage war, or to develop other forms of competition and cooperative ventures (Beck 2007b; Chesson 2007; Craig 2007). Finally, such a group retains the rights to transmission of corporeal and noncorporeal property across generations as defined by the rules of social membership in the house expressed in rules of kinship and/or affinity (Ames 2006; Brown 2007; Gillespie 2007).

Archaeologists have found Lévi-Strauss's conceptualization of the House to be useful given its inherent material correlates. As noted by Gillespie (2000, 2007), it is not without its challenges given that the presence of houses and households does not necessarily implicate the presence of house societies within the Lévi-Strauss definition. Ames (2006) reminds us that Lévi-Strauss's concept of house societies was in part drawn from Northwest Coast ethnography, in particular, the Kwakwaka'wakw concept of *numaym*. He likens the house society concept to Hayden and Cannon's (1982) closed corporate group with its long life, impact on the lives of its membership, and control of property. Ames (2006) notes that given differential member-ship, complex economic activities, and control of property, house societies may also be char-acterized by social ranking. Marshall (2006) however, recognizes that house society and cor-porate group could be separated by definitional emphases respectively on spatial continuity ver-sus the economics of property.

Returning to the Mid-Fraser context, St'át'imc ethnography implicates aspects of the house society model given the presence of clans reflected in village-wide (or multisettlement) membership, clan and family rights to resources that were transmitted between generations, and occupation of multifamily winter houses in permanent villages in which group-level socio-economic and political activities (e.g., feasts and dances) were performed and household and clan traditions transmitted (Kennedy and Bouchard 1978, 1998; Teit 1906). Clan member-ship was not predicated on establishment and maintenance of any single structure as is typical of some house groups elsewhere (Adams 2007; Kahn 2007). Yet membership within a St'át'imc clan did entail both corporate and place ori-ented elements with winter villages, cemeteries, fishing sites, and berry-collecting grounds serv-ing as maintained household and clan spaces.

If at pre-1000 BP dates, as suggested by St'át'imc ethnography, the Bridge River site was organized in a social framework reflecting key aspects of the house society model, then we would expect long occupational histories of houses central to the performance of duties as-sociated with clan membership. Put differently, in this case the house should reflect the history of the House. In contrast, the traditional Pla-teau ethnographic model (Furniss 2004; Harris 2012) would not strongly reflect a house society model despite the presence of houses, given em-phasis on frequent residential moves, unstable social groups, settlement impermanence, mate-rial egalitarianism, and band-like groups with little permanent control of economic resources. There are many ways to measure occupational stability as a marker of long-term House mem-bership and performance. Some of these could include demonstration of residential stability, transmission of knowledge, control over goods production and exchange, and maintenance of political alliances. We focus here on long-term residential stability in order to establish a base-line understanding of Housepit 54 history be-fore undertaking further studies associated with transmission, production, and social alliance. We do note that research at housepits elsewhere in the region does point to transmission of se-lect household traditions (Prentiss et al. 2016), and maintenance of long-lived production and exchange relations (Hayden et al. 1996a).

Occupation and Abandonment

Once constructed, Mid-Fraser pithouses were available for occupation year-round (Alexan-der 1992; Prentiss and Kuijt 2012). Thus groups could occupy the house in any season and en-gage in a potentially wide range of activities with diverse approaches to planning abandon-ment and anticipated return. If occupation patterns varied on annual and seasonal bases, then one would expect some major differences in approaches to artifact discard, house floor cleanup, and treatment of features. In contrast, if houses were used consistently as winter dwellings, we might expect lower inter-floor variability in discard and cleanup of household debris along with consistency in management of features. In order to address questions of variation in occupation and abandonment, we make use of frames of reference developed from a range of historical and actualistic archaeological studies.

A number of scholars have developed expectations for material signatures of occupation cycles and abandonment strategies. Stevenson (1985) identified three phases of occupation in typical hunter-gatherer camps that have equal relevance to occupation of pithouses. The initial phase involves settling in and refurbishing facilities. Exploitation reflects a wide variety of ongoing activities that particularly includes tool maintenance and repair work. Abandonment activities focus on preparations to departure as associated with anticipated needs.

Decision-making associated with abandonment can lead to a variety of outcomes. Drawing ideas from Schiffer (1972), Stevenson (1982) developed and tested a range of general expectations for abandonment under varied conditions. First, he draws a distinction between gradual planned versus less well-planned abrupt abandonments in which the former reflects a higher degree of cleanup and preparation that could include varied accumulations of so-called de facto refuse (items that end up in the archaeological record without the usual use-discard cycle). In contrast, Stevenson expects abrupt abandonment to entail less cleanup and thus better evidence for *in situ* activity areas. Second, he contrasts abandonment with and without anticipated return suggesting that anticipated return leads to greater accumulations of de facto refuse and curated and cached items. He notes however, that enclosed spaces might not receive excess amounts of de facto materials if reoccupation is anticipated. Brooks (1993) adds that in the case of Middle Missouri earth lodges, planned abandonment could include removal of house posts and beams for recycling elsewhere whereas the same items might be left to decay or be burned in an unplanned abandonment. Graham (1993) considers Rarámuri aban-

donment processes and notes that site furniture (*sensu* Binford 1979) would likely be removed in situations lacking expected return while low investment items such as external pens and windbreaks might be left behind. Deal (1985) subdivides abandonment of Mayan settlements into three stages. Pre-abandonment includes caching of items to be retrieved later, cleaning, and dumping of refuse into receptacles and "toft" zones (see also Hayden and Cannon 1983; Scarborough 1989).

Actual abandonment may be gradual or rapid. Gradual abandonment generally includes packing and removal of a range of items including larger tools that can be transported (i.e., not site furniture). In contrast, rapid abandonment might require abandonment of many things, especially larger items. In postabandonment, remaining groups or visitors might scavenge a property. Abandoned structures may also become dumping grounds for residents who remain. LaMotta and Schiffer (1999) offer similar distinctions adding that ritual depletion may also play a role in abandonment processes. Diehl (1998) suggests that in the case of Mogollon houses, given postabandonment scavenging practices, the house with the most accumulated de facto refuse could be those abandoned last. In contrast, Schlanger (1991) argues that frequencies of groundstone tools in abandoned houses could be inverse to length of time since abandonment, assuming that over time others would remove more items in the remaining settlement. Finally, Stevanović (1997) and Gordillo and Vindrola-Padrós (2017) suggest that burning could be a critical ritual marking the final abandonment of a house structure. We have already recognized indicators of ritual roof burnings at Housepit 54 (Prentiss et al. 2020a).

Given knowledge of traditional annual mobility and subsistence cycles in the Mid-Fraser particularly as relevant to understanding the occupation of winter pithouses (Alexander 1992; Lyons et al. 2017; Prentiss 2000; Prentiss and Kuijt 2012; Walsh 2017; Williams-Larson 2017), we can draw on theoretical predictions regarding occupation and abandonment processes to anticipate likely patterns specific to St'át'imc housepits. The warm season in the Mid-Fraser was characterized by significant residential and logistical mobility (*sensu* Binford 1980). Winter houses were likely visited on multiple occasions to deliver foods and other items to be stored for later use. Ill and infirm people unable to maintain vigorous travel could be expected to reside in the winter village during some warm season months. Overall, warm season occupation of winter pithouses could be expected to include use of cooking features and result in discard of food remains. Lithic tools might also be discarded but significant quantities of debitage would be unlikely to be produced. Regular cleanup could be expected that might entail dumping external to the house.

Stevenson's (1985) occupation phases are relevant to imagining the winter cycle of Mid-Fraser pithouse use. By late fall pithouses would be reoccupied with activities focused on refurbishing and repair as might include reflooring (20–25 year cycles) and more typically repair of furniture, house posts, and beams, along with restart or initiation of new hearths and cache pits. Fall gear would be stored, and recently acquired foods and other items would also enter storage. Most of the winter would be spent in Stevenson's exploitation phase in which occupants would remain busy with preparation and consumption of stored foods combined with results of limited winter hunting and gathering. Winter activities would include (but not be limited to) sewing, hide work, lithic tool manufacture and recycling, gearing up for spring fishing, hunting, gathering, and preparation for and participation in winter ceremonial activities. Compared to warm season use and the initiation phase, more debris from lithic tool manufacture would be generated and a high rate of kitchen/work area cleanup would be expected. Such material could end up in pits (for example, former cache pits) or on house roofs and rims. Preparations for spring activities would be in high gear during the weeks of the late winter season. At this point abandonment-related decisions could be considered and made, and these choices are worth considering in some detail.

Late winter activities would focus first on simply making it through the final weeks of cold and extending the utility of stored foods. Tasks could entail final bone grease production from stored bones, preparing soup from stored fish vertebrae ("neckties"), and extending utility of lithic materials using bipolar technology (French 2017; Prentiss 2000). Most critically, final preparations would be underway for springtime mobility, including final gearing up with hunting, gathering, and fishing tools. If lithic tool production was part of this process, we could expect lowest tool to debitage ratios. Then, the actual abandonment could play out in multiple scenarios. In the case of sudden abandonment without anticipated return, we would expect postholes with rotted posts, collapsed roofs with rotted or burned timbers, and relatively intact activity areas. Depending upon cleanup cycles, some evidence for cleaning may also be found. Then, there would not be evidence for cached tools or "placed" (Binford 1978a) curated tools and normal disposal of waste (e.g., in abandoned cache pits). This scenario would only be expected in cases of disasters whether major death, adverse effects of warfare, and loss of access to critical foods. Thus, in general, it is not expected to have been common if the ethnographic pattern was consistently followed.

A variety of planned abandonment scenarios are more likely. The most common scenario would be planned abandonment with anticipated return and reflooring and reroofing expected. In this scenario, we would not expect abandoned and rotting posts and beams. The roof would likely have been cleared but with little or no damage to the previous floor surface. Some site furniture, for example large grinding slabs, might remain, as would some curated positioning items. Given anticipated reflooring during the following fall, we would not expect a significant degree of activity areas cleanup from the last late winter occupation phase. Much evidence for cached items would not be expected, as these tools would likely have been retrieved for continued use.

A variant of the latter scenario would be planned abandonment without reroofing or reflooring. In this situation, a household group would complete a normal winter cycle with a standard springtime abandonment process based on anticipated fall return. However, for whatever reason, that return did not materialize and house is not reoccupied. In this case, we would expect similar closing treatment including extensive cleanup if no reflooring is expected and limited to no final cleanup if reflooring is expected. Then, regardless of anticipated reflooring, we would expect evidence for site furniture and cache tools since return was anticipated but never occurred. Roof posts and beams would have decomposed in place leading to roof collapse but likely without burning. The abandoned house could also have been subject to dumping and scavenging. If the latter occurred, then some curated items and site furniture could have been removed.

A final possible scenario would consist of planned abandonment without expected return and ritual closing of the house. Here we would expect a substantial burned roof deposit with burned or at least partially decomposed posts and beams. Little evidence would be expected of final cleanup of activity area debris. If retaining any utility, site furniture would be removed, as would curated tools (barring idiosyncratic cultural factors that might prescribe leaving select items [e.g., LaMotta and Schiffer 1999]).

Site Structure: Domestic Units and Special Activity Areas

One of the fundamental findings of hunter-gatherer ethnoarchaeology has been the recognition that activity areas may be challenging to reconstruct from archaeological manifestations (O'Connell 1987). While people certainly do engage in work within spatially conscribed spaces, many factors clearly converge to make simple archaeological identifications and reconstructions challenging. First, activities may not leave simple signatures, especially if little evidence survives in the archaeological record (e.g., Binford 1978a, 1991). Second, disposal practices affect the content of debris remaining in activity areas as might occur in the context of "drop" and "toss" zones around hearth features

(Binford 1978a; Stevenson 1991). Third, cleanup practices may remove substantial quantities of debris, particularly those of larger sizes, thus in effect biasing the record toward smaller artifacts and food remains (O'Connell 1987). Fourth, overlapping activities may reduce ease by which simple activity specific reconstructions are possible (O'Connell 1987; Yellen 1977). Finally, archaeologists must be aware of the problem of equifinality in which quite different behaviors generate at least superficially similar distributions of materials. A good example of this issue can be found in debates over the interpretation of activity areas at the French Paleolithic site Pincevent No. 1 as outdoor activity area (Binford 1983) versus tent-like residential structure (Leroi-Gourhan and Brézillon 1966).

Substantial interest has been devoted to the study of site structure in constrained spaces as associated with caves and rock-shelters (e.g., Gorecki 1991; Nicholson and Cane 1991; Spencer and Flannery 1984) and house structures (e.g., Flannery and Winter 1976; Gougeon 2012; Metcalf and Heath 1990; Snow 2012). Most relevant to our considerations are studies that have focused on house floors from the Pacific Northwest region. Long-term research at the Ozette site has been particularly important and has implicated a number of significant concerns for reconstructing indoor activity areas (Samuels 1983, 2006). First, many of the same concerns relevant to hunter-gatherer camps are at play within open house structures. Second, with constrained space, cleanup is especially important, particularly in public spaces. Third, activity areas may be organized around culturally defined conceptions of activity zones. Houses at Ozette were structured around interior floor, hearth area, and bench zones, each with somewhat different expectations as to work and cleanup operations (Samuels 2006). Similar patterns have been recognized in other Northwest Coast houses (Coupland 2006; Grier 2006; Smith 2006). Fourth, activities might also be structured around domestic zones, spaces habitually occupied and used by nuclear to extended family units (Samuels 2006). Hayden (1997; see also Hayden and Spafford 1993) drew from the

Ozette project to develop frames of reference for interpretation of floors at the Keatley Creek site in the Mid-Fraser area. Similar to Ozette, Hayden recognized interior open space, hearth, and bench zones. He and colleagues (Hayden and Spafford 1993; Lepofsky et al. 1996; Prentiss 2000; Spafford 2000) also recognize redundant hearth-centered domestic areas spaced around floor perimeters.

A critical part of our investigation of the Housepit 54 floors is identifying activity areas across the many floors and exploring cultural and contingent factors behind their spatial positions. Hearths are present on every floor from Housepit 54 and serve as a good starting point for exploring activity areas. Thus, we first ask are there hearth-centered activity areas, and if so, are they relatively intact or have they been extensively cleaned or otherwise modified? In a long-term occupied house floor, such activity areas could reflect complex histories that include cleaning (Schmader and Graham 2015). Thus, what appear to be intact activity spaces could be a combination of micro-residues from many accumulated events overlaid by residues from the last cycle of regular use. An essential component to answering these questions will be distinguishing between likely drop and toss zone activities around hearths. If relatively intact hearth-centered activity areas can be defined, we would then ask if these represent a narrower or wider range of actions. Previous research in house contexts (Hayden and Spafford 1993; Samuels 2006; Spafford 2000) and hunter-gatherer camps (O'Connell 1987; Yellen 1977) has shown that accumulated debris in domestic areas can be quite diverse, reflective of multiple activities accumulated over time.

Next, house floors reflect many other spatial options in which artifacts and food remains could accumulate, and we likewise need to determine if these areas reflect secondary refuse as resulting from cleanup and dump events, *de facto* refuse placed in these spaces during an abandonment process, or *in situ* outcomes of specific activities. The latter pattern was common on the Fur Trade period floor at Housepit 54 with spatially distinct zones associated with cooking, stone tool manufacture, socializing, and sleeping (Barnett and Frank 2017; Williams-Larson et al. 2017). Once activity areas are defined and interpreted, we expect to explore questions associated with cultural traditions and contingent problem-solving. Schmader and Graham (2015) demonstrate that groups with quite different cultural traditions will solve spatial dilemmas in common ways.

Occupants of winter pithouses in the Mid-Fraser resolved a number of spatial contingencies within what were likely crowded spaces. Entrances may have been established as ladders from a central hole in the roof structure (Alexander 2000; Kennedy and Bouchard 1978) which would have required central space on the floor clear from hearths and accumulation of excess household goods and refuse. Ethnographies also describe side entrances in some houses ostensibly for women (LaForet and York 1981), and a likely side entrance was indeed documented for the Fur Trade period floor at Housepit 54. Very limited quantities of artifacts, faunal remains, and FCR were recovered from the center and east sides of the fur trade floor, in line with expectations as to the presence of entrances (Williams-Larson et al. 2017).

Another challenge would have been designation of space for heavy-duty and sometimes messy work associated with, for example, wood, bone, antler-working. The northeast portion of Housepit 7 at Keatley Creek appears to have been set aside for this form of work (Prentiss 2000; Spafford 2000). Some evidence also indicates that this work was more routinely conducted around the perimeter of the floor, perhaps in bench zones (Prentiss 2000; Spafford 2000). In contrast, the Fur Trade period floor at Housepit 7 did not have an indoor space obviously designated for this work, though possibly some of this work was conducted outside on the roof, which was effectively an extension of the floor for many activities and a place for dumping household refuse (Barnett and Frank 2017; Williams-Larson et al. 2017). Beyond house roofs and rims, refuse middens are not known from Mid-Fraser villages. Sleeping space can be difficult to recognize if sleeping space was back on the rim under the sloping roof, on wooden platforms, or accomplished by simply spreading sleeping materials on floor spaces used for other activities in the daytime. Empty spaces in the northeast and northwest of the Fur Trade period floor at Housepit 54 could reflect the placement of permanent wooden platforms perhaps in part used for sleeping (Barnett and Frank 2017; Williams-Larson et al. 2017).

An interesting final contingency concerns access to light. During winter, low summer sun would have provided the most direct light in the north to northeast sectors of the Housepit 54 floor. While additional light would have been available via fires, this method was unlikely to be a constant option (Alexander 2000). The question remains as to whether access to light was a significant concern for certain types of work and whether it could have been a social commodity within household groups.

Material Wealth-Based Social Differentiation

Within Northwest Coast villages, ranking was well known to be defined within and between houses (Ames and Maschner 1999; Coupland et al. 2009; Drucker 1955; Matson and Coupland 1995). Whether justified by inheritance or achievement, families negotiated living spaces that reflected their social position within houses (Coupland et al. 2009). Families in Central and South Coast houses typically maintained their own domestic space complete with hearths and sometimes storage features. With most family-specific work centered around those features, these houses have offered some of the best opportunities for reconstructing variation in intra-household relations using archaeological data. The preeminent example is from Ozette where ranking was evident in the spatial positioning of a range of artifacts and food remains within and between houses (Samuels 2006). Other good examples include Tualdad Altu (Chatters 1989), Dionisio Point (Grier 2006), Cathlapotl (Sobel 2006), and Meier (Smith 2006).

Intra-household ranking has been a greater challenge to identify in interior Plateau contexts in part because houses are much smaller and preservation of organics not nearly as good as at some coastal houses (e.g., Ozette). How-

ever, given the overriding assumption that the Plateau was occupied entirely by socially unstable, egalitarian groups, few archaeologists have been willing to explore the question of inter- or intra-house inequality. A major exception has been Hayden's investigation of material wealth-based inequality at Keatley Creek. Hayden and colleagues (Hayden 1997; Hayden and Spafford 1993; Lepofsky et al. 1996) argued that a variety of data pointed to the presence of intra-house inequality in the largest housepit studied (Housepit 7) compared to limited evidence in smaller houses. Based on intra-floor variability in fish and ungulate remains, projectile points, storage pits, and prestige objects, Hayden (1997) argued that the highest ranked family resided in the south portion of the house while lesser-ranked families lived around the rest of the house perimeter. Given abundant evidence in the northeast quarter for heavy-duty wood working efforts and the possibility of a screen separating that area from the rest of the house, Hayden suggested this space could have been used for special activities or lowest status living. While not all scholars agree that material wealth-based inequality existed at Keatley Creek (Harris 2012), social dynamics were clearly at play by ca. 1,200 years ago (Prentiss et al. 2007) in this village that led to variability (however quantitatively limited) within and between houses in the discard and deposition of certain classes of artifacts and food remains.

This study focuses on intra-household inequality at Bridge River. Research to date suggests that significant inter-household inequality may have existed for several generations during the BR3 period. Prentiss and colleagues (2012) found that BR3 houses had significant inter-house variation in nonlocal lithic raw material, prestige raw material (obsidian, nephrite, and steatite), and prestige/display objects (beads, pendants, figurines, pipes, bowls, nephrite adzes). Prentiss and colleagues (2014) added that similar variation could be found in access to deer and the raising and slaughter of domesticated dogs. Finally, Prentiss and colleagues (2015) recognized the same inter-house distinctions on the basis of investment in sawed and distinctly shaped slate scrapers.

TABLE 1.2. Summary of Goals and Measures for Archaeological Analysis of Spatial Distributions on Housepit 54 Floors.

Goal	Measures
Occupation and Abandonment Cycles	stratigraphy (roof and floor sequence); features and architectural materials; artifacts (co-associations between smallest and larger items; evidence for preparations/ gearing up; presence and spatial position of de facto refuse, positioning items, and site furniture)
Site Structure: Communalist and Collectivist Social Strategies	feature positions; co-associated artifact and faunal remains
Material Wealth Distinctions	spatial positions of items indicative of traditional wealth: canids, nonlocal lithic materials (select chert, chalcedony, and obsidian); prestige raw materials (obsidian, nephrite jade, steatite, and copper); prestige objects (stone beads and pendants, nephrite tools, stone bowls, stone pipes, anthropomorphic and zoomorphic figurines in stone or bone)

The question remains however, whether the pattern of wealth-based inequality became manifested on an intra-household basis. Preliminary analysis of Housepit 54 data (drawing from data derived from 2013 and 2014 field seasons) suggests that intra-household inequality did not develop until the IIe floor and may have been accompanied by a reduction in cooperation associated with sharing of household labor (Prentiss et al. 2018a). This conclusion is suggested by variability in Gini coefficients calculated for floors IIg-IIa on nonlocal raw material, prestige objects, salmon, and deer. These conclusions were confirmed using the complete lithics data set for a 12-floor sequence at Housepit 54 (Prentiss et al. 2018b). This study will explore spatial variability in each floor using complete data from all field seasons at Housepit 54 to assess the possibility that material wealth-based inequality developed on an intra-house basis during BR3 times.

Methods

Ultimately, we seek to address the question as to whether the IIa–IIo floors of Housepit 54 accumulated as the result of occupations of repeatedly constructed but largely independent domiciles versus the reoccupations of a long-lived social group as per the House model. We address this question in three ways (Table 1.2).

First, we test alternative hypotheses regarding occupation and abandonment cycles. Second, we assess site structure or more specifically, variability in evidence for activity areas across each floor. In doing so, we ask whether house membership was structured in a communalist or collectivist social strategy. Finally, we develop evidence for variation in accumulated material wealth between occupants of each floor. The independent domiciles hypothesis will be indicated by inconsistency in occupation and abandonment, intra-floor activity area structure, and a distribution of wealth markers. The House hypothesis will be supported by evidence for routine planned abandonment from completed winter occupation cycles, stability or directional change in activity area locations/ functions, and the eventual development of material wealth-based inequality as is recognized in other analyses (Prentiss et al 2018a, 2018b, 2018c).

Occupation and Abandonment Cycle

A variety of data will be required to assess occupation and abandonment cycles. First, we will need to assess architectural materials in the form of postholes and roof materials. In the cases of sudden abandonment without return or planned abandonment without reroofing and reflooring, we would expect intact/rotted posts and evidence for substantial collapsed roof. Planned abandonment with reroofing and reflooring would have evidence for postholes but lack rotted posts. Roof deposits in this scenario would likely not be extensive as we expect that roofs would have generally been dismantled before reconstruction or just partially refurbished. Planned abandonment without expected return would likely include intact, rotted, or burned posts and a substantially burned roof. These data were collected during the excavation and can be assessed on a floor-by-floor basis.

Second, a key factor in assessing occupation and abandonment is variability in artifact size as a marker of *in situ* activities, cleaned spaces, and dumps. Planned abandonment without reflooring or reroofing assumes a scenario whereby the household had expected a return and cleaning likely would have preceded departure. Thus, floor surfaces, particularly around hearth features, would be expected to contain primarily extra-small items that would have been missed in the cleaning process. Sudden abandonment without return could include evidence for cleaning given abrupt abandonment during an active occupation. In contrast, planned abandonment with expected reflooring and reroofing, along with planned abandonment without expected return, should have evidence for limited cleanup, at least of late winter activities. In scenarios involving substantial cleanup, floors would have limited frequencies of larger cultural materials, which when present would appear primarily in discard contexts such as abandoned cache pits or roof deposits. Very small items could still reflect locations of activity areas, most likely clustering around hearth features or in other special activity areas (well-lighted spaces, bench zones, etc.). In scenarios where cleanup did not occur, we would expect co-association of both extra-small and all larger size classes in activity area contexts. Further, in these situations, we might also expect some larger de facto refuse, tool caches, and positioning items placed in various spaces including open areas and bench zones.

Measurement of relationships between smallest and larger items from Housepit 54

floors can be accomplished in two ways. First, we develop maps illustrating distributions of extra-small (less than 1 cm²) lithic artifacts and faunal remains, which are compared to similar maps showing distributions of all larger artifacts and bones. We back up conclusions drawn from examination of the maps with statistical tests for co-associations between smallest and larger cultural items across each floor. Second, we rely upon point provenience and artifact distribution maps to assess the presence of possible positioning items, tool-caching, and de facto refuse.

Site Structure

Our fundamental question regarding site structure on the Housepit 54 floors concerns evidence for communalist versus collectivist organization. The communalist pattern is best indicated by the distribution of artifacts and features on the Fur Trade period floor in which a central hearth was flanked by cooking, toolmaking, sleeping, and socializing areas (Williams-Larson et al. 2017). A collectivist pattern is indicated by redundant hearth-centered activity areas as seen at the *S7istken* (Smith 2014, 2017) and Keatley Creek (Hayden 1997) sites. In each case, artifacts and faunal remains accumulated around hearth features reflect diverse activities as would be expected of family groups during winter.

Our ability to address such questions would not be possible had the floors of Housepit 54 been thoroughly cleaned by original occupants. However, point-provenience maps (see Chapters 2–15) clearly suggest that floors were not likely thoroughly cleaned, thus leaving us with a good opportunity to assess variability in artifact and faunal items across each floor. We approach assessment of house floor sociality via production of a series of maps reflecting distributions of faunal remains (fish, ungulates, and canids), lithic artifacts, and features. Faunal maps include those for smallest size specimens, total faunal remains, total mammals, identifiable ungulates (genus level distinctions), and variation in mammalian elements. The latter distinctions are based on utility index models

(Binford 1978b; Madrigal and Holt 2002) and assume high (upper limbs and scapulae), medium (axial elements), and low (lower limbs and skulls) elements. Lithic artifact maps include smallest items, total lithic artifacts, total debitage, distributions of technologically sensitive flake types (early stage, biface thinning, retouch, and bipolar), and tools as defined within functional classes. These groups consist of hide-working and sewing (end scrapers, spall scrapers, slate scrapers, and piercers), heavy-duty applications (various scrapers on flakes, pièces esquillées, drills, perforators, adzes), hunting and butchering (slate knives, bifaces, and projectile points), groundstone (abraders, hand mauls, manos, and metates), and ornaments, pipes, and statuettes/figurines. Multivariate analysis of artifact data from all blocks and floors indicates a substantial degree of consistency supporting the idea that all floors other than the three deepest (IIm–IIo), thought to be single family occupations, were occupied by two or more domestic groups (Prentiss et al. 2018b).

Wealth Variation

Our final area of study concerns distributions of possessions that might be defined as wealth. Given challenges of measuring noncorporeal wealth associated with ownership and control of stories, songs, images, and the like, we focus instead on material wealth (Coupland et al. 2016; Prentiss et al. 2012). In the case of the St'át'imc, we are able to rely upon ethnographic information to define key foods and artifacts that could be considered material wealth. Success at hunting (especially deer) was an important support for well-off, influential persons and households (Romanoff 1992b). Ethnographers record use of dogs in the hunting process (Teit 1900, 1909), and it is well known that dogs were also eaten (Lamb 1960). Archaeological evidence from other housepits at Bridge River suggests that ownership of dogs was correlated with other indicators of material wealth (Prentiss et al. 2014).

Teit (1900, 1906) documents a wide array of goods made for exchange purposes by Mid-Fraser groups, and archaeological research supports the contention that both specific lithic objects and raw material types were exchanged and that certain classes of items were considered particularly prestigious (Galm 1994; Hayden and Schulting 1997; Rousseau 2004). Inter- and intra-household inequality in material wealth at Bridge River is indicated by variation in dogs, display/prestige objects (beads, pendants, statuettes, nephrite tools), raw material used for display/prestige objects (obsidian, steatite, nephrite, copper), and nonlocal raw materials (many cherts and obsidian; Prentiss et al. 2012, 2014; Prentiss et al. 2018c). Similar to our activity area analysis, we develop maps illustrating distributions of items associated with household material wealth that include canids, display/prestige objects, display/prestige raw materials, and nonlocal raw materials. These maps permit us to visually assess concentrated versus dispersed presence of each class of item. This visual approach is supported by prior multivariate statistical analysis of lithic artifacts that indicates a concentration of material wealth-related items in Block D on floors IIe-IIb (Prentiss et al. 2018b).

GIS Procedures

The distributions of archaeological materials were visualized in two distinct ways. First, artifact categories with larger quantities were visualized through the creation of an interpolated raster surface (e.g., total lithic artifact distributions and total faunal distributions). This raster surface was created by aggregating artifact counts in 50 by 50 cm quadrants of excavation units represented by a single provenience point at the centroid. The next step was to use the "Spline" tool in ArcGIS 10.7, which interpolates a continuous raster (image) surface based on the counts of artifacts (ESRI 2017). In other words, this tool takes point data with numeric values and turns it into a smooth, colored image, interpolating the spaces in between points that contain no data. To ensure that the interpolated surface is as smooth as possible, the spline tool requires that all points (or in this case quadrant centroids) have a numeric value, including the locations that have no data which were assigned a value of zero. The zeros ensure that no data are displayed in areas in which no cultural material was recovered. All spline surfaces were displayed using the "stretched" display option which represents the data on a scale from the minimum number of artifacts (0) to the maximum value. This method was found to be the smoothest and intuitive way to display the distribution of artifacts.

The second way in which data were visualized was with the use of graduated symbols, proportional symbols that are sized based on the quantity of data that's being displayed. This option was used to display the distributions of artifact types and occasional faunal specimens that were found with lower frequency (e.g., hunting/butchery tools). In order to compare different classes or types of artifacts, graduated symbols were consistently symbolized by quantities of one, two, and three or greater. The symbols were based on the artifact counts of excavation unit quadrants, visualized by a point at the centroid and sized according to scale mentioned previously.

Notes

1. *S7istken* site. *S7istken* refers to pithouse or underground house. In this case, *S7istken* is also the traditional name of this particular site. It is sometimes also called the "Little *S7istken*" site (Smith 2017).

2

The Final Floor

Stratum IIa

Stratum IIa is the final floor in the continuous 15-floor sequence from Housepit 54 (Figure 2.1). Consequently, it is also the final occupation within the five-floor group representing Housepit 54 at its maximum size (IIa–IIe). IIa sediments are estimated to be made up of relatively even quantities of silt and clay (total combined approximately 60%) with much reduced and progressively lower percentages of sand, gravel, and pebble-sized clasts. IIa is represented in Blocks A–C, but not D (Figure 2.1). As is evident in Figure 1.7, Block D was purposefully excluded when sediments were laid down to establish IIa. The Figure 1.7 profile illustrates the stratigraphic space in Block D that otherwise would have held IIa sediments was instead filled by six distinct and level layers of rim-like fill. These layers are high in ash and charcoal content and contain frequent pieces of fire-cracked rock (FCR) and lithic artifacts. Such deposits in the rim context surrounding the housepit floors are generally thought to form via accumulation of redeposited roof sediments along with discarded debris cleaned from house floors during occupations. Their presence as fill covering approximately one quarter of the Housepit 54 floor raises the possibility of ritual behavior (see also Prentiss et al. 2018b; Prentiss et al. 2020a).

Unlike deeper floors in Housepit 54, IIa is buried by a thick burned roof deposit (Va). Profiles (Figures 1.5–1.7) illustrate the presence of Va throughout Housepit 54 with particularly thick deposits around the margins of the IIa floor (Supplemental Figure 2.1). Va sediments contain abundant charcoal that includes burned roof beams, extensive quantities of FCR, and a large lithic artifact assemblage. Faunal remains are present though in lower numbers compared to floors. IIa contains six hearths (Figure 2.2), four of which are in Block B while the other two are in Blocks A and C. No obvious cache pits were encountered on IIa in any block, though we now believe that excavators likely did encounter the margin of a clay-filled cache pit on the south end of the west wall in Block A (Figure 1.5). Insufficient material was present to make a final decision on this sedimentary context. A large grinding stone was found within Block B that could be interpreted as site furniture. In the following sections, we draw on maps of artifact and faunal distributions to examine evidence for variation in occupation and abandonment cycles, floor structure, and sociality.

Occupation and Abandonment Cycle

In this section, we examine evidence for the effects of occupation and abandonment cycle on the distribution and composition of materials evident on IIa. We examine occupation phase (initial/settling in, exploitation, and abandonment; Stevenson 1985), drawing on co-associations between major artifact classes, and assuming that settling in is primarily focused on refurbishing architecture and establishing cooking and storage features, while exploitation monitors the daily functioning of the house

Stratum IIa

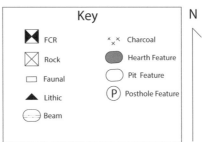

FIGURE 2.1. Comprehensive map of IIa showing point-provenienced artifacts, faunal remains, fire-cracked rock, prior excavations, and features.

Stratum IIa

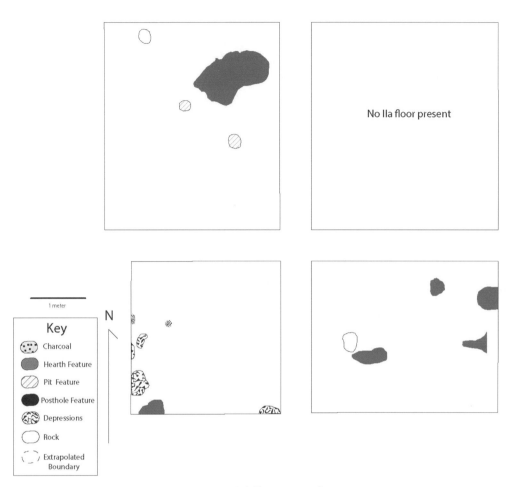

No IIa floor present

Key

Charcoal

Hearth Feature

Pit Feature

Posthole Feature

Depressions

Rock

Extrapolated Boundary

FIGURE 2.2. Features on IIa.

(assuming daily work of cooking, clothing and gear manufacture, and maintenance of social relations). This occupation phase can be largely assessed from previous research into the composition of lithic artifact assemblages on each floor and activity area (Prentiss et al. 2018b). Abandonment should emphasize cleaning out still-usable gear and preparation of equipment for warm season mobility. For an occupation associated with a full winter cycle, we would expect evidence for all phases.

Several divergent scenarios (e.g., Schiffer 1972; Stevenson 1982) complicate recognition of abandonment process. Abandonment may be abrupt or planned. Abrupt abandonment will likely reflect very limited attention to preparation for departure in contrast to normal planning associated with springtime departures for a winter house. Abandonment planning may also be affected by plans for a return. The three most likely scenarios relevant to Mid-Fraser houses would be anticipated return without reflooring or reroofing, anticipated return with reflooring and reroofing, and no anticipated return. The primary archaeological distinctions between these scenarios would be in the degree of cleaning. Anticipated return without reflooring would be associated with cleanup in

TABLE 2.1. Lithic Tools from IIa, Organized by Tool Class and Block.

	Tool Classes																
	A	B	C	D	E	F	G	H	I	J	K	L	M	N	O	P	Q
Block A	0	5	3	2	4	0	0	2	0	0	0	1	4	2	0	0	1
Block B	3	0	1	6	3	1	2	1	2	1	9	1	9	0	0	6	2
Block C	0	0	3	1	2	0	0	0	1	0	0	0	5	2	0	3	0
Total	3	5	7	9	9	1	2	3	3	1	9	2	18	4	0	9	3

Note: A = flake and slate knives; B = bifaces; C = projectile points; D = flake and key-shaped scrapers; E = hide scrapers; F = drills and perforators; G = small piercers; H = pièces esquillées; I = notches and denticulates; J = adzes; K = abraders/groundstone; L = freehand cores; M = bipolar cores; N = slate objects; O = hammerstones; P = used flakes; Q = ritual/social items.

anticipation of reoccupation. In contrast, return with reflooring and no return should not be associated with the same degree of cleaning given the expectation that either the old floor would be buried by new floor sediments or that since no one expected to return, the roof would have been left to rot and collapse or burned and purposefully collapsed over materials remaining from the last occupation.

Distinctions between the reflooring and full abandonment scenarios in the archaeological record would likely be associated with the degree to which site furniture and architectural features were managed. The former could be expected to reflect greater attention to salvaging still useful items including positioning items and site furniture (per Binford 1979), along with architectural members such as roof posts and beams. The latter might also be associated with accumulation of greater amounts of de facto refuse. We explore abandonment process by examining evidence for treatment of house architectural elements, indicators of cleaning as indicated by size distributions in artifact and faunal remains, and variation in the presence of site furniture, positioning items, cached gear, and de facto refuse.

Occupation Cycle

Initiation phase is expected to be particularly characterized by architectural work, along with establishment of critical features such as hearths and storage pits. Thus, it should be indicated by woodworking tools in the form of heavy-duty woodworking—adzes, abraders (for smoothing wood), and flake scrapers and notches/denticulates (for sharpening digging sticks). Exploitation phase would likely be marked by the widest range of tools spanning all major classes given the myriad of work requirements for maintaining a household for several months during winter—heavy-duty woodworking, hunting and butchery (bifaces and projectile points), hide-working (slate, end, stemmed and spall scrapers; small piercers), groundstone (all forms including abraders, grinding slabs and handstones [manos], hand mauls, and stone vessels), stone knapping (cores, hammer stones, billets, pressure flakers), and items dedicated to ornamental and social functions (beads, pendants, pipes, etc.). Abandonment phase should be reflected in investments in production of tools to be transported elsewhere. Gear associated with abandonment phase found items could include tools for hunting (bifaces and projectile points plus byproducts of preparing associated wooden shafts), fishing (nets and frames), and associated lithic byproducts (especially flake scrapers, pièces esquillées, drills, and notches), and gathering (preparation of digging sticks, hide bags, and baskets) and associated lithic byproducts in the form of flake scrapers, knives, and hide scrapers.

Examination of data in Table 2.1 indicates that artifacts accumulated on IIa reflect on all expectations for variation in occupation phases including heavy-duty woodworking (adze) and preparation of wood/bone/antler implements

TABLE 2.2. Lithic Flake Types for Stratum IIa by Toolstone Category.

	Ext	Chal	Cher	Dac	Obs	Intr	Slates	Met.	Total
Biface	4	1	0	40	4	0	0	0	49
Core	4	1	4	22	0	0	2	0	33
Retouch	6	4	9	118	2	0	0	1	176

Note: Ext = extrusives (excluding dacite and obsidian); Dac = dacite; Cher = cherts; Chal = chalcedony; Obs = obsidian; Intr = intrusives plus gneiss; Slates = slate and silicified shale; Met = metamorphic rock inclusive of quartzites, nephrite, and steatite.

(flake scrapers, notches/denticulates, pièces esquillées, drills/perforators), preparation and use of hunting gear (bifaces and projectile points), hide-working (hide scrapers and piercers), and stone knapping (freehand and bipolar cores). The frequent bipolar cores are particularly telling regarding exploitation phase as they likely represent tactics for extending utility of lithic raw material during winter. Variation in major flake types indicates that bifaces were indeed reduced, as were lithic cores, while most effort was expended in late-stage tool reduction and maintenance as represented by retouch flakes (Table 2.2). Thus, the IIa floor likely was occupied through a complete exploitation and planned abandonment phase.

Abandonment Process

The IIa floor was buried by a thick, burned roof deposit, which indicates to us that abandonment did not include an expected return. Further supporting that contention is the presence of an intact roof post on the western margin of Block C discovered during test-trenching in 2008. Otherwise, few postholes or other architectural features were found (Figure 2.1), raising the possibility that many roof posts were simply placed on the floor and did not leave recognizable marks (cf. Alexander 2000; Prentiss 2017b).

Assessment of co-association between different size classes of artifacts can provide insight into cleanup practices (e.g., Metcalf and Heath 1990). This analysis, in turn, can provide information on approaches to household refuse management and the abandonment process. We examined size relationships with a statistical test and by a visual assessment of distribution maps. We assumed that lack of association between

smallest and larger items would reflect cleanup activities. First, examination of mapped distributions of extra-small flakes (Figure 2.3) versus all lithic artifacts (Figure 2.4) illustrates a very close relationship. We recognize a very similar pattern with smallest faunal items (Figure 2.5) versus all faunal remains (Figure 2.6). Second, we ran a Pearson's r correlation coefficient for extra-small flakes versus all larger debitage and achieved a highly significant result ($r = 0.64, p = 0.000$). We ran an additional correlation coefficient for the smallest class of faunal remains against all larger faunal remains ($r = 0.713, p = 0.004$). These results suggest that artifacts and faunal remains were not swept or otherwise cleaned to any significant degree on IIa. This finding fits with a scenario of abandonment without expected return.

Additional insight can be gained from an examination of distributions of materials that could be classified as positioning items (Binford 1979), caches (Binford 1979; Hayden and Deal 1983), site furniture (Binford 1979), and de facto refuse (Schiffer 1972; Stevenson 1982). Maps of IIa artifact distributions do not illustrate obvious positioning items or caches. As noted below, however, certain tools (e.g., hammerstones and cores) may have been set aside on or under benches for later use but never retrieved. De facto refuse is difficult to discern from lithic artifacts alone, though an argument could be made that a cluster or "pile" of larger items away from normal household activity areas and public space (e.g., "toft" areas) could be classified as de facto items. There are no obvious clusters of this nature either. However, the large grinding slab in central Block B could be classified as site furniture (Figures 2.1 and 2.4).

IIa Extra-Small Debitage Distribution

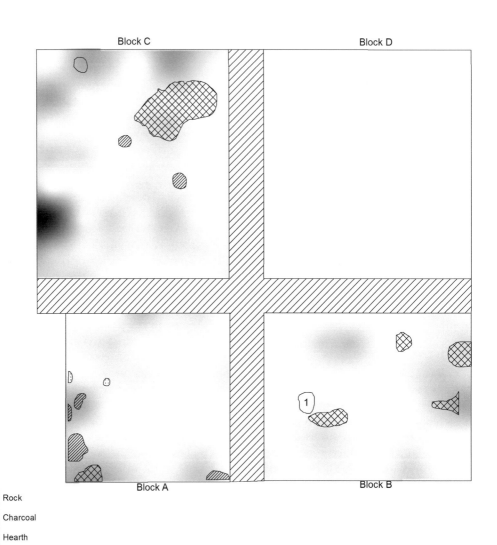

FIGURE 2.3. Extra-small debitage distribution on IIa.

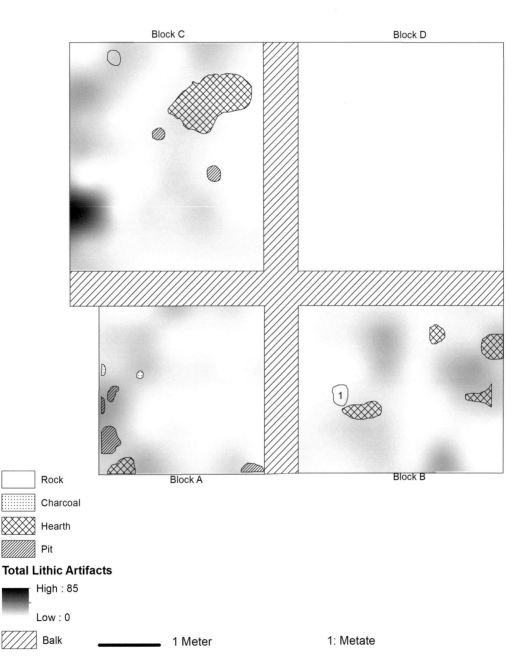

FIGURE 2.4. Total artifact distribution on IIa.

IIa Faunal Specimens Sized 1-9mm

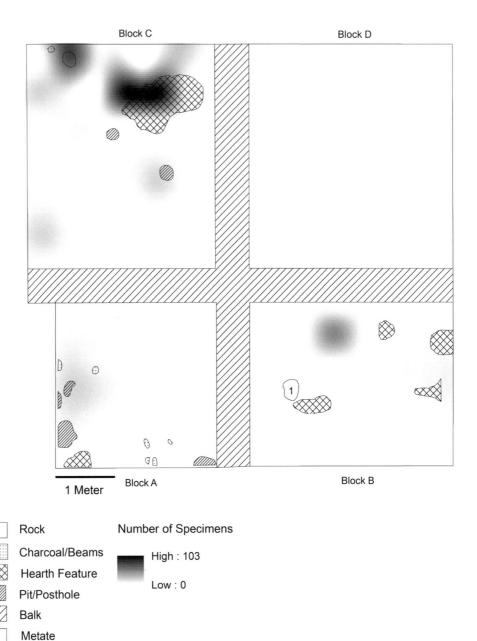

Block C

Block D

Block A

Block B

1 Meter

Rock

Charcoal/Beams

Hearth Feature

Pit/Posthole

Balk

1   Metate

Number of Specimens

High : 103

Low : 0

FIGURE 2.5. Extra-small faunal specimens on IIa.

IIa All Faunal Specimens

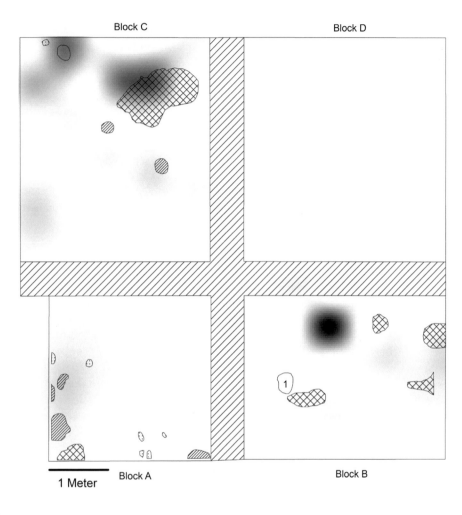

FIGURE 2.6. Total faunal specimen distribution on IIa.

Given the weight of the latter item and the fact that it was buried progressively deeper by users across four floor generations (IId-IIa), it is not surprising that this item remained on the floor after abandonment and burning of the Va roof. In general, other than the one item of site furniture, it would appear that the IIa group likely removed valuable larger items. Then the house was not left open long enough to accumulate debris resulting from discard by neighboring households (e.g., Alexander 2000; Scarborough 1989). In general, these results fit a scenario of fairly rapid, planned abandonment.

Site Structure

In this section, we seek to define variability in the nature and structure of activities across the IIa floor. We have three areas of interest here. First, we examine zonation in the arrangement of floor activities. In particular, we test the hypothesis that the floor is organized into three zones similar to those of many Northwest Coast houses such as Ozette (Samuels (2006). If this were the case, we would expect a central public space, surrounded by a hearth zone where domestic activities were pursued, and a most peripheral bench zone used for select activities, sleeping, and storage. The Housepit 7 floor at Keatley Creek provides a good example of this pattern on the Canadian Plateau (Hayden 1997). A contrasting model would organize the house around a central domestic feature such as a hearth, with a surrounding array of special activity areas and sleeping/storage spaces. The latter pattern was evident on the Fur Trade period floor of Housepit 54 (Williams-Larson et al. 2017).

Second, we seek to understand the nature of variation in specific activity areas. Following from the zonation hypotheses, we could expect two scenarios. One would be a collectivist living pattern with redundant multiple-activity areas most likely associated with domestic units (families) as illustrated at many sites on the Central Coast (Coupland et al. 2009) and on the Canadian Plateau (Hayden 1997; Smith 2017). The alternative would be a communalist

pattern as evident on the Fur Trade period floor of Housepit 54 and as described in Plateau ethnographies (e.g., Teit 1900).

Third, we address questions of contingent problem-solving in the use of space across the house floor. Here we examine the structure of artifact distributions to seek indicators of variation in response to sunlight, space for ladders or side entrances, sleeping space, and specialized (messy) work zones. To accomplish these goals, we assess patterns in lithic reduction as indicated by debitage distributions and then follow with an examination of variation in distributions of major functional tool classes. Finally, we look at distributions of faunal remains, exploring major taxonomic groups and element utility (cf. Madrigal and Holt 2002).

Debitage and Spatial Structure of Lithic Reduction

Debitage vary in their spatial structure between blocks (Supplemental Figure 2.2). Block A flakes occur around the southern and western peripheries associated with a single hearth, while Block B debitage cluster in four concentrations generally associated with several hearth features. In contrast, Block C debitage are not positioned particularly close to the one large hearth, and there is an extremely dense concentration in the southwestern corner. Relatively little debitage is found toward the center of the house. Early stage lithic reduction flakes concentrate along the western margins of Blocks A and C and are most common in north-central Block B (Supplemental Figure 2.3). With the exception of the concentration in southwest Block A, these flakes tend to be away from hearth areas which could be expected given either a concern with avoiding impact on other activities by those using hearths for other activities and/or purposeful removal of larger (core reduction) flakes from hearth-centered activity areas as might be expected of "toss-zones" (Binford 1978a).

Biface thinning flakes are somewhat uncommon and are distributed around all blocks and concentrated to some degree in the southwestern portion of Block A associated with the hearth in that area (Supplemental Figure 2.4). Production of finely made tools such as bifaces would be expected to have occurred in better-lit areas as associated with hearth features (Prentiss 2000). Curiously, r-billet flakes, also typically associated with billet flaking as might commonly be employed with biface manufacture (Hayden and Hutchings 1989), cluster in Block B. Despite the small hearths in this area, Blocks A and B were likely the darker portions of the house and would have made for visual challenges for knappers. One outcome of that would have been impacts from billets removing excess tool margins and thus creating r-billet flakes. Tool retouch flakes are found throughout Blocks A–C (Supplemental Table 2.6) and both adjacent to and spatially separate from hearth features. This location suggests that late stage manufacture and tool resharpening may have been substantially situational or undertaken on an as-needed basis.

Overall, debitage are consistently distributed throughout the house with particularly concentrations adjacent to and occasionally away from hearths. With limited exceptions (small retouch flakes), most debitage is concentrated around the periphery of the house, leaving substantial open space in the center.

Lithic Tools and House Floor Activity Organization

Here we explore the distributions on knapping (cores and hammerstones), heavy-duty (wood/bone/antler working: flake scrapers, key-shaped scrapers, pièces esquillées, notches/denticulates, and drills/perforators), hunting/butchery (bifaces and projectile points), hide-working (hide scrapers and small piercers), and groundstone across the IIa floor. Knapping items concentrate around the western margin of Blocks A and C and in southern margin and north-central portions of Block B (Supplemental Figure 2.7). It is possible that many cores and hammerstones were preferentially placed in marginal contexts, perhaps associated with benches or other storage contexts in anticipation of further use (cf. Hayden 1997).

Heavy-duty tools also concentrate around the margins of the house floor across all Blocks (Supplemental Figure 2.8), fitting a pattern previously recognized in Mid-Fraser houses predating 1,000 years ago, for example at Keatley Creek (Alexander 2000; Hayden 1997; Prentiss 2000; Spafford 2000), potentially associated with male activities (e.g., Teit 1906) undertaken away from kitchen areas and associated with benches. Hunting/butchering tools occur in all blocks and loosely concentrate on the west side of Blocks A and C (Supplemental Table 2.9). Like that of heavy-duty tools, this distribution could reflect gendered activity areas, though this conclusion requires further testing. Hide-working tools are found evenly around Blocks A–C and are not particularly concentrated along margins and are somewhat more common around hearths (Supplemental Figure 2.10). Given the house margin concentrations of traditionally male tool classes (wood/bone/antler working and hunting/butchering), it makes sense that traditionally female tools associated with hide-working and sewing (Teit 1900, 1906) would be mostly found in other spaces, in this case generally associated with hearth-centered activity spaces.

Groundstone tools on IIa include abraders, manos, and a stone bowl fragment. They concentrate in particular around the hearths of Block B, though examples are found in Blocks A and C (Supplemental Figure 2.11). Spatial positions of these items suggest roles in kitchen-related activities that could include food preparation but also potentially using abraders to sharpen tools such as bone awls for sewing or other tools for activities outside of the house (e.g., digging stick tips, bone points, etc.).

Distributional analysis of tools implicates several patterns. First, as recognized elsewhere (e.g., Hayden 1997; Prentiss 2000; Spafford 1993), gender likely affected the spatial organization of activity areas. Second, tools are concentrated on the house floor margin and in adjacent hearth areas. Thus, they are not common toward the center of the house. Third, some tools may have been set aside for later use (e.g., cores and hammerstones) but were lost or otherwise never retrieved.

Faunal Remains and Spatial Organization

The distribution of faunal remains provides insight into how subsistence-related activities were organized on house floors. Fish (primarily salmon vertebrae, ribs, and spines) remains are ubiquitous on Bridge River housepit floors. They concentrate in particular on IIa in the north-central portion of Block C associated with the larger hearth in that area (Supplemental Figure 2.12). Mammals are also found in all blocks and have a particular concentration in north-central Block B (Supplemental Figure 2.13). The latter, however, consist primarily of elements from taxa of little economic importance to IIa residents. In contrast, ungulates (primarily *Cervidae spp.* and in particular, mule deer [*Odocoileus hemionus*]) concentrate most densely along the north wall on Block C with lesser concentrations in Blocks A and B (Supplemental Figure 2.14).

We gain further insight into ungulate processing by examining distributions by element utility. High utility elements (meaty upper limb) concentrate in the north-central portion of Block C and northeast area of Block B (Supplemental Figure 2.15). Medium utility elements (axial skeleton) are relatively common and found primarily across the north end of Block C (Supplemental Figure 2.16). Limited numbers of lower utility elements (primarily lower limb) are found in concentrations within each block (Supplemental Figure 2.17). Collectively, these data suggest that processing of animals for food purposes took place throughout IIa but was particularly concentrated in northern Block C as that space contains the most frequent higher density concentrations of keystone species, salmon and ungulates. This accumulation raises the possibility that this space may have been frequently used for messy work associated with the butchery and cooking of animals, perhaps often for the entire house, and would help to explain the particularly large size to the hearth located in IIc. Another striking pattern is the limited densities of faunal remains toward the center of the house. Clearly animal-related work was conducted around hearths and closer to the edges of floors.

Summary: Site Structure on the IIa Floor

We now return to our initial questions regarding the organization of space on IIa. Our first question concerned zonation in activity areas. Data from all materials point to the likelihood that the house was organized in three concentric zones. With limited exceptions of small flakes and select faunal remains, little debris of any kind were found on the central portion of the floor. Likewise, no features were recovered in that context, raising the possibility that this space was a public zone for household inhabitants. Surrounding that area was a ring of hearths, with hearth-associated activities that included all forms of lithic reduction, use of groundstone, hide-working, and processing of animal resources. Collections of knapping and heavy-duty tools, along with some food remains around the margins of the floor, implicate the strong possibility of a bench zone. The bench itself was likely above the floor, consisting of the top of the rim materials covered by the outer edge of the roof. This space would have been low but potentially deep for storage and sleeping. Its inner margin (close to the house floor) was likely a good place to work, store select items, and socialize.

Second, we asked whether activity areas in the hearth zone were consistently similar or diverse in represented tasks. Results of all analyses point largely to consistency as all major tasks (lithic reduction, wood/bone/antler working, hide-working/sewing, manufacture and use of hunting and butchery items, and work involving groundstone) are represented in every block. However, certain animal-related processing tasks may have been preferentially conducted in northern Block C. This layout distribution raises the possibility of a pattern of inter-family cooperation regarding certain tasks. Such a scenario is also suggested for the concentration of groundstone and heavy-duty tools in Block B.

Third, these data offer implications for how we interpret contingent problem-solving.

First, limited material culture in the center of the house could have provided a space for a roof ladder. The floor lacks postholes, making it hard to envision where roof supports were placed. However, the nearly empty center would have been ideal. We did not find any evidence for a side entrance whether on the wall profiles or within the distributions of materials across the floor. Assuming a central roof entrance, the low winter sun would have provided best light across the north to northeast portion of the house floor. Apparently, available light did not play a major role in structuring IIa activities as nearly the entire Block D area had been retired from further use during the life of this floor and little was found in the northeast portion of Block C.

Virtually no evidence for sleeping space was found on IIa, and we are left to speculate that it existed in bench zones back around the edges of the house up off the floor or that a platform for sleeping was built over the Block D area and used for sleeping there. Given a lack of postholes anywhere on IIa this hypothesis cannot be confirmed. Finally, we likely do have evidence that a particularly messy activity was frequently constrained to one space, that of meat/fat processing in north-northwest Block C. A small portion of the southwestern Block also may have been set aside as a stone knapping area.

Sociality

In a recent study, Prentiss and colleagues (2018b) presented evidence that a pattern of material wealth-based inequality (per Mattison et al. 2016) had developed during occupations of IIe–IIb. They noted that little statistical evidence for inequality on IIa had been found. We explore that conclusion further with an examination of mapped distributions of canids, nonlocal raw materials (cherts and chalcedony not found in the Bridge River Valley; obsidian), prestige items (display items such as beads, pendants, figurines, and stone bowls, along with nephrite jade tools), and prestige raw materials (nephrite jade, copper, steatite, and obsidian). We compare these distributions to those of ungulates and hunting/butchering artifacts.

Ethnographies (Kennedy and Bouchard 1978, 1998; Romanoff 1992a, 1992b; Teit 1906) suggest that successful households in traditional St'át'imc villages required stable subsistence economies capable of sustaining production of surplus to be shared and exchanged for routine acquisition of valuable goods from elsewhere. Consistently successful hunting, fishing, and gathering activities provided a foundation for exchange. Hunting was of particular importance for marking household social status (Romanoff 1992b). Then, abundant food could support producers of valuable display and exchange goods including stone items such as steatite and copper beads and pendants (Prentiss et al. 2017), nephrite jade tools (Morin 2015), and animal products such as hides (Williams-Larson 2017; Teit 1906). Dogs were also important to households as they were served as food for feasts and could be used as assistants in a range of activities associated with hunting and transport (Cail 2011; Crellin 1994; Prentiss et al. 2014). Successful exchange relationships could bring in a variety of items including lithic raw materials from nonlocal sources (Hayden and Schulting 1997).

Canid remains are found exclusively in Block C and associated with the cluster of other faunal remains in the north-central portion of the block (Supplemental Table 2.18). Ungulate remains concentrate in the same general area, though they are also common in Blocks A and B (Supplemental Figure 2.14). We think that the cluster of bones in north-central and northwestern Block C likely developed not due to status signaling but because this space was in part used for preparing meat and fat for consumption perhaps by the entire house group. Hunting and butchering tools are found in all blocks but particularly along the western wall of Blocks A and C near the densest faunal concentrations (Supplemental Figure 2.9). In contrast to the more spatially constrained clusters of faunal material, nonlocal lithic materials are scattered throughout all blocks on IIa (Supplemental Figure 2.19). One particularly dense concentration is found in the southwest corner of Block C, which we have suggested may have been a set-aside space for knapping activities. Prestige items and prestige raw materials are rare and tend to concentrate in Block B (Supplemental Figures 2.20 and 2.21).

Considered in comparison to other research (Prentiss et al. 2018), results of this study confirm little evidence for inequality in access to goods that could be defined as indicators of material wealth. Canid remains are located within a general activity area for animal processing. Nonlocal lithic materials are scattered throughout the house and concentrate in a place where other materials were also knapped. Prestige materials and items are simply too rare to judge them as concentrated in any significant way on IIa. Thus, it appears likely that the IIa house group was cooperative in the sharing of labor. This social arrangement likely also translated into relative equality in sharing of food and material goods.

Conclusions

We examined distributions of features, artifacts, and faunal remains on Stratum IIa with the goals of developing an understanding on occupation and abandonment process, site structure, and sociality. A variety of evidence suggests that the archaeological materials accumulated on IIa during occupation cycles that included initiation, exploitation, and planned abandonment. The abandonment process focused on closing of the house without expected return as indicated by the massive Va roof, an intact house post, and a lack of evidence for cleaning in anticipation of return. Interestingly, a large grinding slab, used for four floor generations in Block B, was not retrieved before abandonment. It may have been left due to its weight though the exact reason is hard to know. Some other still usable items were also abandoned at the close of IIa including cores and hammerstones found around the periphery of floor. These may have been simply discarded or possibly lost amidst other materials associated with the margin of the floor's bench zone.

The IIa floor was clearly structured in a similar way to many Northwest Coast and Interior collectivist houses. A central public space likely was partially surrounded by hearth-based activity areas. One exception is the Block D area that was filled with rim sediments and not used during IIa. Then, we infer the presence of a bench zone peripheral to the hearth areas. Examination of inter-activity area variation in functional artifact classes and faunal remains indicates substantial consistency between areas supporting a conclusion that domestic groups lived in the spaces approximately defined by Blocks A–C. Many forms of work are consistently represented between blocks in the lithic tool and debitage assemblages. However, specialized activity areas may be indicated by clusters of faunal remains in north-central Block C, a dense cluster of debitage in southwestern Block C, and a concentration of groundstone in Block B. If that is the case, it may mean that specific families or family members were often able to pursue particular tasks for the wider benefit of the entire house.

Thus, we conclude that the IIa group lived in a collectivist social arrangement with a probable high degree of sharing in labor and its by-products. The abandonment of the house was purposeful and appears to have centered on a ritual process that precluded a return. We do know, however, that some group did briefly reoccupy Housepit 54 radiocarbon-dated about 100 years later (1004–921 cal BP [Prentiss et al. 2018]). The nature of this occupation (IIa1) is nearly impossible to reconstruct due to removal of much of that material by Fur Trade period occupants about 850 years later (Prentiss 2017b).

3

Final Wealth-Based Distinctions

Stratum IIb

Stratum IIb is the second to final floor in the Housepit 54 sequence and is found in all excavated blocks (Figure 3.1). It has a similar sedimentary profile to that of IIa with relatively even quantities of clay and silt (estimated to vary from 50% to 80% of total sediments) followed by much lower percentages of sand, gravel, and pebbles. Stratum IIb is buried across Blocks A and C by Stratum IIa sediments. However, IIb is buried within Block B by a thin roof deposit designated as Vb1 (Supplemental Figure 3.1). Stratum Vb1 contains abundant charcoal, burned roof-beam fragments, and fire-cracked rock (FCR). Several small patches of sediment resembling Vb1 were also found on IIb in Block D. However, the majority of sediments covering IIb were essentially midden material resembling Stratum III, the house rim. In this context, six level beds were identified suggesting that these sediments were carefully laid down to purposefully bury the IIb floor (Figure 1.7). Prentiss and colleagues (2018b) argue that this event likely reflected a ritual closing of the Block D portion of the IIb floor given that the IIa floor was established and occupied in Blocks A–C.

IIb contains hearth features in Blocks A–C (Figure 3.2). A concentration of charcoal resembling hearth clean-out in central Block D surrounded by dense cultural materials raises the possibility that a hearth feature may have been present in or near this area but was simply missed by our excavation. This concentration

of charcoal also possibly reflects a small, briefly used hearth that did not raise temperatures high enough and/or for a long enough time period to create sediment oxidation.

One shallow cache pit was recovered from the western margin of Block A, and a limited number of narrow width postholes were excavated in Blocks A–C. Block D included one posthole with an intact wooden post cut into a square shape and stabilized with rocks but also chopped off at about 20 cm above the IIb floor surface before abandonment. The large grinding slab evident on IIa in Block B is also present in IIb. In the following sections, we discuss evidence for variation in occupation and abandonment cycles, site structure, and sociality for Stratum IIb.

Occupation and Abandonment Cycle

Occupation and abandonment cycles affect the distribution of materials on archaeological house floors. We outlined expectations for variability in Chapter 2 (Stratum IIa).

Occupation Cycle

We examine evidence for initiation, exploitation, and abandonment cycles drawing upon expectations outlined in Chapter 2 (Stratum IIa).

Data in Table 3.1 demonstrate discard of nearly the full array of tool classes on IIb. We recognize evidence for heavy-duty woodworking in the form of adzes and abraders. Applications to wood/bone/antler items are evident

Stratum IIb

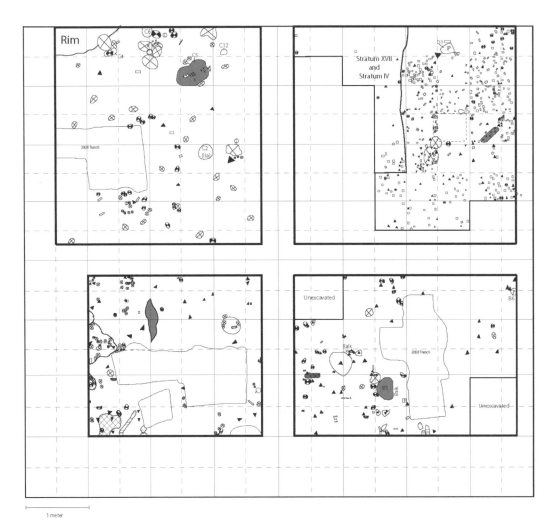

FIGURE 3.1. Comprehensive map of IIb showing point-provenienced artifacts, faunal remains, fire-cracked rock, prior excavations, and features.

Stratum IIb

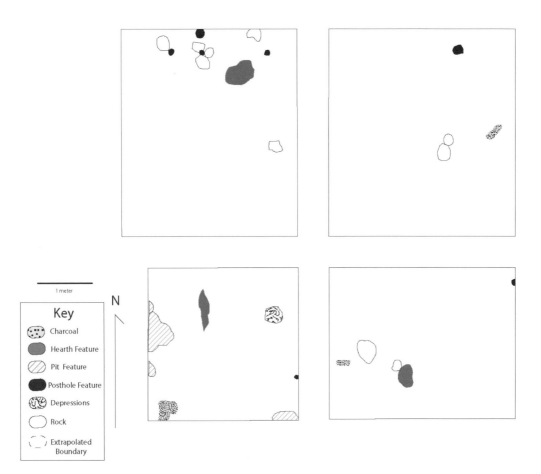

FIGURE 3.2. Features on IIb.

in the presence of pièces esquillées, flake and key-shaped scrapers, and drills and perforators. Interestingly, notches and denticulates are conspicuously absent. Gearing up for hunting is likely reflected in the presence of relatively abundant bifaces and projectile points. Hide-working is also well represented by hide scrapers and small piercers. As with IIa, bipolar cores are common and likely reflected lithic reduction actions directed toward extending the use-life of lithic raw materials during exploitation and abandonment phases. Debitage from IIb reflect a focus on late stage lithic tool retouch followed respectively by biface and core reduction (Table 3.2). Thus, from the perspective of

the lithic assemblage, IIb appears to have been occupied through all occupation cycles.

Abandonment Process

Feature and roof data from IIb point to a process of abandonment with intent to return. The presence of roof deposits covering Block B and rim-like midden deposits covering Block D suggests that two events marked the closure of the IIb occupation cycle. First, the west half (Blocks A and C) of the roof over IIb was cleared as evidenced by a lack of roof deposits in this context, and floor deposits reflect *in situ* activities from the final IIb occupation. The latter would have been disturbed if a burned and collapsed

TABLE 3.1. Lithic Tools from IIb, Organized by Tool Class and Block.

	Tool Classes																
	A	B	C	D	E	F	G	H	I	J	K	L	M	N	O	P	Q
Block A	0	1	2	0	1	0	1	0	0	1	0	0	2	3	2	2	0
Block B	0	1	2	1	4	1	0	0	0	0	1	0	4	1	0	0	0
Block C	2	0	2	1	0	1	0	1	0	0	2	1	5	1	0	1	0
Block D	8	3	8	5	10	3	1	5	0	1	1	1	8	1	0	12	8
Total IIb	10	5	14	7	15	5	2	6	0	2	4	2	19	6	2	15	8

Note: A = flake and slate knives; B = bifaces; C = projectile points; D = flake and key-shaped scrapers; E = hide scrapers; F = drills and perforators; G = small piercers; H = pièces esquillées; I = notches and denticulates; J = adzes; K = abraders/groundstone; L = freehand cores; M = bipolar cores; N = slate objects; O = hammerstones; P = used flakes; Q = ritual/social items.

TABLE 3.2. Lithic Flake Types for Stratum IIb by Toolstone Category.

	Ext	Chal	Cher	Dac	Obs	Intr	Slates	Met.	Total
Biface	0	2	0	47	0	0	0	0	49
Core	5	0	0	16	0	0	4	1	26
Retouch	19	8	6	214	4	0	12	5	268

Note: Ext = extrusives (excluding dacite and obsidian); Dac = dacite; Cher = cherts; Chal = chalcedony; Obs = obsidian; Intr = intrusives plus gneiss; Slate s= slate and silicified shale; Met = metamorphic rock inclusive of quartzites, nephrite, and steatite.

roof had been cleared off the floor. Second, a portion of the roof over IIb was indeed burned and allowed to collapse over the floor across the Block B area and possibly portions of Block D. The logic behind clearing one part of the roof while burning another is not clear, though we might speculate that practical reasons could include excess wood rot or insect infestations. Alternatively, this practice may have had a ritual element that remains elusive to define from an archaeological standpoint. Third, the Block D portion of IIb was then filled with midden sediments and not restarted as the IIa floor. Fourth and finally, all blocks other than D were covered with IIa floor sediment, and the Va roof was constructed after that occurred. Given this history, it makes sense that a house post from Block D was chopped off near its base but otherwise left *in situ*.

We can assess abandonment process by examining evidence for cleanup using relationships between smallest artifacts and faunal remains versus distributions of all items (e.g., Metcalf and Heath 1990). As illustrated on Fig-

ures 3.3 and 3.4, extra-small debitage match nearly exactly the distribution of all artifacts. The relationship between smallest and larger items is confirmed with a correlation coefficient ($r = 0.871$, $p = 0.000$). A similar pattern is evident for the smallest faunal class compared to all larger fauna (Figures 3.5 and 3.6). This result is largely confirmed by a somewhat weaker correlation coefficient ($r = 0.51$, $p = 0.052$). All told, these results demonstrate minimal evidence for sweeping/cleaning of lithic and faunal debris across the IIb floor, fitting a scenario of abandonment with expected return associated with reflooring.

Additional insight can be gained from an examination of distributions of materials that could be classified as positioning items (Binford 1979), caches (Binford 1979; Hayden and Deal 1983), site furniture (Binford 1979), and de facto refuse (Schiffer 1972; Stevenson 1982). Similar to the IIa floor, lithic artifacts on IIb do show any strong evidence for the presence of positioning items or caches. A cluster of cobble-sized rocks on the north side of Block C could be

IIb Extra-Small Debitage Distribution

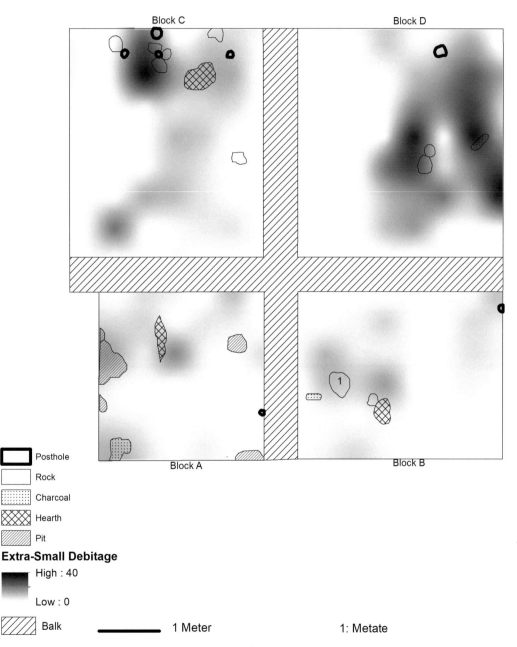

Block C

Block D

Block A

Block B

Posthole

Rock

Charcoal

Hearth

Pit

Extra-Small Debitage

High : 40

Low : 0

Balk

1 Meter

1: Metate

FIGURE 3.3. Extra-small debitage distribution on IIb.

IIb Total Lithic Artifact Distribution

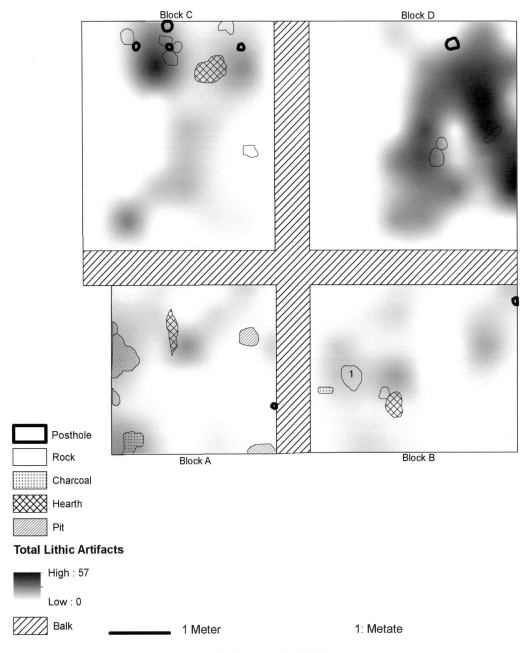

Block C

Block D

Block A

Block B

Posthole
Rock
Charcoal
Hearth
Pit

Total Lithic Artifacts

High : 57

Low : 0

Balk   1 Meter   1: Metate

FIGURE 3.4. Total artifact distribution on IIb.

IIb Faunal Specimens Sized 1-9mm

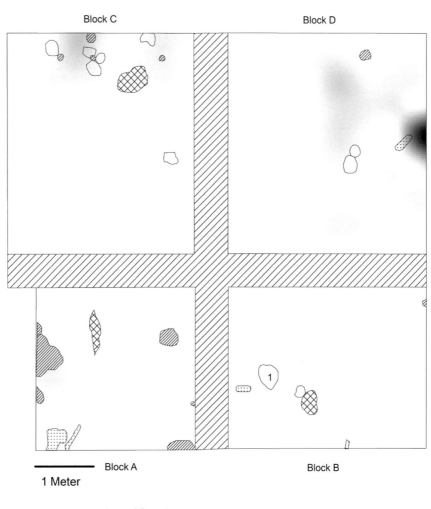

Block C   Block D

Block A   Block B

1 Meter

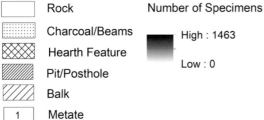

Rock

Charcoal/Beams

Hearth Feature

Pit/Posthole

Balk

1 Metate

Number of Specimens

High : 1463

Low : 0

FIGURE 3.5. Extra-small faunal specimens on IIb.

IIb All Faunal Specimens

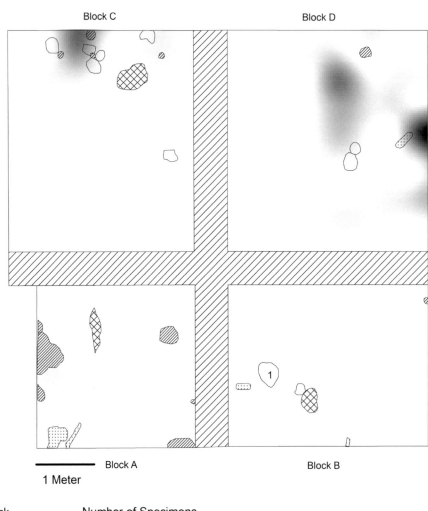

FIGURE 3.6. Total faunal specimen distribution on IIb.

positioning items that remained in their spaces upon abandonment (Figure 3.1). Such items seem unlikely to be de facto refuse dumped in a toft area. Another cluster of cobble-sized rocks was found in the only cache pit feature within IIb (Figure 3.1), and these may have been stored boiling stones, thus providing limited evidence for caching strategies. Also as on IIa, the boulder-sized grinding stone is present in Block B and is best interpreted as site furniture. No evidence for large-scale dumping of random refuse was found, as might be expected had neighbors discarded materials into the temporarily abandoned house (e.g., Alexander 2000; Scarborough 1989). Had this been the case we would have expected to see a cluster of such materials near the center of the floor, assuming dumping occurred through the entrance opening in the roof. All in all, these patterns fit a scenario of planned abandonment without anticipated return to live on this specific floor.

Site Structure

In this section, we explore variability in the structure of house floor space, drawing inferences with the aid of frames of reference explicated in Chapter 2 (Stratum IIa). In the following sections, we consider spatial patterns associated with lithic debitage, tools, and faunal remains.

Debitage and Spatial
Structure of Lithic Reduction

Debitage concentrations are distributed in relation to hearths and concentrations of ash and charcoal (Supplemental Figure 3.2). The charcoal and ash concentrations were interpreted to be hearth clean-out dumps. However, such spaces also possibly represent shallow hearths used briefly such that oxidation of surrounding sediments did not have time to develop. The latter scenario would explain the associated clusters of debitage and other artifacts. Several concentrations of flakes near the margins of blocks raise the possibility of associated hearths external to the excavation blocks. Alternatively, these areas may also simply be knapping areas independent of hearths. Such activity areas

are present on the east side of Block B and the southwest portion of Block C. Interestingly, a similar concentration of debitage was found in approximately the same space on IIa.

The unusually high density of materials on the east side of Block D makes it very likely that a major hearth feature is located just east of the excavated area. Core reduction flakes are found in all blocks, though they occur in highest concentrations in Block D (Supplemental Figure 3.3). In each case, these flakes are generally associated with hearths or charcoal/ash concentrations. Biface thinning flakes are found in low numbers around all blocks (Supplemental Figure 3.4). They occur around hearths in Blocks B and C, while spatially not close to hearths or charcoal and ash dumps in Blocks A and D. R-billet flakes are even rarer on IIb but also occur adjacent to hearths in Blocks B and C (Supplemental Figure 3.5). Tool retouch flakes occur in high numbers and generally follow the overall debitage distribution with particular concentrations around hearths or charcoal/ash clusters in all blocks (Supplemental Figure 3.6). Additional concentrations are found on the east side of Block B, the southwest of Block C, along with particularly high densities along the central and east sides of Block D.

Taken as a whole, debitage is most concentrated in Block D but is otherwise found in clusters particularly around hearths and charcoal/ash clusters elsewhere on IIb. Very little evidence for knapping activities was found in the central portion of the house.

Lithic Tools and House
Floor Activity Organization

Here we explore the distributions on knapping (cores and hammerstones), heavy-duty (wood/bone/antler working: flake scrapers, key-shaped scrapers, pièces esquillées, notches/denticulates, and drills/perforators), hunting/butchery (bifaces and projectile points), hide-working (hide scrapers and small piercers), and groundstone across the IIb floor. Knapping items (cores and hammerstones) appear in approximately the same spaces as debitage concentrations, further supporting our contention little effort was expended in preabandonment cleanup (Supplemental Figure 3.7). Knapping items occur in small concentrations around hearths and charcoal/ash clusters in all blocks and are present in the southwest of Block C that was evidently a knapping activity area. Heavy-duty tools are associated with hearths in Blocks B and C and were densely concentrated throughout the northeast portion of Block D (Supplemental Figure 3.8). Hunting/butchery tools are concentrated around hearths or charcoal/ash areas in Blocks A, C, and D (Supplemental Figure 3.9). Additional clusters are found in the northeast corners of Blocks C and D. Within Block D highest numbers occur on the eastern margin, raising the possibility that this kind of work was generally conducted around the edges of the house or that these tools were discarded or otherwise placed around the periphery perhaps associated with a bench zone along the eastern periphery of Block D. Hide-working/sewing tools are consistently associated with hearths in all Blocks (Supplemental Figure 3.10). Groundstone items are limited in numbers but also associated with hearths and charcoal/ash concentrations (Supplemental Figure 3.11).

Thus tool distribution data suggest that multiple activities were conducted around hearth features including wood/bone/antler working, butchery and food preparation, hide-working and sewing, and preparation of tools likely to be used in those activities. Little evidence suggests separation of activities, in turn suggesting that at least from the standpoint of artifact discard that labor was not clearly segregated by gender (or other principles). One possibly exception is the clustering of hunting/butchery tools on the east margin on Block D. Distributions also suggest that little work was conducted in the central portion of the house.

Faunal Remains and Spatial Organization

Faunal remains provide insight into the structure of subsistence activities on the IIb floor. Fish remains are ubiquitous on all Housepit 54 floors. However, they occur in particularly high concentrations on the north side of the hearth in Block C and partially surrounding the charcoal/ash concentration in Block D (Supplemental Figure 3.12). An extremely high concentration of mammal remains is found on the east-central area of Block D (Supplemental Figure 3.13) that obscures distributions of mammal remains in general as an effect of the GIS program. Thus, it is more informative to explore distributions of mammalian faunal remains within other descriptions.

Ungulate remains consistently surround hearths and charcoal/ash concentrations, again supporting an argument that the latter are actually short-lived hearth features (Supplemental Figure 3.14). Concentrations of high, medium, and low utility ungulate elements are distributed within approximately the same clusters as the overall ungulate distribution (Supplemental Figures 3.15–3.17). This pattern suggests that animal butchery within houses was not segmented spatially but concentrated around hearths within each Block area. Greatest densities of ungulate remains—and thus likely processing activities—occur in Blocks C and D. Small numbers of canid remains are found around the hearths of Blocks A, C, and D (Supplemental Figure 3.18), generally associated with ungulates and fish remains. This location suggests that while canids were not routine food items their presence in food-related concentrations suggests that they were consumed as part of diets of domestic groups within the house.

Distributions of faunal remains offer a number of implications for understanding the structure of activities on the IIb floor. First, faunal remains co-associate with lithic debitage and tools, both consistently distributed around hearth features with spatial patterns resembling drop-zones (i.e., Binford 1978a; Stevenson 1985). Thus, the house does not appear to have any special meat-processing areas outside of kitchen-hearth-associated activity areas. Also similar to the lithics, faunal remains do not concentrate toward the center of the house.

Summary: Site Structure on the IIb Floor

Distributions of features, lithic artifacts, and faunal remains offer several implications for understanding the structure of work on the IIb floor. First, the near-complete lack of lithics or faunal remains in the center of the house couples with clear hearth-associated activity areas around the periphery and supports a zonation structure consisting of central, hearth, and bench zones. We have little evidence for the bench zone as it was likely located above the floor on rim sediments but under the outer edge of the domelike roof. Some lithic artifacts are concentrated along the likely margin of this zone, particularly in Block D where artifacts occur in highest numbers in general.

Second, we are able to recognize four distinct activity areas containing hearths and clusters of artifacts and animal remains. Significantly, lithic reduction of all types (especially tool retouch), all activity classes with applied lithic tools (heavy-duty work, hide-working/sewing, meat-processing, and applications of groundstone) co-occur in each area. Lithic materials associate directly with concentrations of fish, ungulate, and canid remains. Ungulates and fish are found in particularly high numbers in Blocks C and D. Given the multiactivity nature of these spaces surrounding hearth features, we can conclude that these spaces were likely domestic for family groups. Interestingly, pit storage was not important on IIb with only one midsized pit found in Block A and substantially filled with cobble-sized rocks. The latter may have been stored for future use as boiling stones.

Finally, the open space in the center of the floor could have been used to position an entrance ladder, and it likely served as public space for occupants moving between households positioned around the edges. High concentrations of food debris in the northern portions of IIb could reflect groups taking advantage of light from the roof entrance space. However, that hypothesis does not explain the even distributions of all tools and faunal remains around the floor. Highest concentrations of all items in the block with the presence of best light would appear to reflect one family making optimal use of this space. Occupation of this area may reflect status differences within the house, and we explore that in the next section. We do not recognize any special activity areas other than perhaps small knapping areas on the east side of Block B and southwest portion of Block C.

Sociality

In a statistical analysis of lithic artifacts drawing data from all Housepit 54 floors, Prentiss and colleagues (2018b) argued that material wealth-based inequality between domestic groups could be recognized across the IIe through IIb floors. Data presented in that paper implicated Block D as the context whereby excess quantities of measurable material wealth could be detected. Spatial data developed in this study permit us to further examine that hypothesis. As discussed in Chapter 2, we assess spatial variation in lithic artifacts and faunal remains. Lithic-related measures include nonlocal raw material (jaspers and chalcedonies not found in the Bridge River Valley, along with all obsidian), prestige raw material (obsidian, nephrite, steatite, copper), and prestige or display objects (stone beads, pendants, stone and bone figurines, stone bowls, and all nephrite tools). The lithics distributions are also compared to distributions of valuable faunal items including canids and ungulates.

Canid remains are found in Blocks A, C, and D. Highest concentrations are found in the latter context (Supplemental Figure 3.18). In contrast, ungulate remains are distributed more evenly between all Blocks (Supplemental Figure 3.14), though low utility elements concentrate in Block D (Supplemental Figure 3.17). However, evidence for preparation and use of hunting and butchery tools is somewhat (though not exclusively) concentrated in Block D (Supplemental Figure 3.9). Nonlocal lithic raw materials are found in all blocks with highest concentrations in Blocks C and D (Supplemental Figure 3.19). Particularly high concentrations are present in Block D. Prestige raw materials concentrate heavily in Block D (Supplemental Figure 3.20), as do the somewhat rare prestige items (Supplemental Figure 3.20). Clustering in Block D of canid remains, hunting/butchering gear and relatively high proportions of ungulate remains, nonlocal materials, prestige materials, and prestige objects does imply that the occupants of this space maintained a comparatively higher investment in deer-hunting and use of dogs. Economic productivity in the subsistence realm appears to have aided this group in gaining somewhat more regular access to nonlocal materials, and clearly this group was the primary owners and users of prestige materials and objects.

Conclusions

Analyses of the spatial distributions of features, lithic artifacts, and faunal remains provided insight into occupation and abandonment cycles, organization of activity areas (site structure), and intergroup sociality during the occupation of the IIb floor. Stratum IIb features hearth-associated activity areas in each of the four blocks. The large grinding slab present on IIa is also present in IIb within Block B, and one cache pit was found on the western edge of Block A. Abandonment of IIb appears to have been planned following occupation cycles that included initiation and exploitation phases. This hypothesis is supported by the presence of limited roof deposits covering a portion of IIb and an assemblage of lithic tools and debitage reflecting production of tools associated with the full array of expected activities for an extended winter pithouse occupation. Abundant small and larger sized artifacts and faunal remains indicate that debris from the final winter's occupation was not cleaned prior to reflooring (IIa). Some items were left behind including the cache pit filled with cooking stones, while certain items were retained, for example, the Block B grinding slab.

Spatially, we recognize three occupation zones, a nearly empty central space, the hearth-based activity areas, and a probable bench zone, though the latter was not formally excavated. Each hearth area is associated with concentrations of lithic debitage, tools, and faunal remains. Comparison of assemblage variation between these areas suggests that all were multi-activity in nature and thus most likely the result of normal winter activities by domestic (family) groups (Prentiss et al. 2018b). Little evidence for gendered separation of activities was found, though hunting/butchering tools do concentrate along the eastern margin of Block D, raising the possibility of some likely male activities occurring in the bench zone adjacent to the hearth areas. No evidence of a side entrance was indicated. However, plenty of room in the center of the floor could accommodate a ladder associated with a roof entrance. The best-lit portions of the house (particularly Block D) do contain the highest densities of cultural materials and this distribution could reflect practicality. However, domestic groups also clearly occupied the other less well-lit zones, and given variation in distributions of hunting gear, canid remains, nonlocal materials, and prestige items and associated raw materials, control of best living spaces could reflect social standing of families within the house.

4

Persistence during the
Second Demographic Trough

Stratum IIc

Stratum IIc is in effect the middle floor within the five-floor sequence associated with Housepit 54 at its maximum size (Figure 4.1). Sediment composition of IIc is virtually identical with that of IIa and IIb with even representation of clay and silt combined in the range of 60–70% and predictably reduced percentages of sand, gravel, and pebbles. Stratum IIc is buried in all blocks by Stratum IIb sediments, indicating that the roof that had covered IIc was entirely removed without burning prior to the establishment of IIb floor sediments. Hearth features are found in Blocks B–D (Figure 4.2). Block A contains abundant domestic material including scattered fire-cracked rock (FCR), and it is possible that our excavation simply missed a small hearth placed on the margins of this area of the floor. Hearths in Blocks B and C are quite small, particularly in contrast to the two in Block D. The Block D hearths represent spatially extensive areas of burned floor sediment mixed with charcoal and FCR. Consequently, these features appear to have formed as the result of repeated cooking and heating focused actions in this portion of the house (cf. Chatters 1987). One deep bell-shaped cache pit is located in the northeast corner of Block D. Only one posthole is located in Block C. However, a group of small postholes at the north end of Block D potentially reflect the position of a wooden bench or platform. The large grinding slab evident in IIa and IIb in Block B was also in place during IIc. We now discuss evidence for occupation and abandonment, site structure, and sociality.

Occupation and Abandonment Cycle

Our first study of IIc data emphasizes occupation and abandonment cycles. We discuss archaeological expectations for variability in occupation and abandonment in Chapter 2 (Stratum IIa).

Occupation Cycle

Here we assess evidence for three phases of occupation including initiation, exploitation, and abandonment. Stratum IIc lithic tool distributions are very similar to those of IIb (Table 4.1). Heavy-duty woodworking is represented by adzes and possibly abraders. Working of small wood/bone/antler items is reflected in the relatively abundant presence of flake and key-shaped scrapers, pièces esquillées, and drills and perforators. Preparation for hunting is marked by abundant bifaces and projectile points. Hide-working is well represented by various hide scrapers and small piercers. Bipolar reduction reflects extension of raw material utility. Debitage data reflect a reduction focus on late stage tool retouch, followed respectively by biface and core reduction (Table 4.2). These data suggest that all occupation phases likely contributed to the formation of the IIc lithic assemblage.

Abandonment Process

Stratum IIc was not buried by a roof or midden but rather the next floor. Likewise, no intact architectural elements remain, implying that all were removed prior to the establishment of the next floor. These data collectively suggest

Stratum IIc

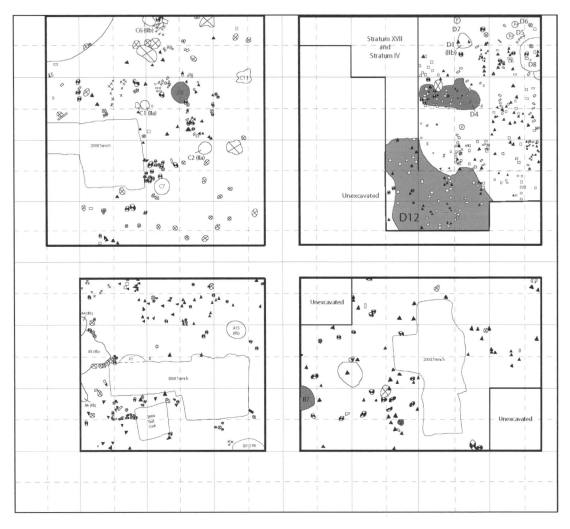

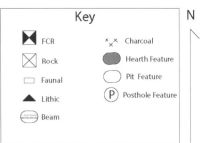

FIGURE 4.1. Comprehensive map of IIc showing point-provenienced artifacts, faunal remains, fire-cracked rock, prior excavations, and features.

Stratum IIc

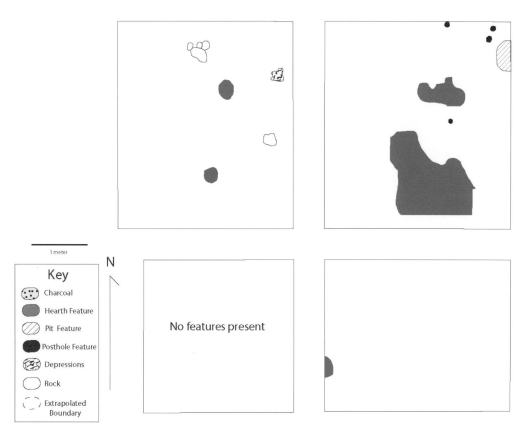

FIGURE 4.2. Features on IIc.

TABLE 4.1. Lithic Tools from IIc, Organized by Tool Class and Block.

	Tool Class																
	A	B	C	D	E	F	G	H	I	J	K	L	M	N	O	P	Q
Block A	2	2	4	4	3	2	1	2	0	0	1	0	5	0	0	1	0
Block B	2	3	2	4	1	2	2	2	0	0	1	0	5	1	0	4	1
Block C	0	0	4	2	4	0	1	1	0	0	2	0	2	6	2	1	0
Block D	7	3	10	7	11	3	1	6	0	2	1	4	7	2	0	14	3
Total	11	8	20	17	19	7	5	11	0	2	5	4	19	9	2	20	4

Note: A = flake and slate knives; B = bifaces; C = projectile points; D = flake and key-shaped scrapers; E = hide scrapers; F = drills and perforators; G = small piercers; H = pièces esquillées; I = notches and denticulates; J = adzes; K = abraders/groundstone; L = freehand cores; M = bipolar cores; N = slate objects; O = hammerstones; P = used flakes; Q = ritual/social items.

TABLE 4.2. Lithic Flake Types for Stratum IIc by Toolstone Category.

	Ext	Chal	Cher	Dac	Obs	Intr	Slates	Met.	Total
Biface	2	0	2	67	0	0	2	0	71
Core	0	1	0	24	0	1	3	1	27
Retouch	21	12	17	342	4	1	15	8	456

Note: Ext = extrusives (excluding dacite and obsidian); Cher = cherts; Dac = dacite; Chal = chalcedony; Obs = obsidian; Intr = intrusives plus gneiss; Slates = slate and silicified shale; Met = metamorphic rock inclusive of quartzites, nephrite, and steatite.

final abandonment of IIc was undertaken with the plan to return with reflooring and likely reroofing.

The next question concerns whether the IIc floor was cleaned before abandonment or if debris from the final winter was simply left in place in anticipation of reflooring. We can assess degree of cleanup by correlating smallest artifacts against all artifacts, assuming that in cleanup situations larger materials would be separated from smaller items missed during sweeping (Metcalf and Heath 1990). We calculated a correlation coefficient for smallest debitage versus all larger debitage returning a significant positive score ($r = 0.688$, $p = 0.000$). A similar calculation was made for smallest versus larger faunal remains ($r = 0.985$, $p = 0.000$). These results can be visualized on distribution maps of smallest debitage (Figure 4.3) versus all debitage (Figure 4.4) and smallest faunal remains (Figure 4.5) versus all faunal remains (Figure 4.6). Similar relationships are evident from the general point-plot map of all materials from IIc (Figure 4.1). These maps collectively demonstrate nearly identical distributions of materials of all sizes, suggesting in turn that no significant cleanup likely occurred prior to closeout of the IIc floor.

Block C contains a number of large cobbles and fire-cracked rock fragments that could be interpreted as positioning items, particularly given their placement surrounding a hearth feature. One item of site furniture, the Block B grinding slab (also used on IIa and IIb), was in use during IIc. Little evidence suggests the presence of de facto refuse in any of the blocks, though substantial numbers of discarded tools

and associated debitage are found throughout much of the IIc floor. Thus, all data considered, we can conclude that closing of the IIc floor was probably an orderly process by which final tools to be removed were manufactured and packed for removal and broken and exhausted items discarded but not removed from primary discard contexts. Some items that may have been useful, such as the large cobbles in Block C, were abandoned while IIb further buried the grinding slab in Block B so that its use could continue.

Site Structure

This section focuses on the structure of space on IIc. Inferences are drawn from study of lithic debitage, tools, and faunal remains using frames of reference outlined in Chapter 2 (Stratum IIa).

Debitage and Spatial Structure of Lithic Reduction

Debitage are found in concentrations largely associated with hearth features in all blocks (Supplemental Figure 4.1). One exception is in northern Block A where there is no hearth. A particularly dense concentration of debitage in central Block D is spatially positioned between two large hearth features. Core reduction flakes are found in each block, though they are particularly concentrated in Blocks C and D (Supplemental Figure 4.2). Biface thinning flakes are also found in each block but concentrate in Blocks A and C (Supplemental Figure 4.3). R-billet flakes are rare but associated with nearby hearths in Blocks A, C, and D (Supplemental Figure 4.4). Tool retouch flakes are found in significant numbers generally

IIc Extra-Small Debitage Distribution

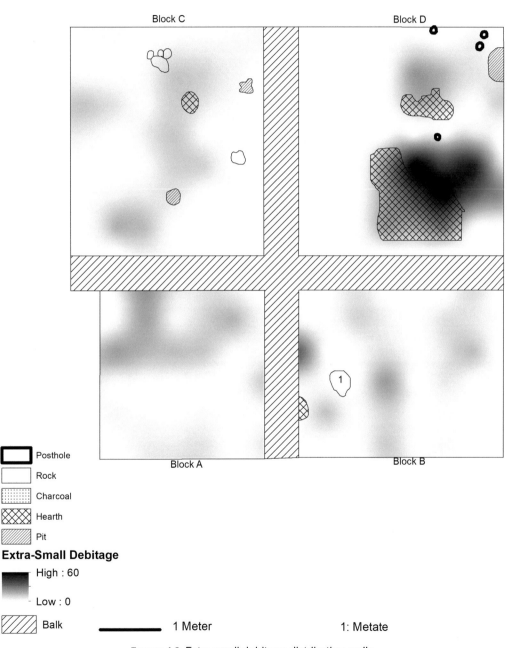

FIGURE 4.3. Extra-small debitage distribution on IIc.

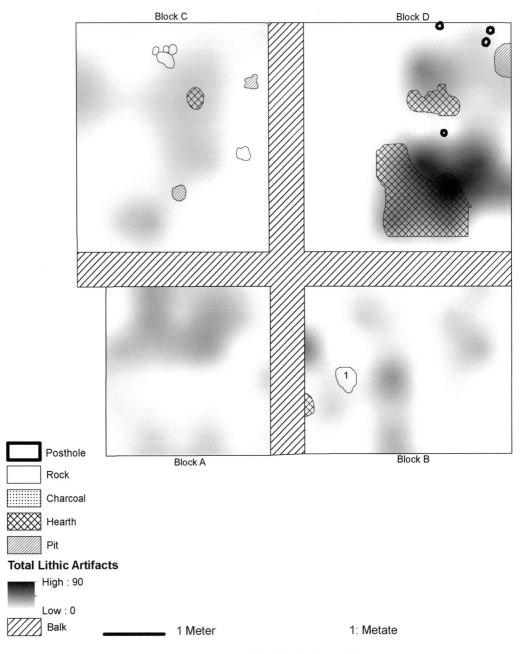

N

IIc Total Lithic Artifact Distribution

Block C

Block D

Block A

Block B

Posthole

Rock

Charcoal

Hearth

Pit

Total Lithic Artifacts

High : 90

Low : 0

Balk

1 Meter

1: Metate

FIGURE 4.4. Total artifact distribution on IIc.

IIc Faunal Specimens Sized 1-9mm

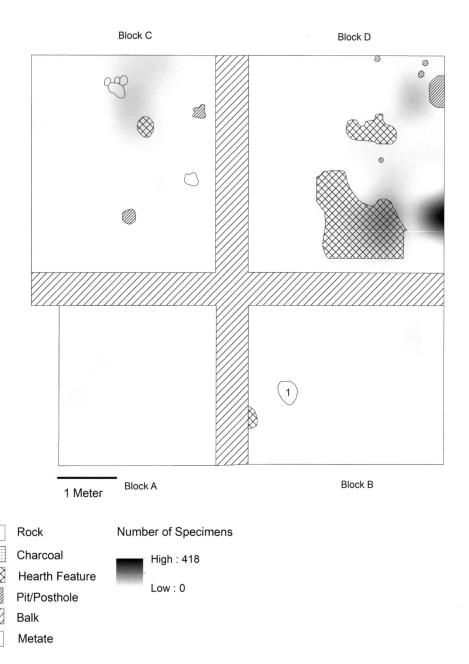

FIGURE 4.5. Extra-small faunal specimens on IIc.

IIc All Faunal Specimens

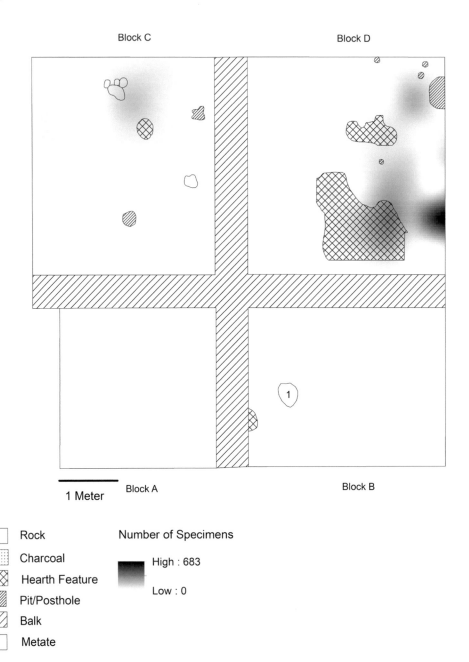

FIGURE 4.6. Total faunal specimen distribution on IIc.

surrounding hearths in Blocks B, C, and D (Supplemental Figure 4.5).

The concentration of retouch flakes in northern Block A raises the possibility that a hearth feature lies just outside of the excavation block, perhaps in the balk between Blocks A and C or to the west of A. Alternatively, northern Block A and southern Block C served as a special area for lithic reduction activities. This possibility is further supported by the extremely low frequencies of faunal remains in this context. Other than this portion of the floor, lithic reduction areas consistently concentrated around hearth features forming apparent drop zones on and adjacent to these features. The densest concentration of flakes developed in Block D. Given concentrations of flakes around hearths, the central portion of the house does not appear to have ever been a focus for lithic reduction activities. No evidence indicated that any single form of reduction was spatially segregated, and from the collective debitage data (Table 4.2) and the distribution maps, clearly the dominant form of reduction was tool retouch/maintenance, regardless of raw material type.

Lithic Tools and House Floor Activity Organization

In this section, we explore the distributions on knapping (cores and hammerstones), heavy-duty (wood/bone/antler working: flake scrapers, key-shaped scrapers, pièces esquillées, notches/denticulates, and drills/perforators), hunting/butchery (bifaces and projectile points), hide-working (hide scrapers and small piercers), and groundstone across the IIc floor. Knapping tools are distributed somewhat evenly through IIc and do not appear to be particularly associated with hearths, raising the possibility that they were often discarded away from hearth-based activity areas (Supplemental Figure 4.6). Heavy-duty tools are found in concentrations relatively close to hearth features in Blocks B through D (Supplemental Figure 4.7). Concentrations are also present in Block A despite the lack of hearth. Hunting/butchery tools occur around the hearths in Blocks B and C, on

the margins of Block A, and in significant concentrations in Block D in and adjacent to the large hearths (Supplemental Figure 4.8). Hide-working/sewing tools are distributed similarly to those of the hunting/butchery tools, with a small cluster in northern Block A and hearth associations in Blocks B through D (Supplemental Table 4.9). Groundstone tools are relatively rare on IIc with individual items found in about the center of each block (Supplemental Figure 4.10).

These data implicate a number of general patterns. As was the case with debitage, little evidence is indicated for regular use of the central portion of the floor, whereas hearths were consistently the focus of lithic tool discards. While heavy-duty, hunting/butchering, and hide-working/sewing tools were generally dropped around hearths and thus, drop zones, knapping and groundstone items were apparently not discarded or removed from direct hearth associated contexts, thus suggesting the practice of "toss zone" behavior (e.g., Binford 1978). Concentrations of heavy-duty, hunting/butchering, and hide-working/sewing tools in north-central Block A once again implicates either the hidden presence of a hearth (in the balk or to the west of the block) or the use of this space as a multiple-activity area. The large numbers of extra-small flakes in this space argue against accumulations here as simply dumps from cleaned-up work elsewhere. The co-association of diverse gear in drop and toss zones around the IIc floor suggests that, at least from the standpoint of tool discard and knapping, behavior gender may have played little role in the spatial organization of activities.

Faunal Remains and Spatial Organization

Distributions of faunal remains provide another source of insight into the organization of activities on IIc. While fish remains are found throughout IIc, they occur in very dense numbers in Block D and to a lesser degree in northern Block C (Supplemental Figure 4.11). The arrangement of mammals is very similar with very high densities in southeastern Block D overlapping with the dense fish remains (Supplemental

Figure 4.12). Faunal remains specific to ungulates also concentrate in one narrow space in southeast Block D with much lower numbers elsewhere (Supplemental Figure 4.13). Given the concentrations of mammals in Block D, not surprisingly high, medium, and low utility elements also concentrate in the same block along with limited numbers elsewhere (Supplemental Figures 4.14–4.16). Finally, canids are found in two concentrations, highest density in central Block D but another low-density area in western Block C (Supplemental Table 4.17).

Spatially faunal processing clearly occurred around hearth features, particularly those of northern Block C and central and southern Block D. As with lithics, the central portion of the house does not appear to have been a regular place for preparing food or tools from animals. Many concentrations of faunal remains are in drop zone contexts immediately adjacent to hearths, also much like the lithic tools and debitage. The concentrations of ungulate and canid remains are slightly removed from the Block D hearths suggesting the possibility that these were preferentially discarded or removed to that position. This location suggests that these larger items could have been placed in a specific dump or that their discard is consistent with the characteristics of a toss zone (Binford 1978).

The concentrations of faunal remains in Blocks C and D clearly indicate the presence of domestic groups in these areas. The hearth-associated activity area in western Block B and eastern Block A also implicate a domestic group. Another is possibly present in northern Block A/southern Block C despite the lack of hearth. However, the low numbers of faunal remains in the latter areas as compared to the former spaces suggests that the numbers of persons using the spaces in Blocks A and B were limited and/or their time in those spaces was comparatively short. Prentiss and colleagues (2018a) argue that the IIc floor occupation was a time when the house's population took a significant dip during the onset of the village-wide Malthusian ceiling associated with subsistence stress. Brief and/or limited occupation of the southerly and least preferred portions of Housepit 54 could reflect this drop in population.

Summary: Site Structure on the IIc Floor

All spatial data from the IIc floor point to a common pattern. The central portion of the floor appears to have been rarely used for any work generating significant quantities of discarded materials. Neither did the center of the house serve as a dump for messy materials (e.g., bones) or as a toft for unwanted gear before or during abandonment. Surrounding the central portion of the floor are four activity areas, three of which include hearth features. Those three include diverse debitage and lithic tools that are co-associated with faunal remains representing fish and mammals. Thus these zones can be interpreted as workspaces for domestic groups (families) inhabiting these portions of the floor.

A fourth activity area, located in northern Block A and south Block C also contains relatively abundant and diverse lithic artifacts, though faunal remains are comparatively limited and no hearth feature is present. As noted previously, this area could reflect another multi-activity domestic space where we simply have not yet found the hearth. Alternatively, it could also be a designated area for diverse activities centered on manufacture and maintenance of lithic tools and activities requiring use of tools designed for butchery, wood/bone/antler working, and sewing/hide preparation. The hearth zone was likely surrounded by a bench zone under the outer portion of the sloping roof. However, excavations did not permit this hypothesis to be verified and distributions of artifacts do not show clusters of items placed around the margins of the house. A group of small postholes in northern Block D does appear to reflect the presence of a bench or platform-like structure on the floor margin.

Finally, the stark contrast between higher density cultural materials in Blocks C and D and the lower counts, particularly in faunal remains along with small hearth features in Blocks A and B, raises the possibility that occupation of this space was either briefer or smaller in population. The distribution of cultural materials from IIc also reflects decisions regarding several contingencies. First, the semi-empty central space would have been optimal for a ladder connecting to a rooftop entrance. If this were the case, then we could expect such a space to have been kept largely free of debris. Second, higher densities of cultural materials at the north end of the house might reflect preferential occupation in this space by long-term residents seeking optimal lighting. Finally, one space on the west central side of the house possibly was set aside for messy work activities though this usage is not fully confirmed, as it may also have simply been another diverse activity domestic space.

Sociality

A pattern of material wealth-based inequality was recognized in a statistical analysis of lithic artifacts from all floors in Housepit 54 (Prentiss et al. 2018b). The latter study focused on distributions of nonlocal raw materials (jaspers and chalcedonies not found in the Bridge River Valley along with all obsidian), prestige raw material (obsidian, nephrite, steatite, copper), and prestige or display objects (stone beads, pendants, stone and bone figurines, stone bowls, and all nephrite tools). Here we compare spatial distributions of these items to those of canids and ungulates, recognizing that successful household subsistence economies could translate into opportunities for production and exchange of valuable goods.

Canid remains occur in clusters within Blocks C and D. The cluster within northern Block D is of much greater density than elsewhere (Supplemental Figure 2.17). Immediately to the south of this area (still Block D) is a similarly dense cluster of ungulate remains (Supplemental Figure 2.13). Clearly, Block D inhabitants routinely gained access to high quality meat resources at greater frequencies than did those elsewhere in the house. Nonlocal lithic raw materials occur in multiple clusters scattered throughout Blocks A, C, and D (Supplemental Figure 4.18). In contrast, relatively little evidence for use of these sources is found in Block B.

Despite the disparity between the Block B materials and those elsewhere, little evidence suggests that the Block D group maintained a lock on access to valuable nonlocal materials. In slight contrast, Block D does include the highest frequencies of prestige raw materials and items (Supplemental Figures 4.19 and 4.20). Thus, while distributions of nonlocal materials do not reflect inequality, all other measures support a distinct difference between the subsistence economies and ability to accumulate valuable stone materials and objects in Block D versus other likely occupants of the IIc floor.

Conclusions

Stratum IIc was established and occupied during a population low during the cycle of final BR3 period floors at Housepit 54. While at least three domestic activity areas have been identified, only one (Block D) appears to have been intensely occupied. To summarize, the central portion of the floor was largely open space and may have provided space for an egress ladder. Surrounding hearth-centered activity areas were probably occupied by domestic (family) groups, though one activity area lacking a hearth could have been a designated space for a variety of uses. Assessment of occupation phases suggests that expectations for initiation are largely met, though there is limited evidence for large-scale woodworking as might be reflected in discarded adzes. Evidence for exploitation phase is abundantly present given the diverse array of activities represented in the hearth-centered areas. Abandonment appears to have been planned with anticipated return associated with reflooring as indicated by removal of architectural elements (i.e., house posts), abandonment of exhausted and broken tools, limited evidence for cleaning, and maintenance of site furniture.

Hearth zones were clearly multiactivity spaces and little evidence indicates special designated spaces for any specific activity. Thus, traditional male and female activities do not appear to have been segregated to any significant degree. Evidence from distributions of canids, ungulates, prestige goods, and to a lesser degree, nonlocal raw materials does support a pattern of material wealth-based distinctions between occupants of the Block D area and those living elsewhere on the floor. This finding supports arguments by Prentiss and colleagues (2018b) that a pattern of inequality measured in accumulations of material goods developed in the final floors of Housepit 54 during the BR3 period.

5

Social Complexity Continues

Stratum IId

Stratum IId is the second established floor in Housepit 54 at its maximum size (Figure 5.1). IId sediments are dominated by clay at up to 70% with the exception of Block D where clay content is generally equal to or slightly less than that of silt. IId sediments in all blocks have typically lower percentages of sand, gravel, and pebbles. Stratum IId is partially buried in Block A by a very thin roof termed Vb, whose sediments are only evident in the western and southern portions of the block (Supplemental Figure 5.1). IId is buried throughout the rest of Block A and all of Blocks B–D. Hearths are found in Blocks A, C, and D (Figure 5.2). Evidence suggests an activity area surrounding the large grinding stone in Block B, though no hearth was located during excavations. IId is the initial resting place of that stone that persists as site furniture through all floors up to IIa.

Two hearths are worth further comment. One hearth in the northern portion of Block C (Feature C15 [2013]) takes a linear path oriented roughly parallel to the wall of the house. The feature contains abundant charcoal including still intact but highly charred timbers. This feature does not appear to serve a clear function other than light and warmth or for open-air roasting of meat. Another large hearth was excavated in Block D on IId. Similar to those of IIc, this feature likely reflects repeated use. One deep cache pit was located in the southeastern portion of Block D, and another shallow pit-depression was excavated in the northeast corner of the same block. We explore occupation and abandonment cycles, site structure, and sociality in the next sections.

Occupation and Abandonment Cycle

In this section, we examine occupation and abandonment cycles drawing on frames of reference outlined in Chapter 2 (Stratum IIa).

Occupation Cycle

The three possible occupation phases are initiation, exploitation, and abandonment. We provide archaeological expectations for each in Chapter 2 (Stratum IIa).

All tool classes are represented on IId, many of which are more abundant than was evident on IIa–IIc (Table 5.1). Tools reflect investments in heavy- (e.g., adzes) and light-duty wood/bone/antler working (flake and key shape scrapers, pièces esquillées, notches and denticulates) such that we can infer the possibilities for work on both architectural elements and smaller tool forms. Bifaces and projectile points are common, particularly in Block D, suggesting activities associated with hunting. Frequent hide scrapers and small piercers may also reflect hunting activities (or trade for hides). Bipolar cores are extremely abundant and, as on other floors, likely indicate a need to extend use-life of lithic raw material during the exploitation and abandonment phase. Lithic debitage reflect a focus on late stage tool retouch, followed to progressively lesser degrees by biface and core

Stratum IId

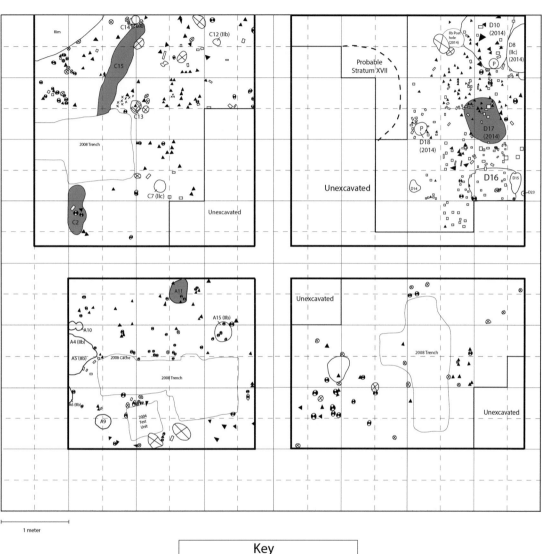

FIGURE 5.1. Comprehensive map of IId showing point-provenienced artifacts, faunal remains, fire-cracked rock, prior excavations, and features.

Stratum IId

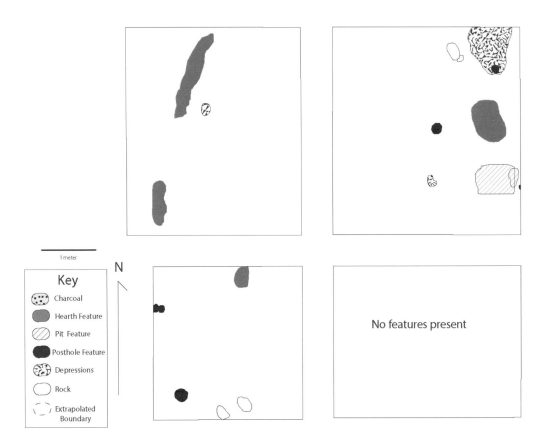

FIGURE 5.2. Features on IId.

TABLE 5.1. Lithic Tools from IId, Organized by Tool Class and Block.

	Tool Classes																
	A	**B**	**C**	**D**	**E**	**F**	**G**	**H**	**I**	**J**	**K**	**L**	**M**	**N**	**O**	**P**	**Q**
Block A	1	1	1	3	0	1	0	1	0	0	0	0	3	2	0	0	0
Block B	4	0	1	3	3	0	0	2	0	0	2	0	2	1	0	2	1
Block C	3	0	7	6	7	2	0	4	1	1	4	1	14	2	0	3	2
Block D	7	5	10	8	12	2	2	3	4	1	4	0	19	0	1	21	5
Total	15	6	19	20	22	5	2	10	5	2	10	1	38	5	1	26	8

Note: A = flake and slate knives; B = bifaces; C = projectile points; D = flake and key-shaped scrapers; E = hide scrapers; F = drills and perforators; G = small piercers; H = pièces esquillées; I = notches and denticulates; J = adzes; K = abraders/groundstone; L = freehand cores; M = bipolar cores; N = slate objects; O = hammerstones; P = used flakes; Q = ritual/social items.

TABLE 5.2. Lithic Flake Types for Stratum IId by Toolstone Category.

	Ext	Chal	Cher	Dac	Obs	Intr	Slates	Met.	Total
Biface	2	0	2	67	0	0	2	0	73
Core	0	1	0	24	0	1	3	1	30
Retouch	21	12	17	342	4	1	15	8	420

Note: Ext = extrusives (excluding dacite and obsidian); Dac = dacite; Cher = cherts; Chal = chalcedony; Obs = obsidian; Intr = intrusives plus gneiss; Slates = slate and silicified shale; Met = metamorphic rock inclusive of quartzites, nephrite, and steatite.

reduction (Table 5.2). Thus, we conclude that IId likely reflects initiation, exploitation, and abandonment phases of occupation.

Abandonment Process

Stratum IId was buried by a small portion of a roof and otherwise by the IIc floor. No intact architectural elements (e.g., wood remaining in postholes) were found. The presence of a very limited roof remnant indicates to us that the bulk of the roof was removed without burning, leaving only a small portion remaining to be burnt and collapsed on to the floor. As with the Vb1 roof over IIb in Block B, the logic behind a partial roof burn is difficult to define though from a practical standpoint we can again point to insect infestations and wood rot. We recognize, however, the possibility of a ritual element that is very challenging to define. All in all, these data suggest to us that the IId abandonment was planned and completed with the intent to return.

Abandonment process can be further assessed through a consideration of cleanup relationships between smallest artifacts and faunal remains and all larger items (e.g., Metcalf and Heath 1990). We accomplish this analysis using a statistical test and a visual assessment of distributions across the IId floor. Extra-small debitage distributions match nearly perfectly that of the total artifact assemblage (Figures 5.3 and 5.4), and this finding is backed by a strongly significant correlation coefficient ($r = 0.933$, $p = 0.000$) for spatial co-associations between extra-small debitage and larger debitage. Extra-small faunal items also demonstrate a similarly strong spatial correlation with larger faunal items as indicated by plotted distributions on maps (Figures 5.5. and 5.6) and statistical results ($r = 0.925$, $p = 0.000$).

We can gain additional insight from an examination of distributions of materials that could be classified as positioning items (Binford 1979), caches (Binford 1979; Hayden and Deal 1983), site furniture (Binford 1979), and de facto refuse (Schiffer 1972; Stevenson 1982). The IId floor includes significant quantities of cultural materials, though none appear to meet the criteria to be classified as positioning items. Caching behavior is evidenced in the form of a shallow pit excavated into the cache pit (Feature D15 [2016]) in the southeast corner of Block D. Within this pit, other finds included two pressure flakers on deer antler tines, an antler billet, and two pieces of chipped slate. These items appear to constitute a stone knapper's tool kit, either retired or set aside for later use and never retrieved. The large grinding stone recognized on floors IIa–IIc rests on IId and thus apparently began its long use-life during this time. This item is the only one that can be classified as site furniture. No obvious evidence for de facto refuse has been found.

Site Structure

A central focus of this study concerns variation in use of space on house floors. In this section, we review data associated with lithic debitage, tools, and faunal remains using frames of reference provided in Chapter 2 (Stratum IIa).

Debitage and Spatial Structure of Lithic Reduction

Debitage are found in all blocks with concentrations associated with hearths in Blocks A, C, and D (Supplemental Figure 5.2). An additional thin concentration of flakes is also found close to the grinding stone in Block B. Core reduction flakes concentrate close to hearths in Blocks C

IId Extra-Small Debitage Distribution

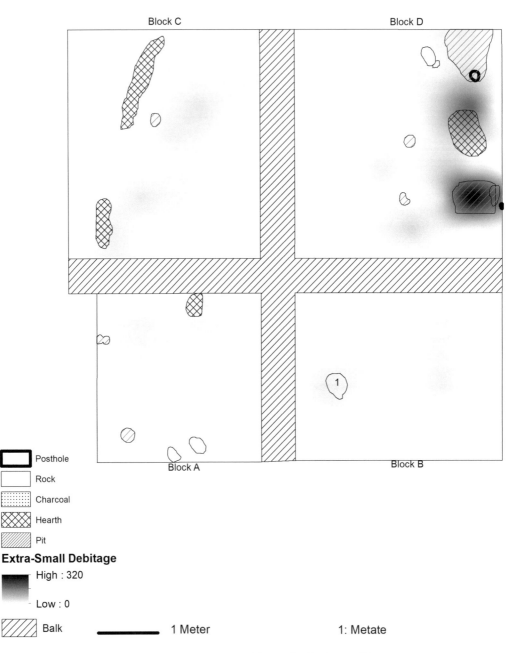

FIGURE 5.3. Extra-small debitage distribution on IId.

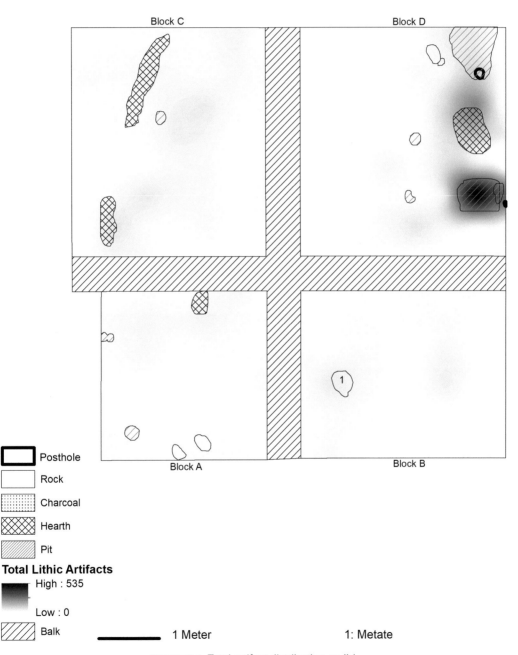

FIGURE 5.4. Total artifact distribution on IId.

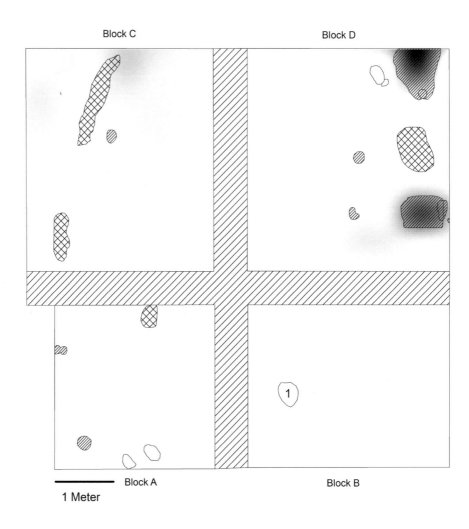

IId Faunal Specimens Sized 1-9mm

Block C   Block D

Block A   Block B

1 Meter

Rock

Charcoal

Hearth Feature

Pit/Posthole

Balk

1 Metate

Number of Specimens

High : 379

Low : 0

FIGURE 5.5. Extra-small faunal specimens on IId.

IId All Faunal Specimens

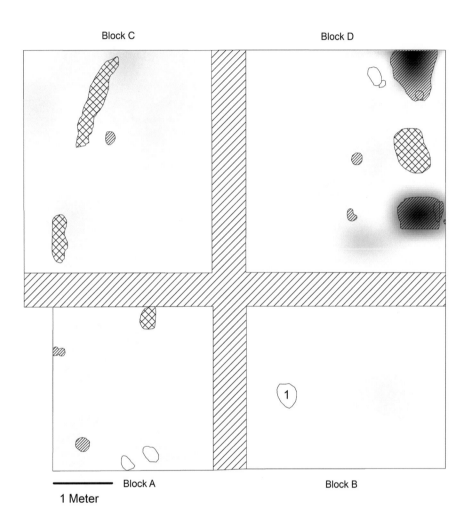

Block C   Block D

Block A   Block B

1 Meter

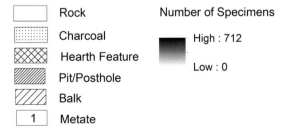

	Rock
	Charcoal
	Hearth Feature
	Pit/Posthole
	Balk
1	Metate

Number of Specimens

High : 712

Low : 0

FIGURE 5.6. Total faunal specimen distribution on IId.

and D (Supplemental Figure 5.3). Biface thinning flakes are found in all blocks and, like core reduction flakes, are most common in Block D, though substantial number do occur in Block C (Supplemental Figure 5.4). R-billet flakes are distributed in similar contexts to those of thinning flakes likewise clustering near features, with higher counts in Blocks C and D (Supplemental Figure 5.5). Small retouch flakes are found throughout all blocks and are most dense in Blocks A, C, and D (Supplemental Figure 5.6).

From these data, lithic reduction activities occurred throughout the IId floor. Block D clearly received the most concentrated work, but hearth-associated reduction areas are present in Blocks A and C as well. Debitage concentrations in Block B are associated to some degree with a large grinding slab, but no hearth feature has been identified during the excavations. Thus, a small hearth existed outside the boundaries of the excavation, this lithic reduction area is not associated with a hearth feature. Further excavations may be required to determine if activity areas exist in the center of the house. However, current data suggest that other than small retouch flakes, most lithic reduction clustered in and around hearths, cache pits, and site furniture.

Lithic Tools and House Floor Activity Organization

In this section, we explore the distributions on knapping (cores and hammerstones), heavy-duty (wood/bone/antler working: flake scrapers, key-shaped scrapers, pièces esquillées, notches/denticulates, and drills/perforators), hunting/butchery (bifaces and projectile points), hide-working (hide scrapers and small piercers), and groundstone on the IId floor. Knapping tools are clustered around the hearth in the northern part of Block C and also associated with the hearth and pit features of the east side of Block D. A thin scatter of additional items is found in Blocks A and B (Supplemental Figure 5.7). Heavy-duty application tools are found in an approximate ring between empty space at the center of the house and the ring of

features and site furniture closer to the margins of the house floor (Supplemental Figure 5.8). The consistency of this discard pattern (at least in Blocks B–D) raises the possibility that the inner side of hearths provided the best space for work of this nature. Although slightly lower in absolute numbers, the distribution of hunting/butchering tools nearly replicates that of heavy-duty tools, further implicating the interior space around hearths and site furniture as good work areas (Supplemental Figure 5.9). Hide-working and sewing tools are distributed in a duel pattern such that the Block C group replicates those of heavy-duty and hunting/butchering tools (Supplemental Figure 5.10).

In contrast, hide-working and sewing tools are found on features or on the wall-sides of features in Blocks B and D. A virtually identical pattern is evident for groundstone tools (Supplemental Figure 5.11). This placement raises the possibility that within Blocks B and D, traditional men's (heavy-duty and hunting/butchering) and women's (hide-working, sewing, and groundstone applications) were kept largely separate, men working toward the center of the house and women busy around the wall-sides of features. Block A has limited numbers of tools and lacks a distinctive pattern. Block C has abundant tools, and in this area, traditional men and women's activities appear to have substantially overlapped. If these patterns represent social dynamics, then these blocks suggest either different gender dynamics or diverging conceptions for the proper organization of workspace. Regardless, the direct center of the house was not generally used for activities leading to discard of stone tools.

Faunal Remains and Spatial Organization

Faunal remains provide a variety of further insights regarding spatial organization of the IId floor. Fish bones are found throughout the IId floor, but concentrations are recognizable in Blocks B, C, and D (Supplemental Figure 5.12). A thin cluster is found in the center of Block B, east of the grinding slab. Fish remains are also found clustered around the long hearth at the north end of Block C. Finally, they occur in particularly dense concentrations associated with the pits of the northeast and southeast corners of Block D that also happen to be the north and south sides of a large hearth feature. Thus, with the exception of the Block B cluster, fish remains tend to be found in kitchen zones of IId. A rare cluster of avian remains is found south of the Block D hearth on and in the sediments of an associated cache pit (Supplemental Figure 5.13). Mammalian remains are found throughout IId and tend to cluster around in a number of spaces (Supplemental Figure 5.14). A small cluster is found in the southwest corner of Block A, and similar to fish remains, a thin cluster occurs in the center of Block B. Mammalian remains are clustered on both sides of the long hearth in northern Block C. Finally, they are most densely concentrated on and in the cache pit feature at the southeast corner of Block D and, to a lesser degree, in the northeast corner. The majority of mammal remains are likely ungulates and thus it is no surprise that the distribution of ungulates substantially replicates that of mammals (Supplemental Figure 5.15).

High utility elements cluster in the southeast corner of Block D and to a less degree at the north end of the long hearth in Block C (Supplemental Figure 5.16). Medium utility elements are found in a series of clusters including central Block B; southwest, west-central and north-central Block C; and northeast and southeast Block D (Supplemental Figure 5.17). Low utility elements are also most concentrated in southeast Block D, which appears to be a major context for meat-processing (Supplemental Figure 5.18). However, low utility elements also appear in north-central Block C and southeastern Block A. Overall the pattern of discard for all ungulate elements is associated with features found in regular concentrations around and on both hearths and cache pits. Little evidence indicates faunal discard immediately around the grinding slab in Block B, though a thin concentration of ungulate remains occurs about one meter to the east. Curiously, canid specimens cluster in northwestern Block A and are not found in Block D (Supplemental Figure 5.19). Considering all faunal remains, a highly

consistent pattern of hearth and pit associations is present, thus implying discard of these items in directly kitchen contexts.

Summary: Site Structure on the IId Floor

While portions of the central IId floor remain unexcavated, data are adequate to recognize a consistent pattern of hearth-associated activity areas. Debitage distributions in hearth areas focused on core reduction and biface thinning. Tool maintenance as reflected in small retouch flakes was likely practiced throughout the house. Tool distributions also clustered around hearths though with some interesting variation. Traditionally male activities of heavy-duty (wood, bone, and antler working) and hunting/butchery-related work consistently occurred on the interior side of hearths and site furniture (grinding slab in Block B). Traditionally female activities of hide-work/sewing and groundstone applications (e.g., food preparation and tool manufacture, such as needles, awls, and other items) occurred on the wall sides of hearths. Subsistence-related activities involving fish and mammals happened around hearths, though not clustered on either wall or interior sides. No direct evidence indicates a bench zone. However, given the density of materials implying diverse activities across the floor, such a zone likely existed for sleeping and storage perhaps on the rim top above the floor and under the outer perimeter of a low sloping roof.

Thus, we conclude that activities were likely structured along the lines of three concentric zones: center, hearth, and bench/periphery. Consistency in the diversity of tools (Prentiss et al. 2018b) and faunal remains between all blocks implies four domestic units on IId. This conclusion is strongly supported for Blocks A, C, and D where hearth features are found with associated hearth-centered activity areas. Block B contains assemblages of debitage, tools, and faunal remains similar to the other blocks but lacks a central hearth. It is therefore unclear whether the Block B space was simply a multi-activity zone for the house or if we simply missed a small hearth just beyond the boundaries of the block. The likely empty space in the center of the house may have provided room for an entrance ladder. By the same logic, the east side of Block B was largely devoid of significant numbers of items, and thus it too could have provided space for an entrance, perhaps from the side. We do not, however, have independent evidence for a side entrance in this space. Distributions of artifacts suggest that, like other floors, the north end of the house was favored for intensive household activities, perhaps due to better light. Other families also occupied less well-lit portions of the house, for example in Block A and possibly Block B.

Sociality

A comprehensive study of inter-floor variability in tool and debitage assemblages from Housepit 54 demonstrated that a pattern of material wealth-based social distinction appears to have developed on the IIe floor and persisted to IIb (Prentiss et al. 2018b). Here we examine the spatial distributions of possible wealth-related items including nonlocal lithic materials, prestige-related raw materials, and prestige-related formed items. We compare these distributions to those of canids and ungulates, which could also help reflect variation in economic wherewithal of families living on IId.

Nonlocal raw materials cluster tightly around hearths and site furniture. Within these distributions, the highest density by far occurred in east-central Block D (Supplemental Figure 5.20). Prestige raw materials are found in Blocks B, C, and D with highest concentrations also in Block D (Supplemental Figure 5.21). Finally, prestige items are found in Blocks C and D but with highest numbers once again in Block D (Supplemental Figure 5.22). Paralleling these artifact distributions, ungulate remains are also most common in Block D (Supplemental Figure 5.15). Differing from floors IIb and IIc, canid remains are primarily found in Block A (Supplemental Figure 5.19). Thus, with the exception of dog remains (which are very sparse in general), all other items suggest that the pattern of differential material wealth persisted on the IId floor with greatest wealth clearly concentrated in Block D, as we also recognized on floors IIb and IIc. Also possibly significant, the only cache pit on IId was in the southeast corner of Block D.

Conclusions

Stratum IId represents the second floor created within the large oval house stage in the history of Housepit 54. The large lithic artifact assemblage provides evidence that the house was occupied across the full range of cycles inclusive of initiation, exploitation, and abandonment. The abandonment was clearly planned with anticipated return as supported by several lines of evidence. A large item of site furniture (grinding slab) was not removed but partially covered by the next floor (IIc). Refuse was not cleaned but left *in situ* reflecting a series of hearth-centered activity areas. One tool cache was buried and abandoned. Given its context within a cache pit, recycled as a refuse pit, this assemblage discarding appears to have been the result of a purposeful action to either hide or otherwise take these items out of circulation. No obvious de facto refuse was noted. Finally, the IId floor was buried in part by a thin, burned roof deposit and elsewhere by the IIc floor.

Site structural studies permitted several conclusions regarding the likely organization of work on IId. Multiple activities were organized around the four hearths and the site furniture item, supporting the multiple zone model (empty center, hearth ring, and outer bench ring). Some evidence for possible gendered workspace was present in the form of select male activities on the interior sides of hearths and site furniture and select female activities on the wall sides. Block D remained a space that appears to have been in use by a domestic group with better connections for access to nonlocal raw materials, prestige goods, and ungulates than those living elsewhere in the house.

The Demographic Peak and Emergence
of Social Complexity

Stratum IIe

Stratum IIe is the first of the series of floors representing Housepit 54 at its maximum size (Figure 6.1). Sediments from IIe contain consistently higher percentages of clay than those of later floors. Clay content ranges from 40% to 60%, followed by silt varying in the 10–30% range, and dramatically lower percentages of sand, gravel, and pebbles. Stratum IIe is partially buried by a thin roof deposit (Vb3) in Block B and otherwise is entirely covered with IId sediments. The Vb3 roof contains oxidized sediment, abundant charcoal, and frequent fire-cracked rock (Supplemental Figure 6.1). It also includes a patch of densely packed possibly woven branches near the south wall of Block B. As was the case in some other sparse roof deposits including Vb and Vb1, this roof appears to have been only a remnant of a much larger roof that was likely cleared prior to burning of the Block B portion and subsequent establishment of the IId floor.

Stratum IIe includes 11 hearth features scattered throughout each block (Figure 6.2). Block A has two very small hearth-like features in its southwest corner. Two hearths are found in Block B, one of which is large though shallow and caps a very large cache pit. The other Block B hearth is a deep cylindrical roasting pit. Block C includes two relatively large hearths, spaced closely together in the northeast corner. Block D has a complex arrangement of five hearth features. Three of these cap cache pits

on the IIe floor, and another is impacted by a IId cache pit. The southernmost of the Block D hearths is also surrounded by an arrangement of postholes. Postholes are otherwise uncommon on IIe with an additional exception of a cluster in the approximate center of Block B and two others in central Block D. A final Block D hearth is located in the southwestern portion of the block and appears to represent an expansive roasting oven.

Stratum IIe also contains six large cache pits and an additional possible cache pit. Cache pits in Block B are arranged in a semicircle and range from 1 to 1.5 m in diameter with similar depths. Two additional cache pits are found in the south and central portions of Block D. Prentiss and colleagues (2018a) project that IIe held the highest number of occupants in the history of Housepit 54. This increase in population could partially explain the investment in cache pits and hearth features. However, extra-storage space and specialized cooking facilities also possibly might be linked to production of food to serve social goals as in feasting. The following discussions focus on occupation and abandonment, site structure, and sociality.

Occupation and Abandonment Cycle

Here we consider occupation and abandonment cycles, making use of frames of reference provided in Chapter 2 (Stratum IIa).

Stratum IIe

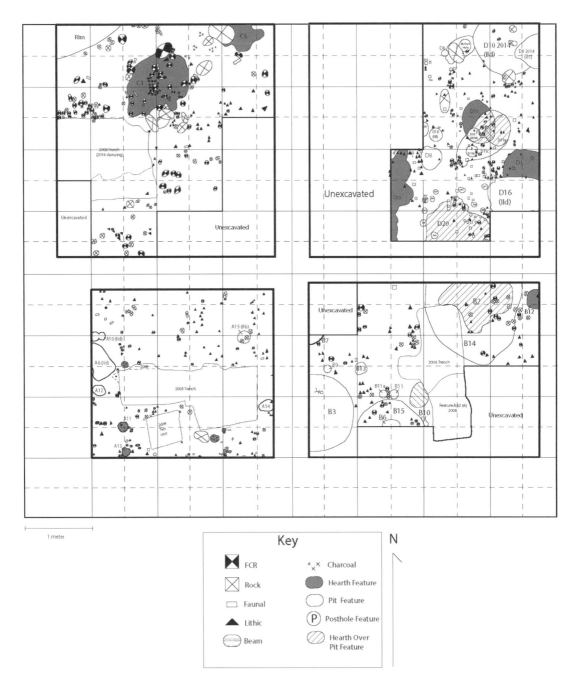

FIGURE 6.1. Comprehensive map of IIe showing point-provenienced artifacts, faunal remains, fire-cracked rock, prior excavations, and features.

Stratum IIe

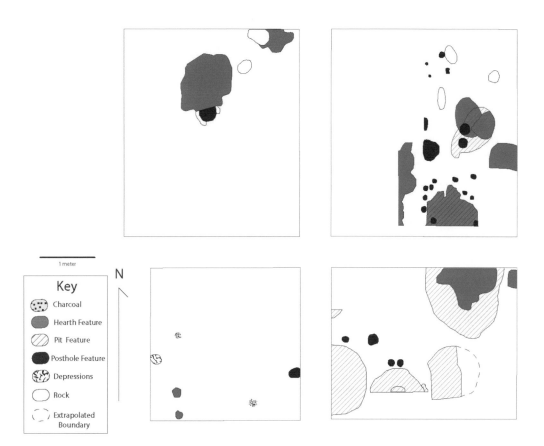

FIGURE 6.2. Features on IIe.

Occupation Cycle

We expect three possible occupation phases termed initiation, exploitation, and abandonment. Archaeological expectations for each are outlined in Chapter 2 (Stratum IIa).

The lithic tool distribution from IIe (Table 6.1) is relatively similar to those of IIa–IId. One major difference is a lack of adzes necessary for house refurbishing. This absence is curious given that IIe was likely associated with major expansion and reconstruction of Housepit 54 from a smaller rectangular shape to the large oval shape of the final floor sequence. Given the intensity of occupations during the IIe cycle, it is entirely possible that indicators of the initiation

phase were substantially obliterated as extremely abundant evidence supports exploitation and abandonment phases. Small wood/bone/antler working tools (flake scrapers, key-shaped scrapers, notches and denticulates, pièces esquillées, drills, and perforators) are highly abundant as are hide-working implements (hide scrapers of all kinds and small piercers). Probable hunting gear also is common (bifaces and especially projectile points). Finally, bipolar cores are highly abundant likely reflecting intensive salvaging of lithic toolstone flakes from otherwise exhausted nodules (including discarded lithic tools). Debitage data suggest that late stage tool retouch is most frequent, followed by biface and

TABLE 6.1. Lithic Tools from IIe, Organized by Tool Class and Block.

	Tool Classes																
	A	B	C	D	E	F	G	H	I	J	K	L	M	N	O	P	Q
Block A	0	0	5	1	3	0	2	0	0	0	1	0	7	0	0	0	0
Block B	1	3	3	5	8	1	1	1	0	0	1	1	5	1	2	9	4
Block C	3	4	7	2	9	4	2	3	2	0	3	1	7	1	1	9	5
Block D	8	5	3	8	6	2	3	2	4	0	7	0	13	0	2	18	2
Total	12	12	18	16	26	7	8	6	6	0	12	2	32	2	5	36	11

Note: A = flake and slate knives; B = bifaces; C = projectile points; D = flake and key-shaped scrapers; E = hide scrapers; F = drills and perforators; G = small piercers; H = pièces esquillées; I = notches and denticulates; J = adzes; K = abraders/groundstone; L = freehand cores; M = bipolar cores; N = slate objects; O = hammerstones; P = used flakes; Q = ritual/social items.

TABLE 6.2. Lithic Flake Types for Stratum IIe by Toolstone Category.

	Ext	Chal	Cher	Dac	Obs	Intr	Slates	Met.	Total
Biface	1	2	2	59	0	1	0	0	65
Core	7	2	1	29	0	4	5	2	50
Retouch	11	5	13	241	1	1	20	9	310

Note: Ext = extrusives (excluding dacite and obsidian); Dac = dacite; Cher = cherts; Chal = chalcedony; Obs = obsidian; Intr = intrusives plus gneiss; Slates = slate and silicified shale; Met = metamorphic rock inclusive of quartzites, nephrite, and steatite.

core reduction (Table 6.2). We conclude that all phases of occupation are likely represented in these data.

Abandonment Process

Stratum IIe was buried by a spatially limited roof deposit and otherwise was entirely covered by the IId floor. One posthole in Block D contained wood from a house-post. Nearly all other postholes were small and located in clusters, reflecting a greater likelihood that they were associated with house furniture or features that could have included cooking stands (e.g., tripods) over hearths (the Block D cluster surrounding the D20[2016] hearth) and supports for benches and cache pit covers (the postholes in central Block B). The fact that IIe is entirely buried by IId sediments makes it very clear that abandonment of IIe was predicated upon intent to return and refurbish the house.

We can also examine abandonment process from the standpoint of cleanup by exploring relationships between smallest artifacts and faunal remains and all larger items (e.g., Metcalf and Heath 1990). We address this analysis by using a statistical test and a visual examination of data from the IIe floor. Extra-small debitage are distributed in a parallel manner to that of larger artifacts (Figures 6.3 and 6.4), and we can confirm that with a significant correlation coefficient between extra-small and all larger flakes ($r = 0.828$, $p = 0.000$). Extra-small faunal items are similarly distributed in relation to larger faunal remains, as illustrated in Figures 6.5 and 6.6 and confirmed with statistical results ($r = 0.993$, $p = 0.000$).

We can gain additional insight from an examination of distributions of materials that could be classified as positioning items (Binford 1979), caches (Binford 1979; Hayden and Deal 1983), site furniture (Binford 1979), and de facto refuse (Schiffer 1972; Stevenson 1982). Stratum IIe is a complex floor in which an earliest period favored creation and use of multiple deep cache pits that were subsequently filled and used as surfaces for hearths, at least by the time of the final season of occupation. Upon abandonment of the floor and before replacement with IId, it

Ile Extra-Small Debitage Distribution

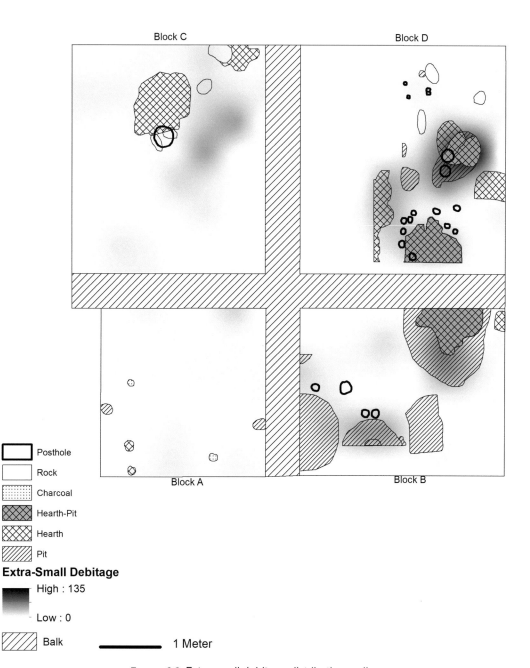

FIGURE 6.3. Extra-small debitage distribution on Ile.

N

Ile Total Lithic Distribution

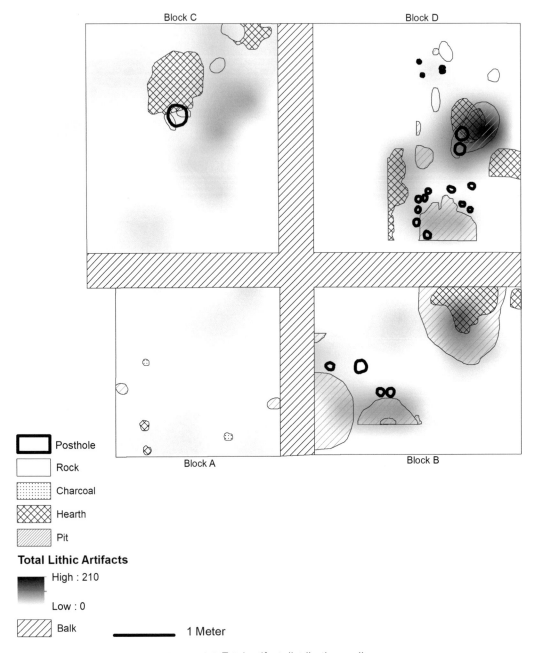

Posthole

Rock

Charcoal

Hearth

Pit

Total Lithic Artifacts

High : 210

Low : 0

Balk

1 Meter

FIGURE 6.4. Total artifact distribution on Ile.

N

Ile Faunal Specimens Sized 1-9mm

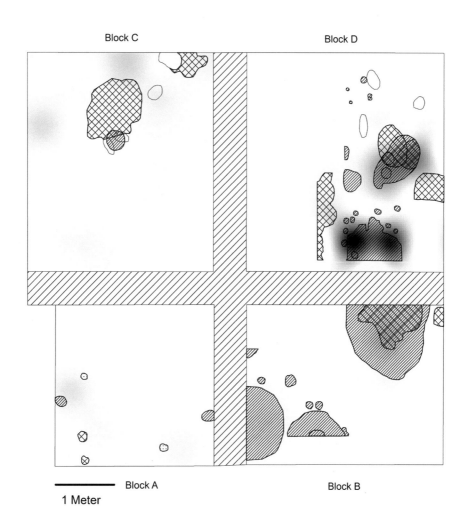

Block C

Block D

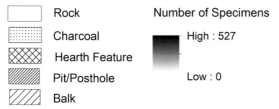

Block A

1 Meter

Block B

Rock
Charcoal
Hearth Feature
Pit/Posthole
Balk

Number of Specimens

High : 527

Low : 0

FIGURE 6.5. Extra-small faunal specimens on Ile.

Ile All Faunal Specimens

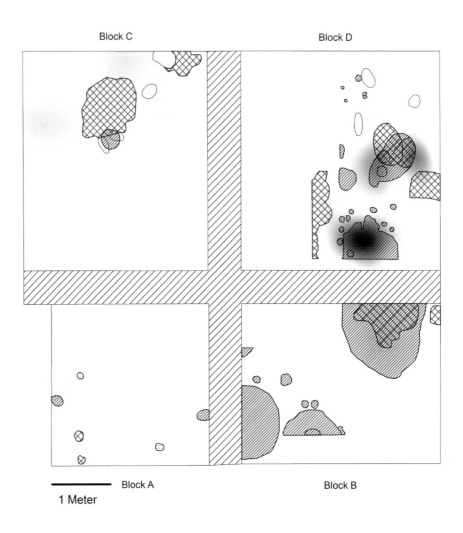

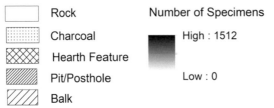

Rock	
Charcoal	
Hearth Feature	
Pit/Posthole	
Balk	

Number of Specimens

High : 1512

Low : 0

FIGURE 6.6. Total faunal specimen distribution on Ile.

is clear that any positioning items (other than large cobbles) were removed and no obvious de facto refuse was dumped on the floor. One bone anthropomorphic figurine was deposited on the surface of feature B3 (2014) in western Block B. However, puncture marks consistent with dog-gnawing suggest that its placement was either deliberate as in discard onto a refuse deposit (cache pit fill) or independent of human intent (left in that space by a canid). Obviously abundant evidence has been found for use of cache pits. However, we do not see any evidence for caching of tools.

Site Structure

This section focuses on the structure of labor across the IIe floor. It draws inferences based upon expectations outlined in Chapter 2 (Stratum IIa).

Debitage and Spatial Structure of Lithic Reduction

Debitage are found in all blocks in concentrations consistently associated with features (Supplemental Figure 6.2). A light concentration is associated with the small hearths in southwest Block A. Debitage concentrate on and adjacent to the large hearth and the cache pits in Block B. Another substantial concentration is found adjacent to hearths at the north end of Block C. Finally, a very dense cluster of flakes is located in the center of the arrangement of cache pits and hearths in Block D. These distributions are consistent with a pattern of hearth-centered lithic reduction behavior and thus the formation of drop zones. Early stage reduction flakes are found in varying though low numbers throughout the house. Concentrations occur around features, particularly in Blocks B–D (Supplemental Figure 6.3). Thinning and R-billet flakes are found in low numbers and generally in spaces not directly associated with features (Supplemental Figures 6.4 and 6.5). Given the lack of good evidence for sweeping and cleanup, this placement suggests that early to mid-stage bifaces were not often manufactured on IIe, but when those activities did occur

they were pursued from positions somewhat removed from hearth-centered activity spaces. In contrast, tool retouch flakes are found consistently throughout the floor, both in hearth areas and open spaces away from hearths and cache pits (Supplemental Figure 6.6). This distribution could suggest that inhabitants simply retouched tools as needed when conducting work scattered throughout the house floor. All debitage data considered, hearth features clearly were attractive places for lithic reduction activities (especially early stage and tool retouch), but lithic reduction, especially associated with tool manufacture and maintenance, could occur anywhere on the floor.

Lithic Tools and House Floor Activity Organization

Here we examine the distributions of knapping (cores and hammerstones), heavy-duty (wood/bone/antler working: flake scrapers, key-shaped scrapers, pièces esquillées, notches/denticulates, and drills/perforators), hunting/butchery (bifaces and projectile points), hide-working (hide scrapers and small piercers), and groundstone on the IIe floor. Knapping tools occur primarily in association with hearths, though a small cluster is also found in the northeast portion of Block A (Supplemental Figure 6.7). Tools for heavy-duty applications are found directly associated with hearth features in Blocks B–D (Supplemental Figure 6.8). Hunting and butchering tools are also associated with hearths in Blocks B and D. They also appear in moderate concentrations in northeastern Block A and southeastern Block C (Supplemental Figure 6.9). If these tools were discarded in work locations, then it implies the possibility that hunting and meat-processing-related activities were conducted around hearths and in other open space. This location would make some sense if such work was at all messy as might be expected with game butchery. However, the scattered hunting/butchering tools in Blocks A and C could also just have been "tossed" into those positions from nearby hearth areas. Hide-working/sewing tools are consistently directly associated with hearths in all blocks (Supplemental Figure 6.10). These activities clearly benefited from the extra light and/or warmth of hearth features. Ground-stone tools are primarily concentrated in associated features (Supplemental Figure 6.11). The pattern is particularly evident in Blocks B–D. However, clusters of groundstone also were found in southern Block C and western Block B, away from hearths. Considering all tool distributions, most household activities generally clustered around features, especially hearths. Scattered hunting/butchering and groundstone tools may have been displaced from feature-associated contexts via need for more space for messy activities or the tools themselves were simply removed from normal work areas forming toss zones (e.g., Binford 1978).

Faunal Remains and Spatial Organization

Faunal remains provide a diverse range of additional insights into the organization of workspace on the IIe floor. Fish bones are found in all blocks but are most densely concentrated in north-central Block D associated with a large hearth feature (Supplemental Figure 6.12). Lower density clusters are found around hearths in the south of Block A and north end of Block C. Additional concentrations appear in the south end of Block C, where no features are found, and west side of Block B, associated with cache pits. The southern Block C area is especially curious given its distance from any known hearths, and it could reflect a dump area or a specific fish-processing zone away from normal cooking space. Mammalian remains are most densely concentrated around two hearths in Block D and one in Block C (Supplemental Figure 6.13). Ungulate remains are found around hearths in all blocks but concentrate in greatest density around one hearth in northern Block C (Supplemental Figure 6.14).

Given that most mammalian remains are ungulate, the difference between the latter two maps likely derives largely from the degree to which elements are specifically identifiable as ungulates, more being located in Block C. This conclusion is confirmed when we consider high utility elements (without concern for specific taxon) that concentrate around hearths primarily in Blocks C and D, with greatest density in the latter area (Supplemental Figure 6.15). Concentrations of medium utility elements are found in or near hearths in all blocks with the densest portion in southern Block D (Supplemental Figure 6.16). Low utility elements are found primarily in Blocks B and C where they cluster by hearths with the exception of one concentration in southern Block C not directly associated with a known hearth (Supplemental Figure 6.17). The difference between the high and medium versus low utility remains is striking and could reflect differential processing in a shared resource with different elements processed in different parts of the house. An alternative scenario is that each portion of the house represented a unique household with its own hunting economy affected by rights of access to hunting spaces outside the village. A third possibility is that Block D was also the context of ritual events involving high quality food as compared to routine food processing elsewhere in the house. In all scenarios, the Block D groups seems to have better access to animal resources than those elsewhere in the house.

Summary: Site Structure on the IIe Floor

Portions of the central area of the IIe floor were not excavated. However, it is still possible to recognize patterns associated with broad patterns of organization across the floor. Debitage data indicate hearth-centered associations for all flake types. However, retouch flakes and, to a lesser degree, biface thinning flakes are also found in areas away from hearths. Tool distributions are also substantially hearth-centered. Limited exceptions occur for hunting/butchery tools and groundstone. Perhaps of significance, biface thinning flakes and bifacial tools are distributed similarly around and away from hearths, thus implying that those activities occurred in diverse spaces within the house. Little evidence suggests a significant segregation of male- and female-oriented activities other than the more widely dispersed hunting and butchery set, and these activities were not necessarily conducted entirely by males. Fish and mammal remains are strongly associated with hearths with the exception of low utility elements in southwestern Block C.

Thus nearly all data suggest that the house was structurally organized into at least two concentric zones including interior space used occasionally for activities related to hunting and/or meat-processing surrounded by an intensely used hearth zone. Given lack of obvious space for storage (other than cache pits) or sleeping, a bench zone likely stretched away from the floor and located under the outer eave of the roof. Given that hearths and consistently similar assemblages of lithic tools are present in each block, four domestic groups appear to have occupied the house during IIe.

However, the history of the floor may be somewhat more complex. The large hearth in the northeast of Block B caps an extraordinarily wide and deep cache pit that was apparently filled gradually and reused multiple times. This implies that this hearth may have only been in use during the final season of occupation of IIe. If that is the case and given the number of other cache pits in this space, the Block B area possibly served as a major storage zone during much of the IIe occupation period, suggesting that IIe was occupied by three domestic groups during much of its history. Further, small hearths and somewhat sparse materials in Block A could imply that, at least during the final portion of the IIe occupation span, this area either was inhabited by a smaller group or this group had a shorter stay compared to those particularly evident in Blocks C and D. The diversity of discarded tools and debitage in this space make it unlikely that Block A was a focused special activity space.

As with other floors so far considered, the low density portion of IIe in the central portion of the house could have served as a space for a roof entrance. No data has been found to adequately support an argument that a side entrance existed. Given low densities of accumulated material in the north-central and northeastern portions of IIe, access to direct sunlight during winter does not appear to have played a major role in structuring activity areas.

However, general concentrations of material in Blocks C and D possibly resulted from the recognition that these spaces were still optimal for natural light.

Sociality

A comprehensive study of lithic artifacts from Housepit 54 (Prentiss et al. 2018b) demonstrated that measurable material wealth-based inequality likely emerged during the IIe occupation. In this section, we assess spatial variation in canids, nonlocal lithic raw material, prestige raw material, and prestige artifacts. Canid remains are found in low numbers in Blocks B–D (Supplemental Figures 6–18). Greatest concentrations occur in northern Block C, while additional clusters are found in southern Block D and western Block B. A concentration of dog coprolites was also recovered from cache pit B14 (2014), located on north-central Block B. Given these distributions, no significant evidence supports differential access to dogs on IIe. Nonlocal lithic raw material is found in all blocks (Supplemental Figure 6.19). However, it is most concentrated in southern Block D and northern Block B. Prestige raw materials and items are found relatively equally in Blocks B–D (Supplemental Figures 6.20 and 6.21).

These data point to a significant disparity between Block A and the rest of the floor. Cumulatively, they also point to greatest concentrations of items around the large hearth and cache pit features of southern Block D and northern Block B. These spatial patterns confirm results derived from lithic data alone, marking Blocks B and D as collectively exhibiting more significant concentrations of material wealth than Blocks A or C (Prentiss et al. 2018b). Given that the IIe floor was likely in occupation for over 20 years (Prentiss et al. 2018a), we suggest that the early periods of IIe were marked by one well-connected group occupying all of Block D and a substantial portion of Block B. By late IIe times, storage pits in Block B were filled with sediment, and this portion of the house became a more typical domestic space. Blocks A and C were likely always distinct domestic spaces. This occupation pattern set the stage for the organization of later floors whereby the spaces sampled by each block became unique domestic living spaces.

Conclusions

Stratum IIe is a critical floor in the history of Housepit 54 as it represented the first occupation of the house at its full oval shape following seven generations of the house in its rectangular form. The house during this time clearly received the full range of cycles inclusive of initiation, exploitation, and abandonment. The final abandonment was no doubt well planned as indicated by a portion of a collapsed roof and complete burial by the IId floor. Cultural materials from the final season were not removed, but no obvious de facto refuse was added either. The early portion of the IIe seasonal occupations likely favored use by no more than three domestic units with the Block B portion of the houses dedicated to pit storage. A distribution of postholes in the approximate center of the block, partially surrounded by cache pits, raises the possibility of racks or even wooden plank covered benches over the storage pits not unlike those of the Meier Site as described by Smith (2006). By the final occupation of IIe, most of the cache pits probably had been filled with either kitchen refuse or bedded layers of clay-loam. A number of them were capped with hearth features, and we suggest that at this point the house likely had space for occupation of all block areas by separate domestic units, which became the standard occupation pattern throughout the span of later occupations.

These results also support the contention by Prentiss and colleagues (2018b) that a pattern of material wealth-based inequality was emergent on IIe with a strong contrast in goods accumulation between Blocks D and B versus Blocks A and C. The large hearth located in the southwest of Block D is a possible candidate for a long-term use roasting oven. Given its size and location near the center of the house, it serves as a possible candidate for use in food-related rituals. If wealth-based inequality first appeared on IIe, this feature suggests that feasting could have played a role in that social process.

A Crowded House

Stratum IIf

Stratum IIf is the final floor of the seven-floor sequence associated with the rectangular variant of Housepit 54 (Figure 7.1). Stratum IIf sediments are clay-dominated in the 35–40% range, followed by silt at 20–30% and subsequent lower percentages of sand, gravel, and pebbles. Stratum IIf is entirely buried by IIe sediments with no evidence for roof deposits. Three hearth features are found on IIf, including a large shallow hearth in the northeast corner of Block C and another large shallow feature in north-central Block A (Figure 7.2). A third small hearth is located in the southwest of Block C. Postholes are extremely abundant and are generally small and parallel the edge of the house in the form of a block of rim sediment trending southwest to northeast in the northwest corner of the Block C. This collection of postholes likely represents support for a wooden bench or bench-like platform. Larger postholes are found in the northern and southern portions of Block C and north half of Block A. This set may reflect roof support posts. One large cache pit was found in the southwest corner of Block A. An additional cache pit was partially excavated in the southwest portion of Block C. The following discussions outline data relevant to understanding variation in occupation and abandonment cycles, site structure, and sociality.

Occupation and Abandonment Cycle

The archaeological manifestations of households are heavily conditioned by variability in occupation and abandonment cycles. This section permits us to evaluate these factors using frames of reference outlined in Chapter 2 (Stratum IIa).

Occupation Cycle

Occupation phases may include initiation, exploitation, and abandonment. Archaeological expectations for each of these are outlined in Chapter 2 (Stratum IIa).

Stratum IIf includes lithic tools from all classes, thus indicating occupation likely spanning initiation through abandonment phases (Table 7.1). Consequently, we find evidence for heavy-duty woodworking (adzes and possibly abraders) and light-duty wood/bone/antler working (flake scrapers, key-shaped scrapers, pièces esquillées, notches, denticulates, drills, and perforators). Hunting is likely evident in the form of bifaces and projectile points. Likewise, hide-working is also indicated by frequent hide scrapers and small piercers. As is typical of shallower floors, bipolar cores are common and likely indicate salvage of lithic raw material. Debitage indicate a focus on late stage tool reduction and maintenance followed by much lesser emphases on biface and core reduction (Table 7.2).

Abandonment Process

Stratum IIf was entirely buried by the IIe floor with no evident roof and very little wood retained in postholes. This finding implies that abandonment was planned and associated with expected reoccupation focused on reflooring and reroofing. In the latter case, this process included doubling the size of the house for the

Stratum IIf

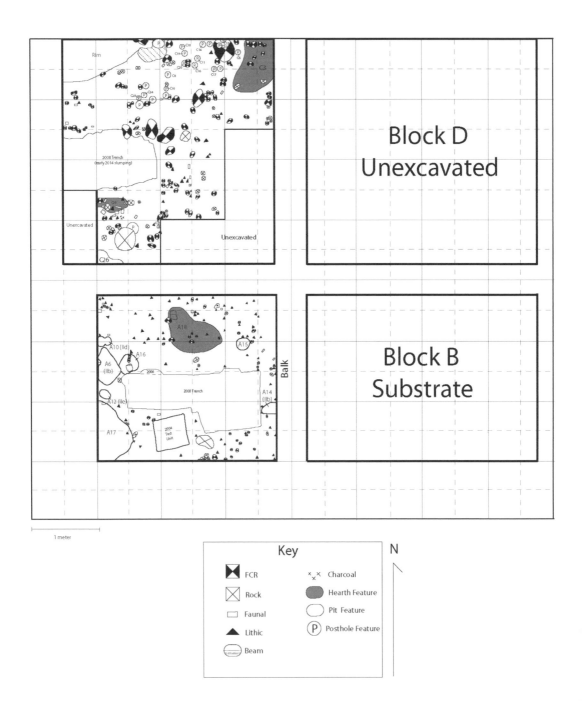

FIGURE 7.1. Comprehensive map of IIf showing point-provenienced artifacts, faunal remains, fire-cracked rock, prior excavations, and features.

Stratum IIf

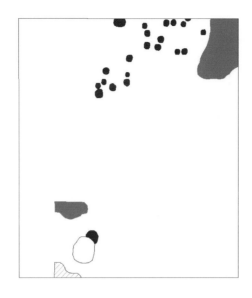

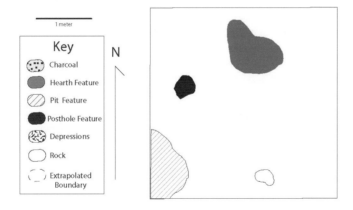

FIGURE 7.2. Features on IIf.

TABLE 7.1. Lithic Tools from IIf, Organized by Tool Class and Block.

	Tool Class																
	A	B	C	D	E	F	G	H	I	J	K	L	M	N	O	P	Q
Block A	3	4	3	8	7	1	3	4	2	1	3	0	11	1	0	12	5
Block C	6	3	4	3	10	3	3	1	1	1	4	2	5	1	1	10	5
Total	9	7	7	11	17	4	6	5	3	2	7	2	16	2	1	22	10

Note: A = flake and slate knives; B = bifaces; C = projectile points; D = flake and key-shaped scrapers; E = hide scrapers; F = drills and perforators; G = small piercers; H = pièces esquillées; I = notches and denticulates; J = adzes; K = abraders/groundstone; L = freehand cores; M = bipolar cores; N = slate objects; O = hammerstones; P = used flakes; Q = ritual/social items.

TABLE 7.2. Lithic Flake Types for Stratum IIf by Toolstone Category.

	Ext	Chal	Cher	Dac	Obs	Intr	Slates	Met.	Total
Biface	2	0	0	12	0	0	0	0	14
Core	1	1	1	6	0	1	0	0	9
Retouch	4	0	3	57	0	1	3	0	68

Note: Ext = extrusives (excluding dacite and obsidian); Dac = dacite; Cher = cherts; Chal = chalcedony; Obs = obsidian; Intr = intrusives plus gneiss; Slates = slate and silicified shale; Met = metamorphic rock inclusive of quartzites, nephrite, and steatite.

IIe occupation. Given the lack of wood remaining in the small postholes at the north end of Block C, occupants in and around the close of IIf probably removed the wooden bench/platform along with its support posts. Interestingly, the IIe floor that followed did not include the same investment in bench space or at least one that would have left the same kind of archaeological signature.

We can gain insight into the abandonment process from an assessment of relationships between very small and larger artifacts and faunal remains (e.g., Metcalf and Heath 1990). This analysis can be accomplished with a statistical test and visual assessment of data from the IIf floor. Distributions of extra-small and larger debitage are virtually identical (Figures 7.3 and 7.4), and this similarity is confirmed by a correlation coefficient ($r = 0.488, p = 0.042$). A similar relationship is evident in the distributions of extra-small and larger faunal remains (Figures 7.5 and 7.6) and confirmed with moderately strong statistical results ($r = 0.557, p = 0.038$).

We gain additional insight from an examination of distributions of materials that could be classified as positioning items (Binford 1979), caches (Binford 1979; Hayden and Deal 1983), site furniture (Binford 1979), and de facto refuse (Schiffer 1972; Stevenson 1982). Abundant cobble-sized rocks are found at the north end of IIf near the likely position of a bench and adjacent to a large hearth in the northeast corner of Block C. Most of these are burned and may have been used in fires perhaps to maintain heat. The largest of these rocks probably was not used for stone-boiling purposes given the unwieldy size. Knapping tools (see below) were found clustered around features, raising the possibility

that these were positioning items. One large cache pit was found in the southwest corner of Block A. This feature was approximately 1 m in width and more than 1 m in depth. Beyond normal pit fit fill, the basal sediments from the pit contained a substantial number of large birch bark rolls possibly originating as liners of the walls and floor of the cache pit. No evidence for de facto refuse was identified.

Site Structure

In this section, we seek to define variability in the nature and structure of activities across the IIf floor. We have three areas of interest here.

First, we examine zonation in the arrangement of floor activities. The IIf through IIl floors are rectangular and thus could be organized like some Northwest Coast long houses, as for example among the Coast Salish (e.g., Coupland et al. 2009). In this model, we would expect a somewhat narrow public space down the center of the floor surrounded by multiple smaller domestic hearth areas as found in the long houses of Ozette (Samuels 2006), select Coast Salish houses (Coupland et al. 2009), and the Lil'wat area (Teit 1906). Another similar possibility would be several hearth-centered activity areas representing the space of two to three families with relatively equal space allocations co-occupying the house. An extreme example of this scenario can be seen at the Meier site in the Lower Columbia Valley (Smith 2006). A contrasting model would organize the house around a central domestic feature such as a hearth, with a surrounding array of special activity areas and sleeping/storage spaces. Coupland (2006) provides a good example from the Tsimshian area of the northern Northwest Coast.

Ilf Extra-Small Debitage Distribution

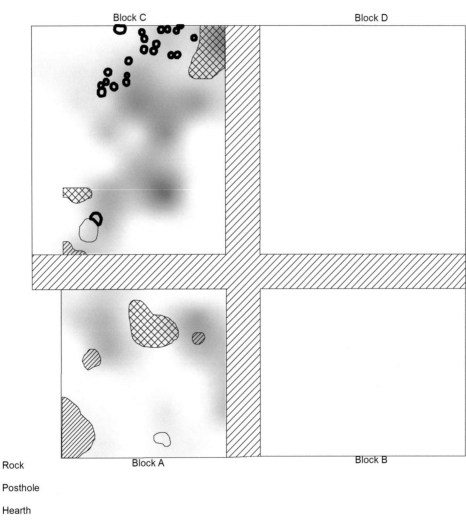

FIGURE 7.3. Extra-small debitage distribution on Ilf.

IIf Total Lithic Artifact Distribution

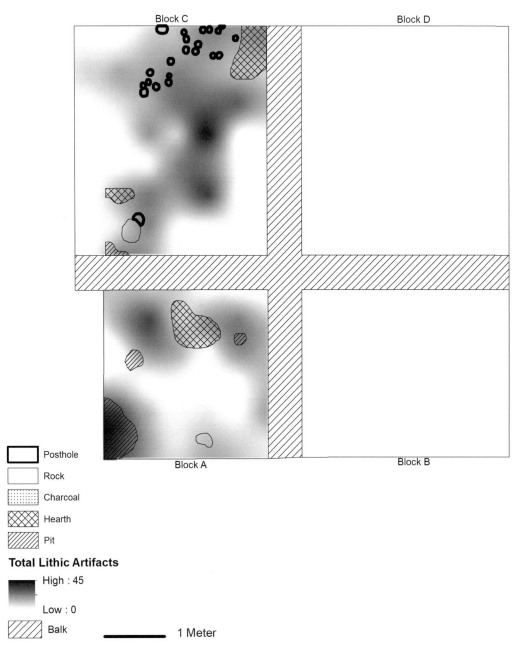

Block C

Block D

Block A

Block B

Posthole

Rock

Charcoal

Hearth

Pit

Total Lithic Artifacts

High : 45

Low : 0

Balk

1 Meter

FIGURE 7.4. Total artifact distribution on IIf.

IIf Faunal Specimens Sized 1-9mm

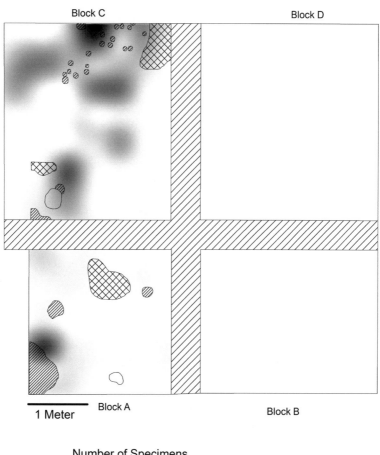

Block C

Block D

Block A

Block B

1 Meter

Rock
Charcoal
Hearth Feature
Pit/Posthole
Balk

Number of Specimens
High : 71

Low : 0

FIGURE 7.5. Extra-small faunal specimens on IIf.

Second, we seek to understand the nature of variation in specific activity areas. Following from the zonation hypotheses, we could expect two scenarios. One would be a collectivist living pattern with redundant multiple-activity areas most likely associated with domestic units (families), as was typical of Ozette/Makah, Coast Salish, and the Lower Columbia models of house floor organization. The alternative would be a communalist pattern as evident in northern Northwest Coast houses and as described in Plateau ethnographies (e.g., Teit 1900).

Third, we address questions of contingent problem-solving in the use of space across the

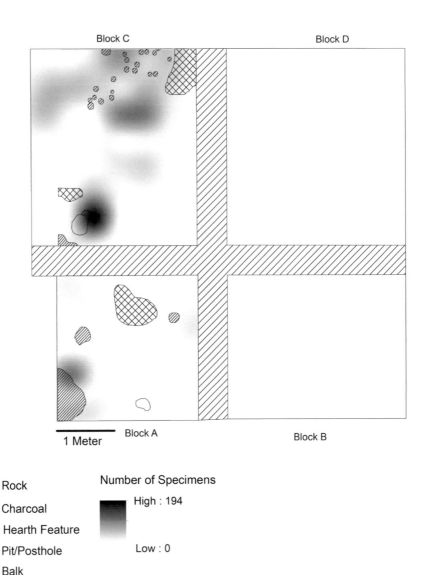

FIGURE 7.6. Total faunal specimen distribution on IIf.

house floor. Here we examine the structure of artifact distributions to seek indicators of variation in response to sunlight, space for ladders or side entrances, sleeping space, and specialized (messy) work zones. To accomplish these goals, we assess patterns in lithic reduction as indicated by debitage distributions. Follow with an examination of variation in distributions of major functional tool classes. Finally, we look at distributions of faunal remains, exploring major taxonomic groups and element utility (cf. Madrigal and Holt 2002).

Debitage and Spatial Structure of Lithic Reduction

Debitage are found at relatively high densities throughout the IIf floor. The empty spaces in Supplemental Figure 7.1 correspond to unexcavated areas or 2008 test trench locations. Evidence for early stage lithic reduction is relatively sparse with flakes clustered to the east of the small hearth in southwest Block C and in and around the hearth and cache pit in Block A (Supplemental Figure 7.2). Thinning flakes likely representing biface reduction concentrate entirely around the major features in Block A (Supplemental Figure 7.3). Tool retouch flakes in contrast are found throughout the floor (Supplemental Figure 7.4). No R-billet flakes were identified. Clearly, tool retouch was the primary lithic reduction activity on this floor, conducted likely on an as-needed basis in all sectors, both adjacent to and away from hearths. In contrast, the limited engagement with early stage reduction and biface thinning focused around hearths and the cache pit.

Lithic Tools and House Floor Activity Organization

Here we examine the distributions of knapping (cores and hammerstones), heavy-duty (wood/bone/antler working: flake scrapers, key-shaped scrapers, pièces esquillées, notches/denticulates, and drills/perforators), hunting/butchery (bifaces and projectile points), hide-working (hide scrapers and small piercers), and groundstone on the IIf floor. Knapping tools cluster around features through the IIf floor (Supplemental Figure 7.5). These items may have been routinely used on an as-needed basis, repositioned after each use event, and eventually discarded upon abandonment of the floor. Heavy-duty tools also concentrate around hearths and cache pits (Supplemental Figure 7.6), implying that activities requiring scraperplanes, notches, drills, and perforators required light for successful completion.

Hunting and butchery tools (bifaces and projectile points) are generally found in the center of the house both near and away from hearths and the cache pit (Supplemental Fig-

ure 7.7). As has been seen on other floors, this distribution raises the possibility that this kind of work was sometimes conducted away from hearths perhaps to gain the advantage of workspace. This exception would not be surprising for messy butchering activities. Hide-working and sewing tools are found at even greater distances from features (Supplemental Figure 7.8), suggesting that, similar to hunting/butchering activities, spatial constraints may have played a critical role. We can imagine this scenario to be particularly the case if this work focused on hide-working, as is suggested by the large number of hide scrapers. Groundstone tools cluster in the center of the house near the hearth in southwestern Block C and also in a small concentration on the cache pit in southwestern Block A (Supplemental Figure 7.9).

Thus, from the standpoint of tool distributions, we recognize several patterns. First, hunting/butchering and hide-working activities appear to have been primarily conducted in more open spaces somewhat removed from hearth features. Second, knapping, heavy-duty, and groundstone tools are generally associated with features. Third, all hearths developed clusters of discarded tools reflecting multiple activities, making it likely that each represents a general domestic space.

Faunal Remains and Spatial Organization

Faunal remains provide important insights into the organization of food-related activities on the IIf floor. Fish remains are found in three concentrations associated with features in the north and south of Block C and in the southwest of Block A (Supplemental Figure 7.10). They are particularly dense on the east side of the hearth and cache pit in southwestern Block C. A thin scatter of faunal remains is found between the line of small postholes and the north wall of Block C, raising the possibility that some remains were discarded or even set aside for later use under a bench or platform at the north end of the house. A number of these remains consisted over partially articulated postcranial salmon remains.

Not unlike the hunting/butchery and hide-working tools, mammalian remains are found both adjacent to and somewhat disjunct from hearths and the cache pit in Blocks C and A (Supplemental Figure 7.11). Mammalian remains are particularly dense throughout much of the northern end of Block C, suggesting the processing activities may have been particularly frequent here. Identifiable ungulate remains mirror those of mammals in general but concentrate most highly on the east side of the hearth in Block A (Supplemental Figure 7.12). High utility mammalian elements (meat/fat rich upper limbs) are found around each of the three hearth groups, but occur at greatest density at the north end of Block C behind the row of small postholes (Supplemental Figure 7.13). Either these items were discarded consistently in this location or they were placed under the bench or platform in storage for possible later use as could be expected if these elements retained some food (e.g., bone grease) or tool utility. Medium utility bones (generally axial parts) are found in three relatively even clusters located in the north and southwest of Block C and the southwest of Block A, all associated with hearths and cache pits (Supplemental Figure 7.14). Low utility elements (generally lower limb and some cranial parts) are found in the same spaces but concentrate at greatest density just outside the line of small postholes in northern Block C (Supplemental Figure 7.15). This signature is an interesting one, raising the possibility that either these elements were collected in this spot as associated with work around the hearth just to the east or that one or more persons sat at the edge of the bench implied by the postholes and worked on limbs, discarding the low utility set in front of the bench.

Summary: Site Structure on the IIf Floor

Activities on the IIf floor are clearly organized around three hearth features and two associated cache pits. The northernmost hearth is the largest and is associated with what was likely a wooden bench support by a series of posts. The central hearth is relatively small and is located adjacent to an equally small cache pit. Finally, another large hearth is found in central Block

A near a large cache pit located in southwestern Block A. Each set of features is associated with a relatively similar distribution of debitage, stone tools, and faunal remains. This placement suggests that each area formed as the result of diverse activities associated with potentially three domestic units living and working on this floor.

Hearths and associated activity zones are not evenly positioned down the center of the floor. Neither are they consistently positioned along the lateral margins. Rather, one is in the northeast corner, another is west-central, and the last in south central. Although a portion of eastern Block C is yet unexcavated, we raise the possibility that the eastern side of the house might have been a side entrance to this rectangular living space. The small scale of the southwest Block C hearth and its associated cache pit suggests that this feature group was not occupied by as large a group for as long as those on either side. Further, if it was opposite the doorway, this location would have been the least desirable portion of the floor in which to live. This position suggests that such a group might have been a late addition to the IIf house, perhaps in the final winter(s) before the house was reorganized to develop the IIe floor.

Thus, we can conclude that in its final occupation period three households inhabited IIf. If any open public space existed, it might only have been on the east-central side associated with a hypothesized entrance. The three-zone pattern recognized on the later floors (IIa–IIe) is not upheld on IIf. Rather we see what appears to have been a single domestic activity zone that we can surmise was probably surrounded by raised bench space on the rim but the inner eaves of a sloping roof. Neither a roof entrance nor a probable sunlit zone has been found on IIf, supporting the higher probability of a side-entrance.

Sociality

A comprehensive study of differential material wealth on the Housepit 54 floors demonstrated a signature for relatively even distribution of prestige items, raw materials, and nonlocal tool-stones on IIf (Prentiss et al. 2018b). We explore those patterns further here and consider canid remains.

Canid elements are found in association with each cluster of features (Supplemental Figure 7.16). They are sparse in southwestern Block A, but appear at surprisingly high densities in southwest, central, and north-central Block A. Given general abundance around both hearth zones and the bench area of Block C, it does not appear that any single group retained exclusive access to canid elements. Nonlocal lithic raw materials are distributed relatively evenly between the three feature clusters (Supplemental Figure 7.17). Prestige raw materials are also found around each feature cluster, though several are located in more open space in east-central Block C (Supplemental Figure 7.18). Finally, prestige items are found in approximately similar quantities between all feature areas as well (Supplemental Figure 7.19).

Canids, nonlocal raw materials, and prestige objects of all kinds are found at slightly higher numbers in Block C. However, this distribution may be largely due to the presence of two domestic activity areas in this space compared to only one in Block A. Given that the hearth/cache pit activity area in southwest Block C is positioned in the center of the house, it is tempting to view it as somehow reflective of a lower status group. However, this space has equivalent food remains and goods to the other areas. Thus, we conclude little evidence for material wealth-based inequality has been found on the IIf floor.

Conclusions

Stratum IIf represents the final of seven floors associated with the rectangular form of Housepit 54. Analysis of occupation and abandonment cycles suggests a complete cycle from initiation to planned abandonment and burial under the IIe floor. The feature layout included three distinct activity areas including a major hearth and concentration of small postholes in the north, a small hearth and cache pit in the center, and another large hearth with cache pit in the south. Artifacts and faunal remains suggest that each cluster of features accumulated a similar array of materials reflecting food preparation and consumption, lithic tool maintenance (and to a lesser degree, core reduction and tool manufacture), and work on hides and various other materials.

Thus, we conclude that at least during the final season of occupation, floor IIf held at least three family groups. Given the simultaneous presence of three family compartments, IIf would appear to have operated in a collectivist social strategy. The single very large cache pit in southwestern Block A raises the possibility that some storage facilities could have been shared between families and would conform to our conclusion that status relationships were economically egalitarian. Overall, we gain the impression that IIf was a busy and crowded space on the eve of its abandonment and replacement with the much larger and apparently socioeconomically ranked IIe house. This hypothesis supports the arguments of Prentiss and colleagues (2018b) that populations were steadily rising during the period after occupation of the IIi floor, culminating perhaps in pressure to build a much bigger house.

8

The Collectivist House Strategy

Stratum IIg

Stratum IIg is the sixth of seven rectangular floors from Housepit 54 (Figure 8.1). Stratum IIg sediments are virtually identical to those of IIf with clay-dominated at around 30–40% followed by silt in the 15–25% range and then dramatically lower percentages of sand, gravel, and pebbles. Stratum IIg is entirely buried by IIf sediments with no evident roof deposits. Seven hearth features are found on IIg, of which five are in Block C and two in Block A (Figure 8.2). One expansive shallow hearth is adjacent to another smaller though similarly configured feature in north-central Block C. Three small hearths are located in the southwest corner of Block C. These closely packed hearth features would not necessarily have been in use simultaneously, and we can imagine that their contiguous positions reflect shifts in the organization of space during the occupation of IIg (e.g., Binford 1978a). Two small hearths are located on the eastern margin of Block A. One of those hearths caps a somewhat narrow pit feature. One large cache pit was excavated in the south-central portion of Block A. Stratum IIg includes a cluster of very small postholes similar to those of IIf in the north-central portion of Block C. We interpret these similarly to IIf as remains of a wooden platform or bench at the north end of the house.

Found south of the large hearth in Block C, one additional pit (Feature C28 [2014]) resembles a large posthole with a stone collar and slab base as might expected to support a major

house post (Alexander 2000). However, the pit also contained a large number of metate and abrader fragments, along with several unmodified (though some burned and others not) portions of cobbles. After the post was removed (if it served that function), the pit appears to have been converted into a receptacle for groundstone fragments. One reason for placing such a collection of broken tools in a single place would be to recycle them for another purpose. A possibility is that they were destined for use as cooking stones, as this practice was common on some of the deeper floors. However, apparently neither the IIg or IIf occupants utilized this resource. We mention IIf in this context as the feature was so brimming with rock that a few projected into the IIf floor, and thus we would expect those later occupants to be fully aware of these materials. We review evidence for occupation and abandonment cycles, site structure, and sociality in the following sections.

Occupation and Abandonment Cycle

As elsewhere in the Housepit 54 floor sequence, we begin with an assessment of occupation and abandonment cycles drawing upon expectations in Chapter 2 (Stratum IIa).

Occupation Cycle

Occupation phases include initiation, exploitation, and abandonment. Archaeological expectations for each are reviewed in Chapter 2 (Stratum IIa).

Stratum IIg

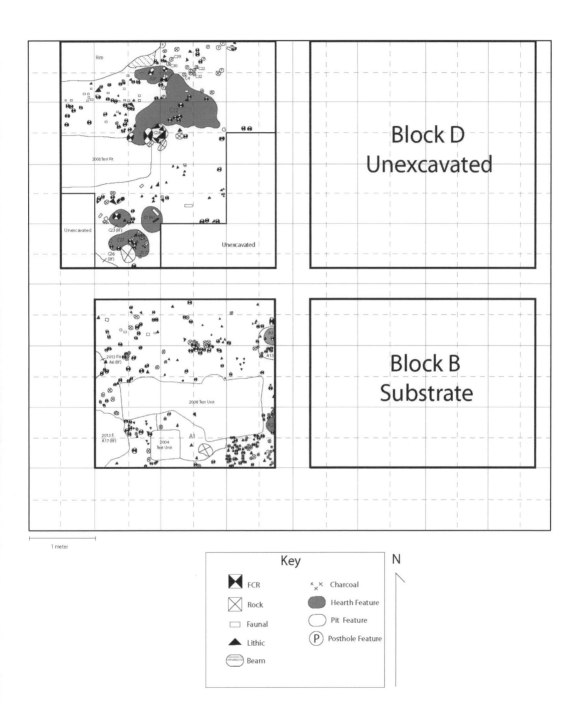

FIGURE 8.1. Comprehensive map of IIg showing point-provenienced artifacts, faunal remains, fire-cracked rock, prior excavations, and features.

Stratum IIg

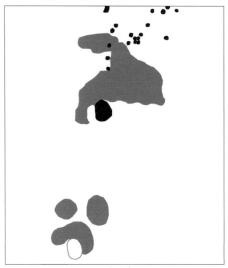

Block C

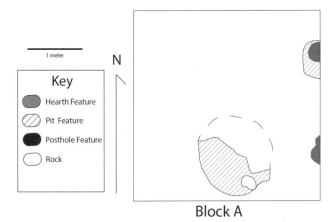

Block A

FIGURE 8.2. Features on IIg.

TABLE 8.1. Lithic Tools from IIg, Organized by Tool Class and Block.

	Tool Class																
	A	B	C	D	E	F	G	H	I	J	K	L	M	N	O	P	Q
Block A	5	1	2	6	9	4	1	3	0	2	3	1	7	6	0	11	1
Block C	3	3	4	1	3	2	0	2	1	0	42	4	6	6	4	4	4
Total	8	4	6	7	12	6	1	5	1	2	45	5	13	12	4	15	5

Note: A = flake and slate knives; B = bifaces; C = projectile points; D = flake and key-shaped scrapers; E = hide scrapers; F = drills and perforators; G = small piercers; H = pièces esquillées; I = notches and denticulates; J = adzes; K = abraders/groundstone; L = freehand cores; M = bipolar cores; N = slate objects; O = hammerstones; P = used flakes; Q = ritual/social items.

TABLE 8.2. Lithic Flake Types for Stratum IIg by Toolstone Category.

	Ext	Chal	Cher	Dac	Obs	Intr	Slates	Met.	Total
Biface	0	0	0	13	0	0	1	0	14
Core	1	0	2	5	0	0	0	1	9
Retouch	2	3	4	70	0	0	13	0	92

Note: Ext = extrusives (excluding dacite and obsidian); Dac = dacite; Cher = cherts; Chal = chalcedony; Obs = obsidian; Intr = intrusives plus gneiss; Slates = slate and silicified shale; Met = metamorphic rock inclusive of quartzites, nephrite, and steatite.

The lithic assemblage from IIg is very similar to that of IIf and later floors, and from that standpoint, we can conclude that the floor was occupied across initiation, exploitation, and abandonment phases (Table 8.1). Evidence was found for heavy-duty (adzes and possibly abraders) and light-duty (flake scrapers, key-shaped scrapers, notches, denticulates, pièces esquillées, and drills/perforators) tool-use on wood/bone/antler. Hunting and hide-working were practiced as indicated by bifaces, projectile points, various hide scrapers, and small piercers. Abundant bipolar cores support activities designed to extend the use-life of lithic raw materials. Finally, we point to the very high frequency of groundstone (abraders and metates). While this pattern is atypical pattern for the post-IIg floors, it is more common on some deeper floors (IIh and IIm for example). We suspect that this has less to do with the need for more groundstone and more to do with a practice of recycling groundstone tools as cooking rocks. Debitage reflect a focus on late stage tool reduction and maintenance followed by a much lower respective emphasis on biface and core reduction (Table 8.2).

Abandonment Process

Stratum IIg was entirely buried by stratum IIf sediments, and none of the features within the stratum contained preserved architectural materials. Feature C28 (2016) contained what was effectively a cache of broken rock that might have been saved for use as boiling stones (and/or some other functions). All of these data reflect positively on the inference that was abandoned with the intent to return and to refloor and reroof the house.

We gain further insight into abandonment process by assessing relationships between smallest artifacts and all larger items (e.g., Metcalf and Heath 1990). The correlation coefficient between extra-small and all larger sized debitage demonstrates a high degree of correlation (r = 0.883, p = 0.000), and this relationship is clearly evident on mapped distributions of extra-small debitage (Figure 8.3) and total lithic artifacts (Figure 8.4). A similar correlation is recognized for faunal remains (r = 0.867, p = 0.000) and is clearly visible on plan view maps of extra-small (Figure 8.5) and all faunal items (Figure 8.6). Clearly, IIg was not significantly swept before abandonment.

Caches (Binford 1979; Hayden and Deal 1983), positioning items (Binford 1979), and de facto refuse (Schiffer 1972; Stevenson 1982) provide additional insight into the abandonment process. Two cache pits filled with refuse are found in Block A. Clearly neither held goods that could be used during or after the IIg abandonment process. Feature C28 (2014), the pit filled with groundstone items and burned and unburned cobble-sized rocks, is an interesting case. We think it likely that this feature held a cache of items that might have been useful to occupants during and after the abandonment process, as well as during the subsequent IIf occupation. This feature therefore implies the possibility of anticipated need for a future generation. The uppermost rocks from the feature even protruded into and slightly above the surface of IIf. Yet it was never reopened possibly due to either a lack of need or a cultural prohibition against reawakening such a collection of items.

Cores and groundstone items are common on IIg and cluster around hearths. While

Ilg Extra-Small Debitage Distribution

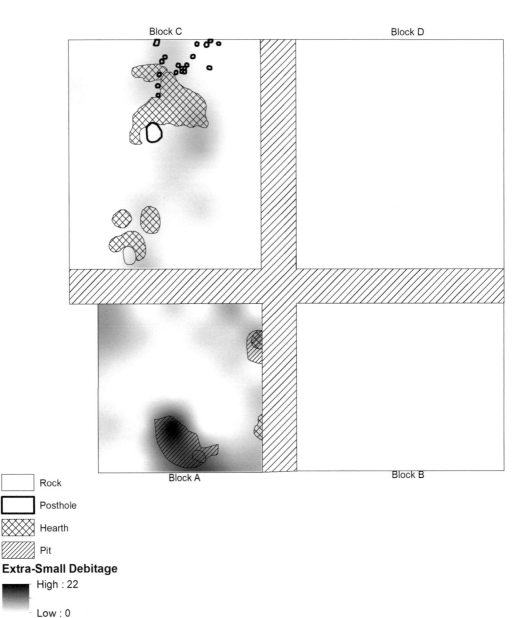

FIGURE 8.3. Extra-small debitage distribution on Ilg.

IIg Total Lithic Artifact Distribution

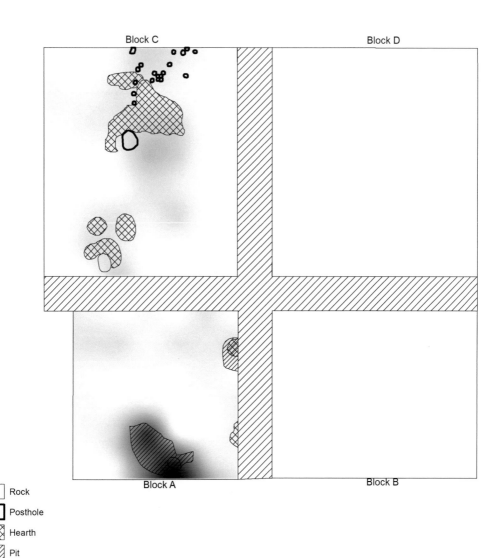

FIGURE 8.4. Total artifact distribution on IIg.

Ilg Faunal Specimens Sized 1-9mm

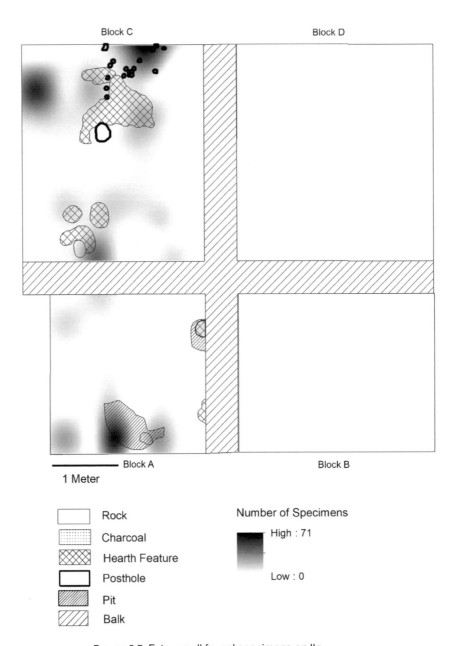

FIGURE 8.5. Extra-small faunal specimens on Ilg.

Ilg All Faunal Specimens

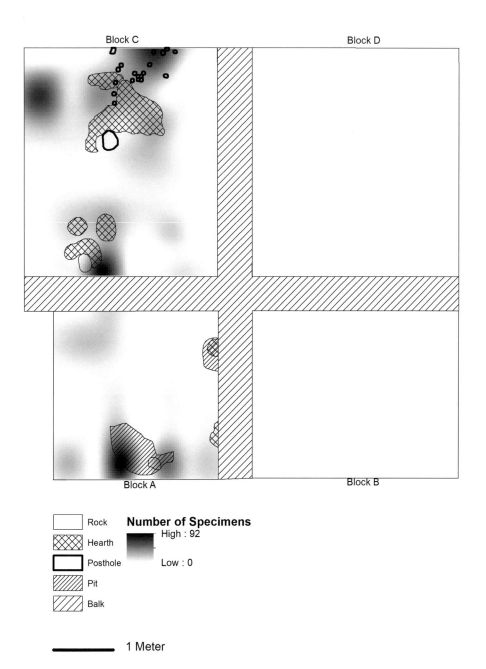

FIGURE 8.6. Total faunal specimen distribution on Ilg.

ultimately abandoned, many of these may have been moved about as positioning items during the IIg occupation. Large rocks are also found at the south end of Block C and the same in Block A, both adjacent to hearths. These stones give the appearance of site furniture as items that could have received use as anvils (though anvil-wear was not recognized) and even boundary markers. Whatever their specific role, these items remained in place and were used again during the IIf occupation. No indicator of de facto refuse was noted, other than possibly the rock-filled feature. But if this material was truly de facto, we would expect it to have simply been dumped on the floor prior to reflooring.

All data considered, several conclusions are warranted. While the house was not formally swept or otherwise cleaned prior to abandonment and reflooring, clear evidence indicates some intent to leave resources for the next generation. A pit filled with still usable stones could have provided a resource for grinding slabs or cooking rocks. Two boulder-sized rocks were left in place, presumably for similar uses during the subsequent occupation. Thus, the IIg abandonment clearly was carefully planned with the expectation of return and reuse of the house, which did occur as reflected in the development of the IIf floor.

Site Structure

In Chapter 7 (Stratum IIf), we outlined a number of scenarios as to how space might be allocated and organized within a rectangular house. Briefly, within a collectivist scenario we proposed that we would expect multiple families with independent living space, either organized in compartments running the length of the central portion of the house or as living spaces along the walls with open space remaining down the center. We contrasted that with a communalist model, whereby the house might be organized by special activity areas such that no single-family space would be recognizable. Finally, we noted that activity spaces could be structured around contingencies including entrances, access to light, sleeping space, and need

for workspace associated with messy activities. We explore these possibilities with examinations of spatial variation in lithic reduction, lithic tools, and faunal remains.

Debitage and Spatial Structure of Lithic Reduction

Debitage are found throughout the IIg floor and occur in densest concentrations around the large cache pit in southern Block A, but also in low to moderate concentrations associated with hearths in both blocks (Supplemental Figure 8.1). Limited numbers of early stage reduction flakes are found exclusively around features in Block A (Supplemental Figure 8.2). Biface thinning flakes are also rare and concentrate in southern Block A (Supplemental Figure 8.3). Low numbers of R-billet flakes are associated with features in both blocks (Supplemental Figure 8.4). As with other floors, small retouch flakes are found throughout much of the floor. However, they particularly concentrate around the hearths and cache pits in both blocks (Supplemental Figure 8.5). These data suggest that lithic reduction activities occurred throughout the IIg floor often but not exclusively associated with hearths. Concentrations of most flake types are found in south-central and southwestern Block A where no hearths are present. In contrast, clearly some spaces (e.g., northwest and northeast Block C) were not used for lithic reduction.

Lithic Tools and House Floor Activity Organization

Knapping items (cores and hammerstones) cluster around features in Blocks A and C (Supplemental Figure 8.6). Heavy-duty tools (wood/bone/antler working: flake scrapers, key-shaped scrapers, pièces esquillées, notches/denticulates, and drills/perforators) occur primarily in Block A and are not particularly associated with hearth features (Supplemental Figure 8.7). In contrast, hunting/butchering tools (bifaces and projectile points) are consistently associated with hearths (Supplemental Figure 8.8). Hide-working/sewing tools (hide scrapers and small piercers) are found in both blocks but not specifically around hearths (Supplemental Figure 8.9). Groundstone items are clearly associated with hearths in Block C but not in Block A (Supplemental Figure 8.10).

Tool distributions are similar in some ways and different as well from IIf. Like IIf, the full array of IIg tools occur in both blocks, and given the presence of hearths in each area, each block clearly contained feature-centered multi-activity spaces consistent with our expectations for domestic areas. However, in contrast, heavy-duty and hide-working/sewing tools are found scattered away from hearths. This placement could make considerable sense if we assume that tools were discarded where generally used given that wood/bone/antler working and hide preparation were likely messy activities. Hunting/butchering tools could have been discarded around hearths if lighting was critical for manufacture and maintenance of these items. Concentrations of groundstone around hearths are best explained by the likelihood that many groundstone tools were purposefully fractured and recycled as heating/cooking stones.

Faunal Remains and Spatial Organization

Fish remains occur in clusters around features at the north, central, and southern portions of IIg (Supplemental Figure 8.11). This pattern is replicated by mammalian and ungulate remains, which also cluster around the same features (Supplemental Figures 8.12 and 8.13). Ungulate remains are particularly dense in association with the three hearths of southern Block C. Interesting variability is observed in the positions of high, medium, and low utility ungulate remains. High utility elements (meaty limb parts) occur around features but are found in greatest numbers at the south end of Block A (Supplemental Figure 8.14). In contrast, medium utility (generally axial parts) occur in nearly equal numbers within clusters at the north, central, and southern areas of IIg (Supplemental Figure 8.15). Low utility elements (lower limb and some cranial parts) occur nearly exclusively in the northwest of Block C (Supplemental Figure

8.16). Overall, these results confirm the strong likelihood that three domestic groups lived on IIg since both fish and mammalian prey were processed and presumably consumed around the three feature areas.

The consistent presence of faunal remains, lithic tools, and debitage along the southern margin of Block A raises the possibility that a hearth feature may be present in this area but just beyond the bounds of our excavation. Curiously the hearth in northeast Block A has virtually no associated artifacts or faunal remains. Given its presence capping a refuse-filled pit, perhaps it was exclusively used for hygienic purposes (e.g., reducing olfactory impact of discarded materials). The concentration of high utility parts coupled with abundant tools and the large storage feature in southern Block A raises the possibility that a domestic unit of particular importance could have resided in that space.

Summary: Site Structure on the IIg Floor

Artifacts and faunal remains cluster around features at the northern, central, and southern portions of the IIg floor. Like IIf, the spatially extensive northern hearths are also associated with an array of small postholes, suggesting a platform or bench was used at times during this occupation cycle. In addition, somewhat like IIf, we found another cluster of hearths in southern Block C with abundant evidence for multiple activities and, unique to IIg, a likely associated cache pit. Finally, we recognized overlapping concentrations of artifacts and faunal remains along the southern margin of Block A in association with a large cache pit and a hearth just to the east. Considering all data, 11g appears to have three domestic units, spaced relatively evenly down the center of the floor. This placement suggests that domestic groups may have inhabited relatively equally sized spaces. Similar to IIf, the central cluster of hearths (southern Block C) are positioned somewhat to the west side of the house. Given the dense materials at either end, this location raises a possibility of a side entrance on the east-central side of the house. If that is the case, then the only real public space on this floor was that entry area as no spatial evidence of a roof entry has been found.

Sociality

Our previous study of material wealth variation within and between floors suggested that IIg was relatively even in terms of nonlocal lithic materials, prestige materials, and prestige objects (Prentiss et al. 2018b). This study provides an opportunity to assess these conclusions in light of spatial organization that considers these same data classes but also canid remains. Canids are found at low density near the central hearths of IIg (Supplementary Figure 8.17). Nonlocal lithic materials area are found in all three domestic zones but occur in particularly high density at the south feature group in Block A (Supplementary Figure 8.18). Prestige raw materials occur in even numbers across all three domestic areas (Supplementary Figure 8.19). Finally, prestige items are rare but found in the north and south domestic areas (north Block C and south Block A).

The combination of concentrated high utility elements and highest concentrations of nonlocal lithic materials implies the possibility of some importance to the group in south Block A. However, this significance did not apparently translate into greater access to dogs or prestige goods. Thus, while clearly areas exhibit some differences in materials, this disparity does not appear to reflect the same degree of social differentiation we recognize on IIb–IIe.

Conclusions

Stratum IIg is the sixth of seven rectangular floors in the Housepit 54 sequence. The floor was established following the closing of IIf and was intensely occupied, leaving evidence for a complete occupation and abandonment cycle. The distribution of features indicates three areas with concentrated hearths and in two of three spaces, associated cache pits. Similar to IIf, a cluster of small postholes at the north end suggests that a bench or platforms had been constructed there. Artifacts and faunal remains generally cluster around each concentration of features, implying that each space was used for multiple activities spanning cooking to preparation of hunting gear. Some more messy activities (wood/bone/antler-working and hide preparation) may have been undertaken in spaces between hearths.

Overall, these data suggest the presence of three domestic units on IIg positioned in relatively equal spaces from north to south across the floor. Given that no single obvious communal space is evidenced, we suggest that the IIg human group was organized in a collectivist strategy. The southernmost group appears to have had frequent access to high utility elements from deer-sized game and to have gained the most frequent access to nonlocal lithic materials. No other data back up an argument for material wealth-based inequality, and this group simply could have had one or more particularly good hunters whose successes led to more frequent contact and trade opportunities with neighboring villages. This expectation could have been verified from ethnography, where households clearly benefited from having good hunters (Romanoff 1992b).

9

The Final Communalist House

Stratum IIh

Stratum IIh is the fifth of seven floors associated with the rectangular form of Housepit 54 (Figure 9.1). Stratum IIh is stratigraphically the most complex of the Housepit 54 floors because effectively two occupations occurred within this stratum. Level 3 of stratum IIh is dominated by two very large roasting ovens, one 2+ m in diameter (C3[2016]) and the other (A5[2014]) at least 1.5 m in diameter. The larger of the two is at the south end of Block C and is paired to the north with a 5–10 cm thick layer of charcoal and fire-cracked rock spanning about 1 × 2 m in area. We believe the latter is clean-out material from the large oven just to the south. The other large oven is in the northwestern portion of Block A. This early occupation on IIh is not our primary focus given our interest in residential occupations. The early occupation of IIh appears to have been a specialized focus on large-scale cookery and thus is examined elsewhere (e.g., Lyons et al. 2018). The level 3 period, when IIh was narrowly focused on large scale pit cooking, was relatively short.

We infer that at the initial establishment of the IIh floor, occupants used the house for a singular specialized activity, that of food preparation on a scale unlike any other known floor at Bridge River or other Mid-Fraser villages. Following that, Stratum IIh occupants added more sediment to fill in the oven depressions and occupied the floor as a standard residential pithouse. As was the case with Stratum IIg, IIh sediments are clay-dominated, though somewhat more variable according to field estimates (25–70%), followed by silt (10–30%), sand (10–35%), and eventually low percentages of gravels and pebbles. The upper levels of IIh contain seven hearths, three in central and south Block C and three in northern Block A, along with one on the southern edge of Block A (Figure 9.2). The northernmost in Block C (C6[2016]) is reminiscent of the linear hearth feature from Block C on IId as it consists of a 10–15 cm deep trench filled with charcoal and charred timber fragments of various sizes. The southern hearth in Block C is actual three superimposed hearths (C9, C11, and C13 [all 2016]), likely reflecting different periods of use on the same feature. The southernmost in Block A (A6[2014]), as excavated, appears to be a portion of a cylindrical roasting oven. The others are more typical, shallow bowl-shaped hearths. One large cache pit (diameter is at least 1.5 m) was found in the north-northwest portion of Block A. Postholes are extremely rare on IIh. One unique feature was a literal pile of burned and unburned rocks and abrader fragments in central Block C. Stratum IIh was buried in part on its south side (Block A) by a thin roof (Vc) and the IIg floor elsewhere (Supplemental Figure 9.1). The following discussions outline evidence for variation in occupation and abandonment cycles, site structure, and sociality associated with the upper occupation of IIh.

Stratum IIh Levels 1-2

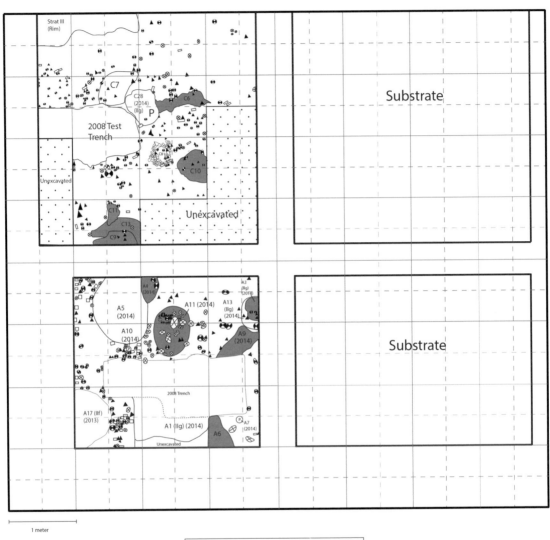

FIGURE 9.1. Comprehensive map of IIh showing point-provenienced artifacts, faunal remains, fire-cracked rock, prior excavations, and features.

Stratum IIh Levels 1-2

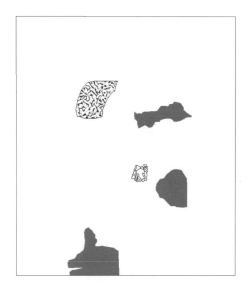

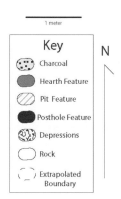

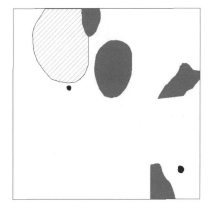

FIGURE 9.2. Features on IIh.

Occupation and Abandonment Cycle

We examine IIh occupation and abandonment cycles using expectations outlined in Chapter 2 (Stratum IIa).

Occupation Cycle

Occupation cycles consist of initiation, exploitation, and abandonment. We provide archaeological expectations for each in Chapter 2 (Stratum IIa).

The Stratum IIh lithic assemblage (Table 9.1) closely resembles that of IIg with representation of heavy-duty woodworking tools (adzes and possibly abraders) and light-duty wood/bone/antler working tools (flake scrapers, key-shaped scrapers, notches, denticulates, pièces esquillées, and drills/perforators). Evidence for hunting is present in the form of bifaces and projectile points, while hide-working is indicated by numerous hide scrapers and piercers.

TABLE 9.1. Lithic Tools from IIh, Organized by Tool Class and Block.

	Tool Class																
	A	B	C	D	E	F	G	H	I	J	K	L	M	N	O	P	Q
Block A	2	3	4	3	11	0	1	3	1	1	12	5	15	8	1	14	2
Block C	5	1	4	4	8	2	0	1	3	6	70	2	6	2	5	15	5
Total	7	4	8	7	19	2	1	4	4	7	82	7	21	10	6	29	7

Note: A = flake and slate knives; B = bifaces; C = projectile points; D = flake and key-shaped scrapers; E = hide scrapers; F = drills and perforators; G = small piercers; H = pièces esquillées; I = notches and denticulates; J = adzes; K = abraders/groundstone; L = freehand cores; M = bipolar cores; N = slate objects; O = hammerstones; P = used flakes; Q = ritual/social items.

TABLE 9.2. Lithic Flake Types for Stratum IIh by Toolstone Category.

	Ext	Chal	Cher	Dac	Obs	Intr	Slates	Met.	Total
Biface	2	1	0	26	0	0	0	0	29
Core	3	0	0	10	0	2	1	0	16
Retouch	4	6	4	87	0	0	23	4	128

Note: Ext = extrusives (excluding dacite and obsidian); Dac = dacite; Cher = cherts; Chal = chalcedony; Obs = obsidian; Intr = intrusives plus gneiss; Slates = slate and silicified shale; Met = metamorphic rock inclusive of quartzites, nephrite, and steatite.

Bipolar cores are common, reflecting the practice of extending raw material use-life. Groundstone also is extraordinarily common, primarily a consequence of these items being pre-formed as cooking/heating rocks and either used in hearths or stored for later use (note the pile of abraders and other rocks in central Block C). Debitage reflect a focus on late stage tool reduction and maintenance, with progressively lowered emphases on biface and core reduction (Table 9.2). The diversity of tools and debitage on IIh informs us that the upper portion of this floor was likely occupied through initiation, exploitation, and abandonment phases. The early occupation (level 3) of IIh likely did not adhere to the same occupation cycles as it may have had a specialized use in communal cooking.

Abandonment Process

The residential occupation surface of IIh was buried by sediments from a thin roof termed Vc, containing charcoal, small fragmentary roof beams, and abundant fire-cracked rock. Sediments from Stratum IIg then buried the latter roof and the rest of the final IIh surface. No evidence was found for preserved architec-

tural members on IIh. The Vc roof is our earliest example of a partially cleared and partially burned roof. As with the other such roof deposits (Vb, Vb1, and Vb3), we note that both practical and ritual explanations could be relevant. Regardless, the subsequent burial of all with a new floor layer (IIg) and the lack of abandoned architectural elements (posts and beams) tells us that the end of the IIh occupation came with a commitment to refloor and reroof the house.

Cultural debris from the final cycle of occupation on IIh does not appear to have been systematically cleaned. A correlation coefficient for the relationship between extra-small versus larger sized debitage returned a very high score ($r = 0.844$, $p = 0.000$). This pattern is visually evident on Figures 9.3 and 9.4 where distributions match very closely. A similar pattern is evident from the faunal remains ($r = 0.891$, $p = 0.000$), as illustrated on Figures 9.5 and 9.6.

Distributions of positioning items (Binford 1979), caches (Binford 1979; Hayden and Deal 1983), site furniture (Binford 1979), and de facto refuse (Schiffer 1972; Stevenson 1982) provide additional insight. While no obvious examples of site furniture or de facto refuse were found,

IIh (Levels 1-2) Extra-Small
Debitage Distribution

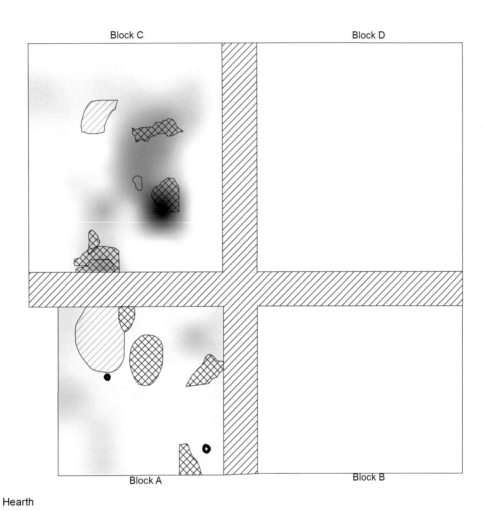

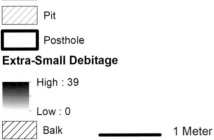

Hearth

Pit

Posthole

Extra-Small Debitage

High : 39

Low : 0

Balk

1 Meter

FIGURE 9.3. Extra-small debitage distribution on IIh.

IIh (Levels 1-2) Total Lithic Artifact Distribution

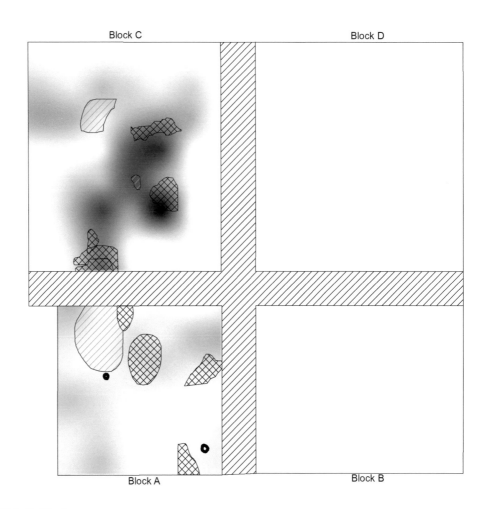

Block C

Block D

Block A

Block B

Total Lithic Artifacts

Hearth

Pit

Posthole

High : 77

Low : 0

Balk

1 Meter

FIGURE 9.4. Total artifact distribution on IIh.

Ilh Faunal Specimens Sized 1-9mm
Levels 1 and 2

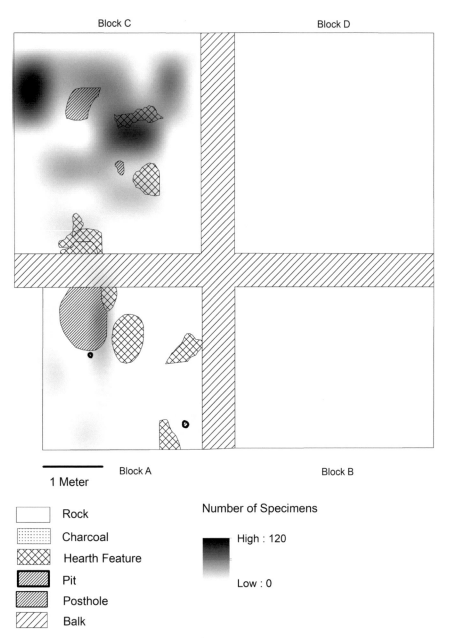

FIGURE 9.5. Extra-small faunal specimens on Ilh.

IIh All Faunal Specimens
Levels 1 and 2

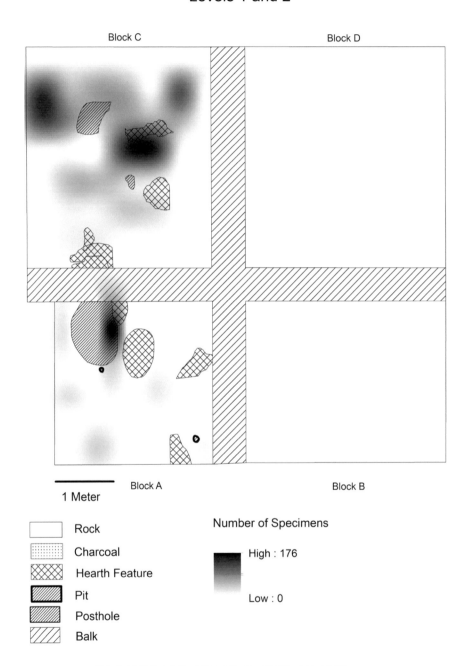

FIGURE 9.6. Total faunal specimen distribution on IIh.

we do have a possible cache and some positioning items. A circular cluster near the center of Block C consists of vesicular basalt rocks that appear to be cracked both via knapping and thermal cracking. Given their relatively small size (all about 5 cm in maximum diameter), these rocks likely were utilized for stone boiling and set aside after and or in anticipation of use, as well as being not of enough importance to be salvaged before reflooring with IIg sediments. A large cache pit was used for a period within Block A. However, during the final occupation cycle(s), it was clearly converted to a refuse receptacle. Lithic cores are relatively abundant across the IIh floor, and while many were likely discarded, they also represent a source of lithic material that may have been moved around as positioning items during the occupation period. Finally, we recognize an abundance of groundstone, in part because abrader tools were often recycled as heating/cooking stones on this floor.

Site Structure

As with the previous chapter, we are interested in three aspects of site structure: zonation of floor activities, variation in the nature of activity areas, and contingent problem-solving. We address these interests by examining distributions of debitage, tool forms, and faunal remains.

Debitage and Spatial Structure of Lithic Reduction

Debitage are found throughout the IIh floor (Supplemental Figure 9.2). Early stage reduction flakes are found in low numbers throughout the house but occur in highest frequency adjacent to hearths in Block C (Supplemental Figure 9.3). Biface thinning and R-billet flakes are uncommon and scattered throughout the house without any particular feature associations (Supplemental Figures 9.4 and 9.5). In contrast, tool retouch flakes are found throughout the IIh floor and in particularly high numbers in Block C (Supplemental Figure 9.6). These results are largely in line with those of later floors, suggesting that tool retouch was the most common lithic reduction activity on

IIh and practiced throughout the floor with no consistent association with hearths. Only early stage reduction appears to have occurred closer to hearths, though sample sizes are small.

Lithic Tools and House Floor Activity Organization

Knapping items (hammerstones and cores) are found throughout the IIh floor, and cores and hammerstones appear to have been discarded both near and away from hearths and pits (Supplemental Figure 9.7). In contrast, heavy-duty tools (wood/bone/antler working: flake scrapers, key-shaped scrapers, pièces esquillées, notches/denticulates, and drills/perforators) are found consistently in or adjacent to features, raising the possibility that these activities benefited from access to light and warmth (Supplemental Figure 9.8). Although sample sizes are lower, hunting/butchery tools (bifaces and projectile points) and hide-working/sewing tools are also typically associated with features (Supplemental Figures 9.9 and 9.10). Finally, groundstone items are highly clustered around features, particularly in Block C (Supplemental Figure 9.11). One reason for this distribution is that the majority of these items are abraders recycled as heating/boiling stones. To accomplish this purpose, each item was knapped or otherwise broken to form a somewhat cuboid shape before use. Many are blackened and also have thermal fractures.

Distribution of tool forms illustrates two general patterns. First, knapping items pattern similar to that of debitage without clear association with house features, thus confirming that during the IIh occupation, knappers were not concerned with accomplishing their work in proximity to fires. Indeed, given the focus of those spaces with other activities, staying somewhat apart from hearth areas may have been preferred for knapping activities. Second, virtually all other tool forms tend to be found in association with features, especially hearths. The fact that all tool classes are present around features in Blocks A and C supports an argument that a domestic group engaged in similar household work occupied each area. Given consistently higher densities of items in Block C, we suggest that this area may have held a somewhat higher number of people.

Faunal Remains and Spatial Organization

Fish remains are found in several distinct clusters, three of which occur at the north side of Block C and one in north-central Block A (Supplemental Figure 9.12). Two of the Block C clusters are associated with a hearth feature, as is the Block A cluster. Curiously hearths at the south ends of each block do not have strong numbers of fish elements. Mammal remains are found throughout much of the IIh floor but occur in particularly high densities in the northwest of Block C and southwest of Block A (Supplemental Figure 9.13). These areas do not have the highest concentrations of fish, which could imply different work and/or discard zones for each. The fact that each area is positioned away from hearths suggests that this work may have not required extra light or was perceived as messy or needing extra space. Identifiable ungulate remains are found in small clusters associated with hearths and cache pits in both blocks (Supplemental Figure 9.14). Hearths on the east side of Block A did not accumulate ungulate remains. High and medium utility elements from mammals occur in two high-density clusters in northern Block C (Supplemental Figures 9.15 and 9.16). Lower density clusters are found adjacent to hearths elsewhere on the floor with the exception of southeast Block A. Low utility elements are distributed lightly around the floor, while a particularly dense concentration is found in northeast Block C (Supplemental Figure 9.17).

Fish and mammals are represented in each block, supporting the idea that each cluster of hearths and associated food remains could reflect the activities of distinct domestic groups. However, as with the lithics, the higher densities of faunal remains in Block C could suggest that more people occupied this portion of the house. Some variability in discard location of elements could reflect distinct activity areas for processing and cooking of different prey packages.

Summary: Site Structure on the IIh Floor

Three hearths are found in association with a large cache pit, the latter in northern Block A. Each block also has two smaller hearths positioned in somewhat removed spaces from the central cluster of features. Artifact and faunal remains occur in consistently high densities in the northern (Block C) and central areas. Much fewer numbers of each are found around the hearths of eastern and south Block A.

We suggest that the central cache pit and its hearths may have served as a communal activity area space for two domestic groups. The north Block C group appears to have been larger and perhaps more persistent in terms of longevity in this space. In contrast, the Block A group appears to have been much smaller in size and likely less persistent in terms of continuous reuse of this space. We do not see any indicators of a roof entrance, which implicates the use of an entrance from the side. The east-central portion of the house seems most likely. However, further excavation is necessary to confirm this conclusion.

Sociality

Previous research into variability in markers of differential material wealth indicated that the IIh floor was likely egalitarian (Prentiss et al. 2018b). Here we further evaluate this conclusion in light of spatial variation in distributions of canid remains, nonlocal lithic raw materials, prestige raw materials, and prestige objects. Canid remains concentrate in the center of the house (northwest Block A) and in low numbers on the north side of Block C (Supplemental Figure 9.18). Nonlocal lithic raw material is found in clusters loosely associated with hearths and pits throughout the IIh floor (Supplemental Figure 9.19). These materials occur in greatest density in southern Block C associated with the central cluster of features. Prestige raw materials and items are rare and are generally found around the central cluster of features in southern Block C and northern Block A (Supplemental Figures 9.20 and 9.21). Considering all data, indicators of material wealth appear to co-occur in the center of the house, further supporting an argument that this floor was likely communalistic in social organization and egalitarian.

Conclusions

The upper portion of IIh (levels 1 and 2) included an extensive quantity of occupation debris and clear indicators of all occupation phases, as well as a planned abandonment process with intent to reoccupy. The IIh floor included a complex distribution of features, artifacts, and faunal remains. A cluster of three hearths and a large cache pit are found in approximately the center of the floor, while additional hearths are also scattered in Blocks A and C. This distribution raises the interesting possibility that domestic groups occupied each end of the rectangular floor and shared cooking and storage space in its center. The co-association of lithic retouch flakes, all tool types, and fish and mammal remains indicates that multiple activities were conducted in the center of the house. Equally diverse activities occurred in areas of the floor north and south of the fea-

ture cluster, though discarded materials are particularly dense on the north side in Block C. Some evidence also indicates dispersed special activity zones, particularly associated with mammal processing.

We suggest that this floor may have been organized in a communalistic strategy with distinct domestic areas and a major shared work, storage, and, eventually, refuse disposal zone. If that is the case, the north Block C domestic area also appears to have held a preferred position as it contains by far the greatest densities of all forms of material culture and food remains as compared to Block A. The concentration of material wealth-markers in the central area of the house suggests that despite differences in quantities of materials between the two blocks and their implications for population and occupational persistence, the house was probably egalitarian in nature. The Block A group was just likely smaller, and perhaps this portion of the house was occupied less consistently than that of Block C.

10

Survival during the First Demographic Low

Stratum IIi

Stratum IIi is the fourth of seven floors associated with the rectangular form of Housepit 54 (Figure 10.1). Some portions of IIi were removed by features excavated during the occupation of IIh. In particular, the roasting oven in the southwest portion of Block C (C3[2016]) and the cache pit in the northwest sector of Block A (A5[2014]) collectively removed about two square meters of IIi deposits. Stratum IIi sediments are somewhat variable between excavated units and blocks. Units in Block A can be silt- or clay-dominated with highly variable percentages. In contrast, Block C sediments are consistently clay-dominated. All have low percentages of sand, gravel, and pebbles. Given consistency in the excavation teams working in these Blocks, these estimates are unlikely to be the result of error. Thus we may conclude that source material for the IIi sediments varied to some degree between the Block A and C portions of the floor.

Three hearths were excavated in IIi, two in Block C and one in Block A (Figure 10.2). The Block C hearths consist of a trench-like linear hearth similar to those in IId and IIh and a shallow bowl-shaped form. One broad, though shallow, hearth is found in Block A. The pair of hearths in Block C are positioned within about one meter of the other, raising the possibility that positions shifted during the life of the floor. Alternatively, if the hearths had different functions, then they might have been used

simultaneously. One cache pit was found in the northeast corner of Block A. Two small postholes are located close to the north wall of the house in Block C. Four additional small postholes are found along the east wall of Block A. Three of these are directly adjacent to the cache pit. Given small sizes and positions along walls, we think that all postholes in IIi likely reflect construction and use of wooden benches or platforms in these areas. The floor is entirely buried by sediments from Stratum IIh. In the following sections, we explore evidence for variation in occupation and abandonment cycles, site structure, and sociality.

Occupation and Abandonment Cycle

This section focuses on defining occupation and abandonment cycles using IIi data. We accomplish this analysis, drawing upon frames of reference outlined in Chapter 2 (Stratum IIa).

Occupation Cycle

Our assessment of IIi occupation cycles focuses on evidence for initiation, exploitation, and abandonment phases using expectations outlined in Chapter 2 (Stratum IIa).

Occupation materials in the form of fire-cracked rock (FCR) and lithic artifacts are somewhat sparse on IIi (Table 10.1). Limited FCR densities and equally limited cache pit volume (relative to floor volume) permitted Prentiss and colleagues (2018a) to argue that

Stratum IIi

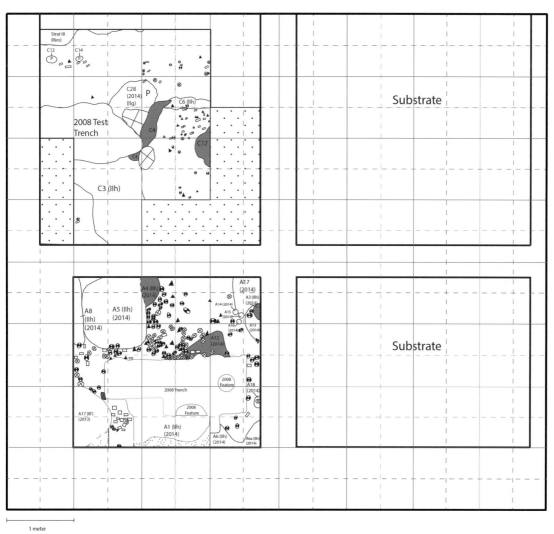

Substrate

Substrate

1 meter

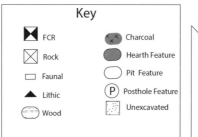

Key

FCR

Rock

Faunal

Lithic

Wood

Charcoal

Hearth Feature

Pit Feature

Posthole Feature

Unexcavated

FIGURE 10.1. Comprehensive map of IIi showing point-provenienced artifacts, faunal remains, fire-cracked rock, prior excavations, and features.

Stratum IIi

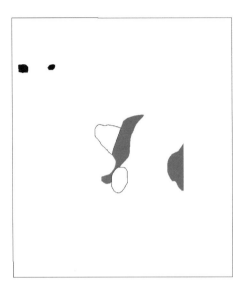

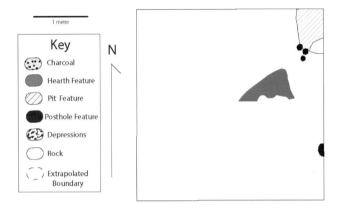

FIGURE 10.2. Features on IIi.

low population correlated with limited investment in storage at this time. Artifacts illustrate a pattern somewhat different from later floors. Very little evidence indicates any investment in gearing up for hunting as only one biface and no projectile points are found. In contrast, a small set of hide scrapers and one piercer does suggest limited access to hides. Likewise, only sparse evidence has been found for production of wood/bone/antler tools (two flake scrapers but no drills/perforators or pièces esquillées).

Further contrasting with later floors, no bipolar cores are present. Debitage are also quite sparse, though as typical for other floors, remains are dominated by late stage retouch flakes and much lower counts of biface and core reduction flakes (Table 10.2).

All evidence considered and recognizing low sample size, we cannot conclude that occupants of IIi completed exploitation and planned abandonment phases. Put differently, final occupants of IIi appear to have left much earlier

TABLE 10.1. Lithic Tools from Iii, Organized by Tool Class and Block.

	Tool Class																
	A	B	C	D	E	F	G	H	I	J	K	L	M	N	O	P	Q
Block A	0	1	0	1	1	0	1	0	0	0	4	1	0	1	1	2	2
Block C	2	0	0	1	3	0	0	0	0	0	3	0	0	1	1	2	0
Total	2	1	0	2	4	0	1	0	0	0	7	1	0	2	2	4	2

Note: A = flake and slate knives; B = bifaces; C = projectile points; D = flake and key-shaped scrapers; E = hide scrapers; F = drills and perforators; G = small piercers; H = pièces esquillées; I = notches and denticulates; J = adzes; K = abraders/groundstone; L = freehand cores; M = bipolar cores; N = slate objects; O = hammerstones; P = used flakes; Q = ritual/social items.

TABLE 10.2. Lithic Flake Types for Stratum Iii by Toolstone Category.

	Ext	Chal	Cher	Dac	Obs	Intr	Slates	Met.	Total
Biface	0	0	0	6	0	0	0	0	6
Core	1	0	0	1	0	0	2	0	3
Retouch	0	0	2	31	0	1	1	2	37

Note: Ext = extrusives (excluding dacite and obsidian); Dac = dacite; Cher = cherts; Chal = chalcedony; Obs = obsidian; Intr = intrusives plus gneiss; Slates = slate and silicified shale; Met = metamorphic rock inclusive of quartzites, nephrite, and steatite.

and more abruptly than later occupants had done and thus failed to leave significant evidence for preparation of gear or extension of raw material use-life. Given limited reliance on storage, winter survival during the final season on IIi possibly required residential mobility.

Abandonment Process

Despite the apparent early and hurried abandonment of IIi, findings overall indicate a planned intent to return. Stratum IIi is entirely buried by IIh sediments inclusive of the large ovens and later large cache pit. No architectural elements (wooden posts, etc.) remain on IIi. Thus, while the occupants of Housepit 54 may have suffered one or more difficult winter seasons during late IIi, they clearly still retained the house and perhaps even briefly during the following season reconfigured it as a communal cooking facility (IIh lower level) before occupying it again in a residential fashion (IIh upper levels) that is very close in structure to that of IIi.

No evidence suggests that the IIi floor was cleaned before abandonment. A correlation coefficient for extra-small versus all larger debitage was very strong ($r = 0.779$, $p = 0.000$), and the same pattern is visible on Figures 10.3 and 10.4. A somewhat similar correlation was achieved for extra-small versus larger faunal items ($r = 0.683$, $p = 0.021$). These relationships are visually evident in Figures 10.5 and 10.6.

Excavation reveals little evidence of positioning items (Binford 1979), caches (Binford 1979; Hayden and Deal 1983), site furniture (Binford 1979), and de facto refuse (Schiffer 1972; Stevenson 1982). Two large cobble- to small-boulder-sized rocks remain in place around the central Block C hearth. Groundstone, hammerstones, and cores are rare and, when present, fragmentary or exhausted. During the life of the floor, some of these items may have been treated as positioning items. However, by abandonment they had clearly become refuse. One cache pit, located in the northeast corner of Block A, was converted to a refuse receptacle. No direct evidence for de facto refuse is indicated. All told, the IIi floor clearly was occupied for a comparatively short period and abandonment may not have included a high degree of advanced planning in terms of floor preparation or gear development.

N

Ili Extra-Small Debitage Distribution

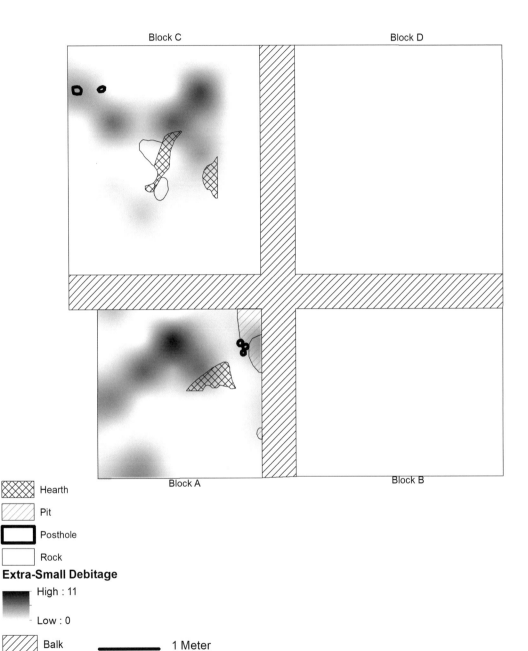

FIGURE 10.3. Extra-small debitage distribution on Ili

Ili Total Lithic Artifact Distribution

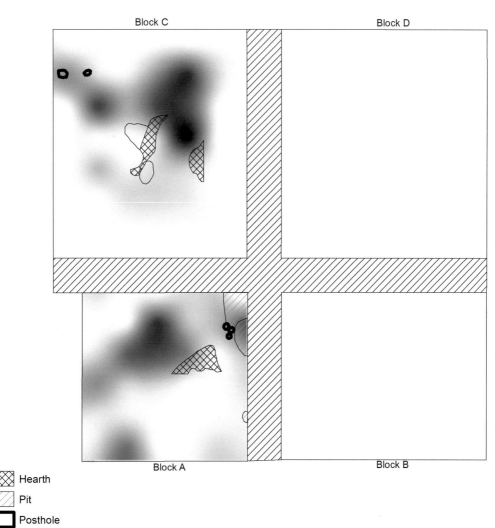

FIGURE 10.4. Total artifact distribution on Ili.

Ili Faunal Specimens Sized 1-9mm

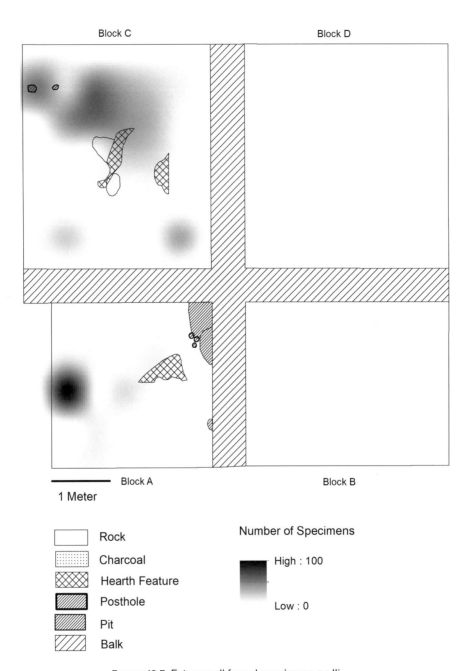

FIGURE 10.5. Extra-small faunal specimens on Ili.

Ili All Faunal Specimens

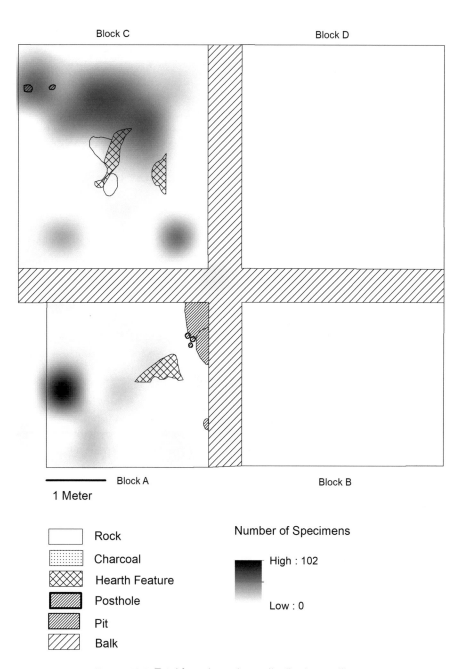

FIGURE 10.6. Total faunal specimen distribution on Ili.

Site Structure

Expectations for variation in the spatial organization of a rectangular house are provided in Chapter 7 (Stratum IIf). In the following sections, we explore spatial data regarding lithic reduction activities, lithic tool use and discard, and food preparation as indicated by faunal remains as means to assess house floor activity zonation, activity areas, and contingent use of space.

Debitage and Spatial Structure of Lithic Reduction

Debitage are found in distinct clusters within central Blocks A and C (Supplemental Figure 10.1). These clusters are somewhat artificial, due to constraints imposed by sediments removed by features associated with later floors and the 2008 test trenches. However, the shapes of the high-density debitage clusters still suggest particular favored knapping areas close to hearth features. Early stage reduction flakes are rare and are found adjacent to hearths in Blocks A and C (Supplemental Figure 10.2). Biface thinning and R-billet flakes are also rare and most common around the central hearth in Block A (Supplemental Figures 10.3 and 10.4). Similar to other floors, tool retouch flakes are found throughout the IIi floor with the common implication that tool retouch was practiced throughout the house (Supplemental Figure 10.5). Tool retouch was clearly the dominant lithic reduction activity on Iii, while other reduction activities were rare and spatially constrained to hearth areas.

Lithic Tools and House Floor Activity Organization

Knapping items (hammerstones and cores) are uncommon on IIi and found scattered in Blocks A and C (Supplemental Figure 10.6). Heavy-duty tools (wood/bone/antler working: flake scrapers, key-shaped scrapers, pièces esquillées, notches/denticulates, and drills/perforators) are most common in a cluster associated with the hearths in Block C, though two are found in Block A (Supplemental Figure 10.7). Hunting-butchering (bifaces and projectile points), hide-working/sewing (hide scrapers and small piercers), and groundstone (abraders) all cluster in low frequencies in association with the hearths in Blocks A and C (Supplemental Figures 10.8 to 10.10). These data suggest that no single activity was practiced in a very intense way on IIi. Further, no evidence suggest segregation of space for particular work. With the exception of knapping items and tool retouch, all activities appear to have been concentrated around the hearths on the house floor. The co-association of these items implicates dual domestic activity areas on the IIi floor.

Faunal Remains and Spatial Organization

As with lithic artifacts, the distribution of faunal remains from IIi are constrained by excavation limits, test trenches, and features excavated by post-IIi occupants of the house. Nonetheless we can still recognize some general patterns particularly addressing the question of associations with features in both Blocks A and C. Fish remains are most intensely concentrated across the north end of Block C adjacent to the linear hearth feature (Supplemental Figure 10.11). Likewise, a dense concentration of fish remains, with lower numbers, is found on the west side of Block A closer to the Block A hearth. Fish remains appear to be generally discarded around features in both Blocks. Evidence also suggests that some fish remains were processed or at least dumped at slight distances away from hearth-centered activity areas. The latter scenario is most likely to have occurred in Block A.

Mammalian remains are scattered throughout Block C but occur in greatest density in the northwest corner (Supplemental Figure 10.12). Mammalian remains also occur in Block A with lower densities clustering near the hearth feature and higher numbers present in the southwest corner. As with the fish remains, mammals were clearly processed in two hearth-centered spaces in Blocks A and C. However, some work clearly was completed and/or remains dumped slightly away from hearths. We can gain a better understanding of mammal distributions by more closely considering variation in ungulate remains. Ungulate remains occur in small clusters both directly adjacent and slightly away from hearths. Quantities in Block C are relatively low compared to the somewhat higher density cluster in southwestern Block A (Supplemental Figure 10.13). High utility faunal elements are found in several small discrete clusters near and away from hearths in Block C, including the east-central, northwest, and southwest areas (Supplemental Figure 10.14). Very few are found in Block A. Medium and low utility faunal elements occur most densely across northern Block C, though small clusters also are present in west and southwest Block A (Supplemental Figures 10.15 and 10.16).

Summary: Site Structure on the Ili Floor

Hearths are found in roughly central positions in each block. Each hearth area is associated with similar distributions of lithic tools and debitage. A moderate sized cache pit also is present in the northeast corner of Block A. In contrast, virtually all faunal remains are in Block C, with most dense concentrations in its northern half. Thus, from the standpoint of basic floor structure, there would appear to be spaces for two domestic units living on Ili. However, some activity segregation also is indicated, with animal resources not only clearly processed around hearths but also slightly away from hearth areas. The latter is also explainable by reference to cleanup and dump zones. However, overlap between size classes suggests that cleanup or classic drop and toss zones was not a typical practice. Thus, spatial variation in faunal clusters seems more likely to represent diverse work and possibly consumption zones that accumulated discarded animal refuse.

No obvious space is set aside for a roof entrance, though this possibility is difficult to evaluate given constraints in reconstructing the entire floor area. Neither is it clear where a side entrance might have been located. However, given the cluster of hearths and cache pits on the east side of both Blocks A and C, a west side entrance might have been possible.

Sociality

Previous research into variation in distributions of material wealth items suggested that Ili was characterized by little evidence for social inequality (Prentiss et al. 2018b). We can explore that conclusion further with spatial data

on artifact classes reflecting access and rights to wealth.

Only one canid bone was recovered, found adjacent to the hearth in Block A (Supplemental Figure 10.17). The distribution of nonlocal lithic raw materials is clustered relatively evenly around the hearths in each block (Supplemental Figure 10.18). Only one prestige item made from a prestige material (steatite) is present in Block A (Supplemental Figures 10.18 and 10.19). These data suggest no wealth distinctions between hearth groups on Ili, and we can assume a high likelihood of intrahouse cooperation.

Conclusions

Stratum Iii appears to represent a time when winter occupations were shorter and perhaps sometimes truncated as compared to those of later floors. Despite limited evidence for the extensive abandonment phase activities, the abandonment process still appears to have been planned. The Iii floor accumulated central hearths in its north and southern areas (Blocks C and A respectively), along with a cache pit in northeast Block A. Large cobble- to small-boulder-sized rocks may have been used to constrain some spaces, specifically the central hearth in Block C. Lithic debitage accumulated evenly around both hearth areas, as did a sparse scatter of lithic tools. Faunal remains cluster in a similar manner with particularly high abundances in northern Block C and west to southwest Block A. This distribution suggests that the house probably held two domestic groups. The single cache pit context in northeastern Block A could suggest use of a common storage facility, thus implying some degree of communalist organization. Neither artifacts nor faunal remains are highly abundant (compared to other floors) on Iii, raising the possibility that the floor was not used at the same intensity as others. The lack of bipolar cores could indicate that winter stays were never long enough to require tactics for extending the use-life of lithic raw materials.

Short Winter Occupation Cycles

Stratum IIj

Stratum IIj represents the third floor of seven associated with the rectangular manifestation of Housepit 54 (Figure 11.1). Stratum IIj sediments are consistently clay-dominated though variable in estimated percentages (30–85%), followed by silt (0–30%) and subsequent low percentages of sand, gravel, and pebbles. Stratum IIj includes five hearths, three located in Block C and two in Block A. The southern Block C hearths are relatively large, while the northern Block C hearth is small but associated with an ash and charcoal dump and an adjacent posthole (Figure 11.2). On the southeast corner, feature C18(2016) spans more than 1 m in diameter and might be described as a small roasting oven. In contrast, the hearths in northwest and north-central Block A are comparatively small and shallow. Evidence for storage is limited to one small cache pit located in the northeast of Block A. The feature (A19 [2014]) was impacted by excavation of the cache pit from IIi (A17 [2014]). Two postholes were found on IIj, one in each block. Despite their positions, they seem unlikely to have been roof supports, given narrow width of each posthole. Stratum IIj is entirely buried by IIi sediments. We discuss the evidence for occupation and abandonment cycles, site structure, and sociality in the following sections.

Occupation and Abandonment Cycle

This section focuses on occupation and abandonment cycles drawing from expectations outlined in Chapter 2 (Stratum IIa).

Occupation Cycle

Occupation phases include initiation, exploitation, and abandonment. Archaeological expectations for each are provided in Chapter 2 (Stratum IIa).

Like Stratum IIi, IIj contains relatively sparse cultural materials compared to many later floors (Table 11.1). Also like IIi, occupation of the floor appears to have been terminated during exploitation phase without major investments in gear that would be expected for a slow planned abandonment phase. Heavy-duty woodworking is indicated by one adze and a large collection of abraders (recognizing that numbers of the latter were likely inflated by recycling some as cooking/heating rocks). Very sparse numbers of bifaces, projectile points, and hide-working tools suggest limited engagement with hunting but not a significant effort in gearing up for extended activities of this nature. Likewise, virtually no evidence was found for manufacture of wood/bone/antler implements given the lack of flake scrapers, notches/denticulates, drills/perforators, or pièces esquillées. Finally, only one bipolar core was recovered from IIj, and thus extension of raw material utility could not have been a major concern. As with IIi, debitage are relatively sparse but continue to reflect the common focus on late stage tool maintenance and retouch followed by a lesser focus on biface and core reduction (Table 11.2).

These results raise the possibility that for perhaps two generations (IIi and IIj) occupations

Stratum IIj

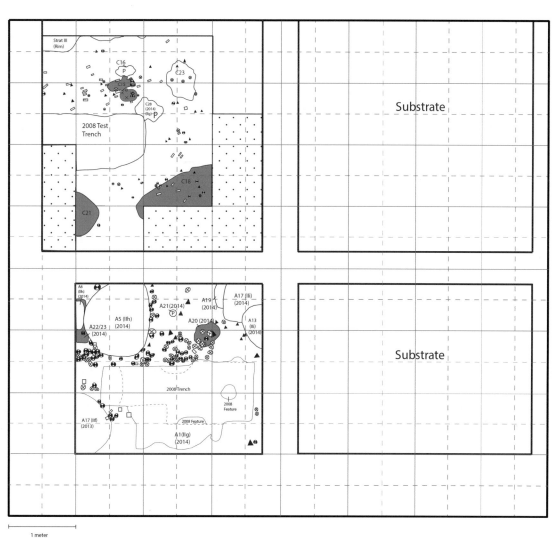

FIGURE 11.1. Comprehensive map of IIj showing point-provenienced artifacts, faunal remains, fire-cracked rock, prior excavations, and features.

Stratum IIj

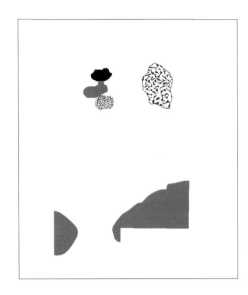

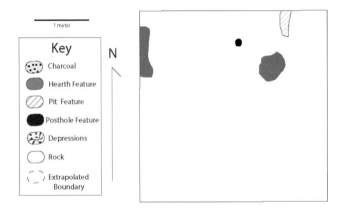

FIGURE 11.2. Features on IIj.

TABLE 11.1. Lithic tools from IIj, Organized by Tool Class and Block.

	Tool Class																
	A	B	C	D	E	F	G	H	I	J	K	L	M	N	O	P	Q
Block A	0	0	0	0	1	0	0	0	0	0	12	1	0	0	2	2	1
Block C	3	1	1	0	1	1	0	0	0	1	9	1	1	1	2	2	0
Total	3	1	1	0	2	1	0	0	0	1	21	2	1	1	4	4	1

Note: A = flake and slate knives; B = bifaces; C = projectile points; D = flake and key-shaped scrapers; E = hide scrapers; F = drills and perforators; G = small piercers; H = pièces esquillées; I = notches and denticulates; J = adzes; K = abraders/groundstone; L = freehand cores; M = bipolar cores; N = slate objects; O = hammerstones; P = used flakes; Q = ritual/social items.

TABLE 11.2. Lithic Flake Types for Stratum IIj by Toolstone category.

	Ext	Chal	Cher	Dac	Obs	Intr	Slates	Met.	Total
Biface	0	0	0	1	0	0	0	0	1
Core	0	0	1	0	0	0	2	0	3
Retouch	1	0	3	29	0	0	4	0	37

Note: Ext = extrusives (excluding dacite and obsidian); Dac = dacite; Cher = cherts; Chal = chalcedony; Obs = obsidian; Intr = intrusives plus gneiss; Slates = slate and silicified shale; Met = metamorphic rock inclusive of quartzites, nephrite, and steatite.

of winter houses were relatively brief with limited investment in storage and recurrent necessity to pursue winter residential mobility to gain adequate subsistence returns (see also Prentiss et al. 2018a).

Abandonment Process

Stratum IIj was fully buried by IIi sediments with no remaining architectural elements associated with IIj features. This evidence implies that, despite a comparatively brief stay on the final surface of IIj, occupants planned a return that would have included reflooring and likely rerooting after removal of the old roof. Distributions of extra-small debitage are virtually identical to overall lithics distributions (Figures 11.3 and 11.4), and this finding is supported by a significant correlation coefficient for extra-small versus larger debitage ($r = 0.677$, $p = 0.008$). Similar patterns are evident when we compare spatial distributions of extra-small to larger faunal remains ($r = 0.707$, $p = 0.076$; see Figures 11.5 and 11.6). Thus, IIj was probably not significantly swept prior to abandonment.

Caches (Binford 1979; Hayden and Deal 1983), positioning items (Binford 1979), and de facto refuse (Schiffer 1972; Stevenson 1982) allow additional insight into the abandonment process. One cache pit is found in northeastern Block A, but little remains of it as much of the fill from this pit was removed and refilled by later occupants creating their own cache pits. The most abundant artifacts on IIj are groundstone items, which cluster around hearths. These items were functional tools, but many were recycled as heating or cooking rocks likely in the associated features. These tools were likely

moved around as needed, and thus many could be classified as positioning items. However, by abandonment, they collectively appear to have become refuse left on the old floor and subsequently buried by addition of IIi sediments. No other items on IIj can be classified as positioning items or de facto refuse.

Site Structure

We developed expectations for variation in the organization space and its social implications within Chapter 7 (Stratum IIf). The following sections consider evidence for spatial organization with regard to lithic debitage, tools, and faunal remains.

Debitage and Spatial Structure of Lithic Reduction

Debitage cluster around the five hearths on IIj and occur in particularly high densities around the two large hearths in southern Block C (Supplemental Figure 11.1). Early stage reduction and biface thinning flakes are rare and occur close to the large hearths in southern Block C (Supplemental Figures 11.2 and 11.3). Only one R-billet flake occurs in central Block A (Supplemental Figure 11.4). Small retouch flakes are found in three distinct clusters associated with the small north hearth and large southern hearths in Block C and the northeastern hearth in Block A (Supplemental Figure 11.5). Clearly, the major emphasis in lithic reduction was late stage tool manufacture and maintenance, and those activities were conducted around household hearths. This pattern is different from many other floors where lithic retouch flakes are virtually ubiquitous. If IIj was occupied for shorter

Ilj Extra-Small Debitage Distribution

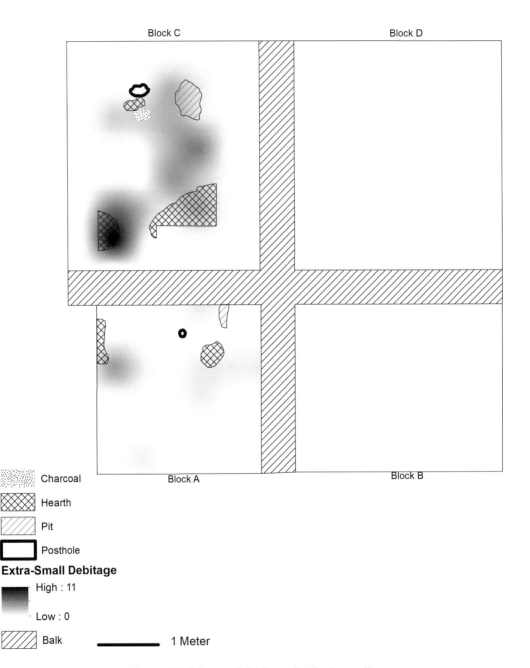

FIGURE 11.3. Extra-small debitage distribution on Ilj.

Ilj Total Lithic Artifact Distribution

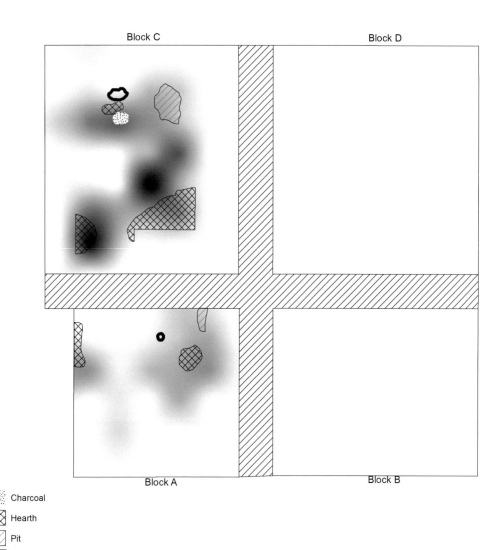

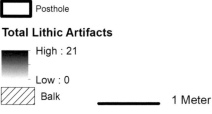

FIGURE 11.4. Total artifact distribution on Ilj.

Ilj Faunal Specimens Sized 1-9mm

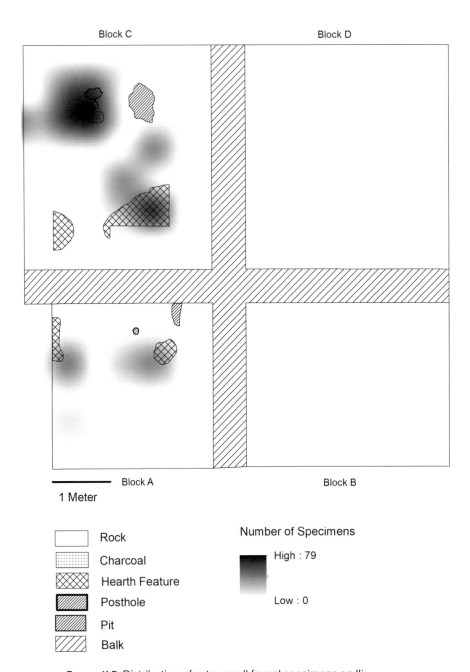

Figure 11.5. Distribution of extra-small faunal specimens on Ilj.

Ilj All Faunal Specimens

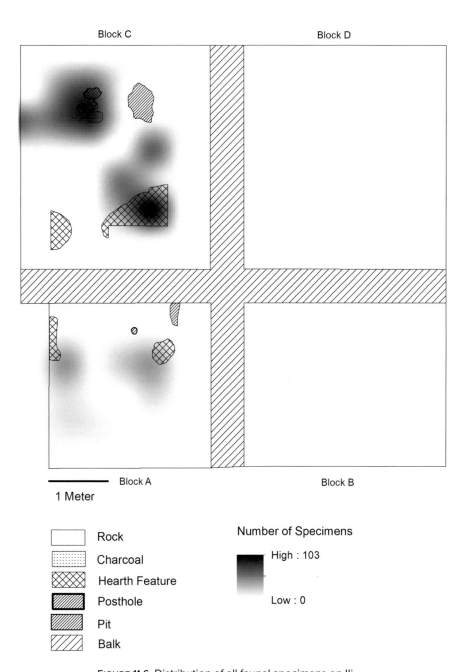

FIGURE 11.6. Distribution of all faunal specimens on Ilj.

periods, there may not have been enough time in any given winter for debitage to accumulate beyond the hearth drop zones.

Lithic Tools and House Floor Activity Organization

Knapping items (cores and hammerstones) occur in low numbers around the north Block C hearth and the northeast Block A hearth (Supplemental Figure 11.6). Heavy-duty tools (drills/perforators and adzes) are rare and occur exclusively at the north end of Block C (Supplemental Figure 11.7). Hunting/butchery tools are limited in number and occur in central Block C between the north and south hearths (Supplemental Figure 11.8). Hide scrapers are present, though rare in IIj sediments but not discarded in open floor contexts. Groundstone are common and consist primarily of fragmentary abraders clustered around the northeast Block A hearth and the large hearth in southeast Block C (Supplemental Figure 11.9). Several others occur in southwest Block A. As with other floors, clustering of groundstone around hearths is not surprising, given that these items were commonly also used as cooking or heating stones. Lithic data confirm that similarly diverse activities clustered around the three hearth areas, implicating the likelihood that each area reflected occupation by a domestic group.

Faunal Remains and Spatial Organization

As with lithic artifacts, faunal remains tend to cluster around IIj hearths. Fish remains occur at greatest densities associated with hearths in the northwest and southeast of Block C and in the northeast of Block A (Supplemental Figure 11.10). Mammal remains are similarly distributed, though the highest concentration is found adjacent to the hearth in northwest Block A (Supplemental Figure 11.11). Ungulate remains cluster in central to southwest Block A such that the area between and slightly south of the Block A hearths seems to be particularly focused on ungulate processing (Supplemental Figure 11.12). High, medium, and low utility mammalian elements co-associate around

all hearths with the exception of the southwest Block C feature (Supplemental Figures 11.13 to 11.15). These data are similar to lithics distributions with the exception that faunal processing does not appear to have occurred around the southwest Block C hearth.

Summary: Site Structure on the IIj Floor

Stratum IIj has an interesting distribution of features with its four major hearths forming corners of a square in the center of the house flanked on the north by an additional small hearth in Block C. The single cache pit in northeast Block A is small, though also impacted by a later cache pit from IIi. Artifact and food remains tend to cluster around these features though with some variation. Fish remains are more prominent in the north and identifiable ungulate remains in the south. Overall, IIj appears to have been structured to permit cohabitation of two domestic groups, each with two central hearths and adjacent open space for work and other activities. The small hearth in northern Block C was clearly the center of a busy activity area likely operated by the domestic group whose space was sampled by Block C. However, the hearth's small size (despite an evident clean-out event) suggests that it was not in use throughout the history of the floor. Possibly the two domestic groups shared all features and to some degree used each for different work, thus processing fish in northern Block C, ungulates in central Block A, and intensive lithic reduction in south-central and southwestern Block C. In either scenario, we argue for the likelihood of extensive cooperation between house members and a probable communalistic living scenario. The entrance to this house floor is not clear from current data.

Sociality

Previous analyses of inter- and intra-floor variability in lithic artifacts suggested that IIj occupants were relatively egalitarian and highly cooperative (Prentiss et al. 2018b). Our spatial data confirm this conclusion. Only one canid bone was recovered from central Block A (Supplemental Figure 11.16). Concentrations of non-local lithic raw materials were found around all hearths (Supplemental Figure 11.17). Prestige items were not identified.

Conclusions

In several ways, Stratum IIj is similar to that of IIi. Compared to other floors, fire-cracked rock, lithic artifacts, and faunal remains are low in number. Bipolar cores are rare. We do not recognize significant gearing-up for major subsistence activities. Likewise, only limited evidence was found for investment in underground food storage. These data support the likelihood that IIj (like IIi) was occupied for shorter periods during winter cycles. Virtually no evidence suggests cleaning/sweeping of floor materials. Thus, the spatial structure of activity areas is very clear. Four large hearths are found in the center of the floor (north Block A and south Block C). Three of four accumulated food remains and lithic debris. The fourth collected lithic materials. A fifth hearth was found in north Block C, which clearly was reused at least once and served as a central space for various activities, especially fish processing.

We conclude from these data that two domestic groups likely shared IIj and lived in a relatively communalistic fashion during the winter portion of their annual cycles. They probably did not stay in this house for entire winters.

12

Large Scale Storage and
Hints of a Shorter Winter Cycle

Stratum IIk

Stratum IIk is the second of seven floors associated with the rectangular manifestation of Housepit 54 (Figure 12.1). Stratum IIk sediments are heavily clay-dominated (55–90%) with substantially lower percentages of silt, sand, gravel, and pebbles. Six hearths are found on IIk, two in Block C and four in Block A. The Block C hearths consist of a shallow bowl in the southwest corner and a small remnant (impacted by the IIk cache pit) in the south-central portion of the block (Figure 12.2). The Block A hearths include a cluster of three shallow features in the north-central portion and a large shallow feature in the west-central area (against the block wall). The former three hearths may have formed via repositioning of activity areas, while the latter probably expanded from repeated use. We note evidence for hearth clean-out in the form of charcoal clusters adjacent to hearths in both Blocks A and C. One very large cache pit (Feature C5[2016]) was identified in the central portion of Block C. This feature is the only one of its kind found on any Block C floors spanning the entire Housepit 54 sequence. Postholes are limited with one found on rim material slightly above the IIk floor in northwest Block C and two other very small ones located along the southern wall of Block A. As has been the case on other floors, these small features positioned around the margin of the floor most likely reflect supports for benches or platforms. Stratum IIk was entirely buried by IIj sediments. In the following sections, we discuss evidence for vari-

ation in occupation and abandonment cycles, site structure, and sociality.

Occupation and Abandonment Cycle

As on the other Housepit 54 floors, we expect the IIk lithic assemblage to reflect variability in occupation and abandonment cycles. Archaeological expectations for these phenomena are outlined in Chapter 2 (Stratum IIa).

Occupation Cycle

Here we assess alternative scenarios for occupation cycles including initiation, exploitation, and abandonment, drawing from expectations outlined in Chapter 2 (Stratum IIa).

Lithic artifacts from IIk have similarities to those of IIj in several ways (Table 12.1). Both stratums have very fewer bifaces and projectile points, as well as limited numbers of hide-working tools. Likewise, no piercers, drills/perforators, or notches/denticulates, and only one pièce esquillé are present. Bipolar cores also are limited in frequency. Abraders are relatively common, primarily due to breakage and recycling as cooking/heating stones. These data suggest to us that while the exploitation phase probably did not end catastrophically, the winter exploitation cycle during IIk was likely not as long as on floors at IIh and later. Some evidence suggests gearing up for late winter/spring hunting and gathering, but it is very limited. Likewise, four bipolar cores do imply some efforts at extending raw material use-life, but with

Stratum IIk

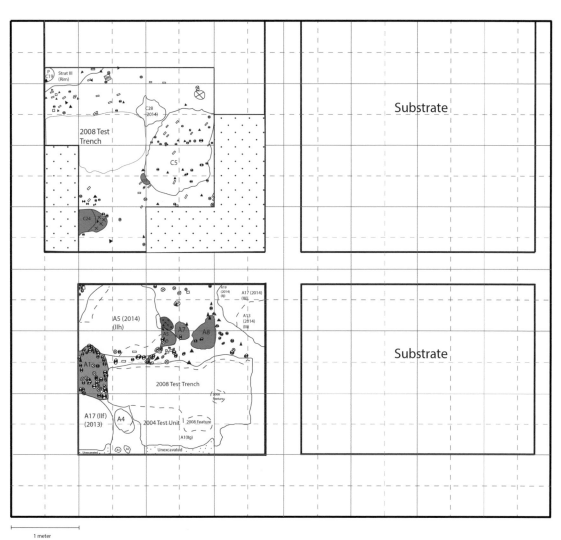

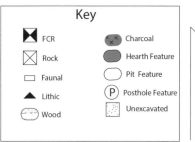

FIGURE 12.1. Comprehensive map of IIk showing point-provenienced artifacts, faunal remains, fire-cracked rock, prior excavations, and features.

Stratum IIk

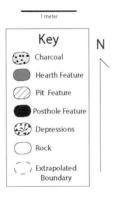

FIGURE 12.2. Features on IIk.

TABLE 12.1. Lithic Tools from IIk, Organized by Tool Class and Block.

	Tool Class																
	A	B	C	D	E	F	G	H	I	J	K	L	M	N	O	P	Q
Block A	0	0	0	0	0	0	0	0	0	0	5	0	1	0	5	6	0
Block C	5	1	1	7	7	0	0	1	1	0	15	1	3	1	2	11	4
Total	5	1	1	7	7	0	0	1	1	0	20	1	4	1	7	17	4

Note: A = flake and slate knives; B = bifaces; C = projectile points; D = flake and key-shaped scrapers; E = hide scrapers; F = drills and perforators; G = small piercers; H = pièces esquillées; I = notches and denticulates; J = adzes; K = abraders/groundstone; L = freehand cores; M = bipolar cores; N = slate objects; O = hammerstones; P = used flakes; Q = ritual/social items.

TABLE 12.2. Lithic Flake Types for Stratum IIk by Toolstone Category.

	Ext	Chal	Cher	Dac	Obs	Intr	Slates	Met.	Total
Biface	0	0	0	3	0	1	0	0	4
Core	0	1	1	5	0	1	1	4	13
Retouch	6	4	11	117	0	0	5	1	144

Note: Ext = extrusives (excluding dacite and obsidian); Dac = dacite; Cher = cherts; Chal = chalcedony; Obs = obsidian; Intr = intrusives plus gneiss; Slates = slate and silicified shale; Met = metamorphic rock inclusive of quartzites, nephrite, and steatite.

a high count of used flakes compared to few formally retouched flake tools, it is hard to sustain an argument that raw material access ever was a significant concern on IIk. Debitage data reflect a reduction focus on late stage retouch with very limited attention to core or biface reduction (Table 12.2). We would expect such a pattern if winter occupation was relatively short and not characterized by intensive preparation of gear to be transported elsewhere.

Abandonment Process

Stratum IIk was fully buried by IIj sediments, and we did not encounter any architectural elements preserved in postholes or elsewhere on this floor. Thus, when abandonment happened at the end of the IIk generation, probable plans were made to reoccupy the house with an updated floor (IIj) and also likely roof. Comparing distributions of extra small debitage to larger lithic artifacts, significant overlap is clear (Figures 12.3 and 12.4). This assessment is further confirmed by a significant correlation between extra-small and larger lithic debitage ($r = 0.918$, $p = 0.000$). The same pattern is strongly confirmed by faunal data ($r = 0.942$, $p = 0.000$, and as illustrated on Figures 12.5 and 12.6).

These data suggest that the debris from the final occupation cycle on IIk was not likely to have been swept or otherwise cleaned. We can derive additional insight by examining spatial variation in caches (Binford 1979; Hayden and Deal 1983), positioning items (Binford 1979), and de facto refuse (Schiffer 1972; Stevenson 1982). No tool caches are found on IIk, though one quite large cache pit is present in central Block C. However, this feature was filled with household refuse prior to abandonment of IIk.

Hammerstones, cores, and groundstone cluster around features in southern Block C and northern Block A. As these items were probably intermittently used and periodically recycled for alternative functions (e.g., groundstone becoming cooking or heating rocks), their positions probably were moved regularly. While they were undoubtedly positioning items during the IIk occupation period, they appear to have been discarded and not retrieved at the time of abandonment. Finally, typical of Housepit 54 floors, we do not see direct evidence of de facto refuse.

Site Structure

Expectations for variability in floor spatial structure within a rectangular house are outlined in Chapter 7 (Stratum IIf). Here we review the spatial distributions of lithic debitage, tools, and faunal remains.

Debitage and Spatial Structure of Lithic Reduction

Debitage occur throughout the IIk floor, including a small cluster around the hearths in north-central Block A, and then at relatively high density associated with the hearths and cache pit in Block C (Supplemental Figure 12.1). Low numbers of early stage reduction flakes are present in all of these spaces (Supplemental Figure 12.2). The two biface thinning flakes and two other R-billet flakes are found in the southern portion of Block C near the two hearths and/or on top of the filled cache pit (Supplemental Figures 12.3 and 12.4). In contrast, small retouch flakes are found at high density throughout nearly all of the excavated space in Block C and in smaller clusters around the hearths in north-central and southwest Block A (Supplemental

Ilk Extra-Small Debitage Distribution

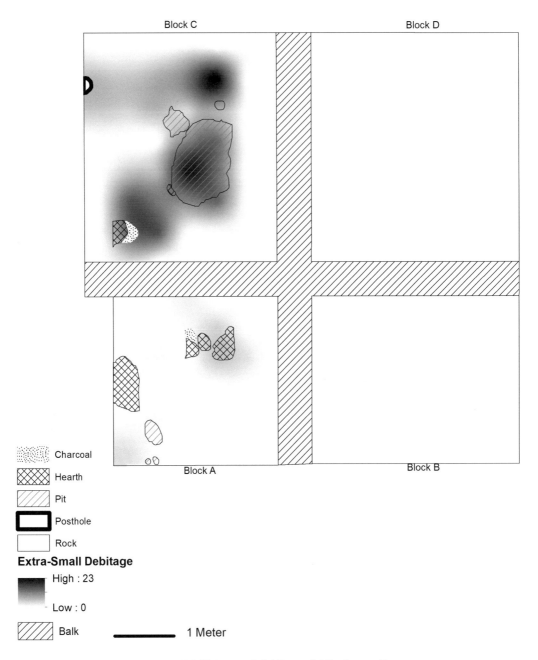

Charcoal

Hearth

Pit

Posthole

Rock

Extra-Small Debitage

High : 23

Low : 0

Balk   1 Meter

FIGURE 12.3. Extra-small debitage distribution on Ilk.

N

Ilk Total Lithic Artifact Distribution

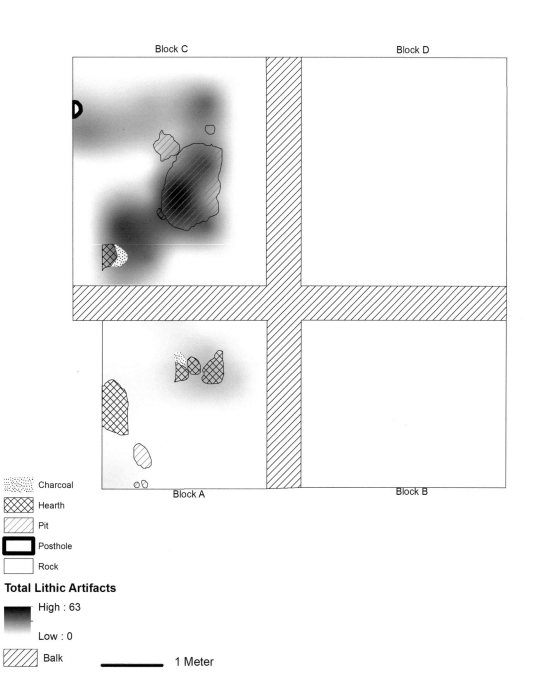

Block C

Block D

D

Block A

Block B

Charcoal

Hearth

Pit

Posthole

Rock

Total Lithic Artifacts

High : 63

Low : 0

Balk

1 Meter

FIGURE 12.4. Total artifact distribution on Ilk.

Ilk Faunal Specimens Sized 1-9mm

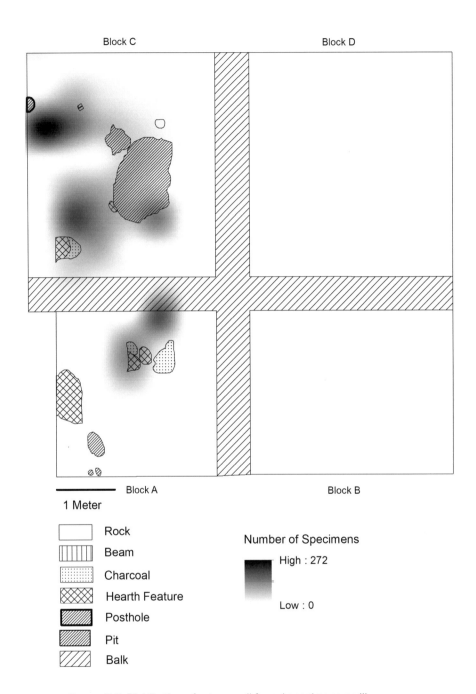

FIGURE 12.5. Distribution of extra-small faunal specimens on Ilk.

Ilk All Faunal Specimens

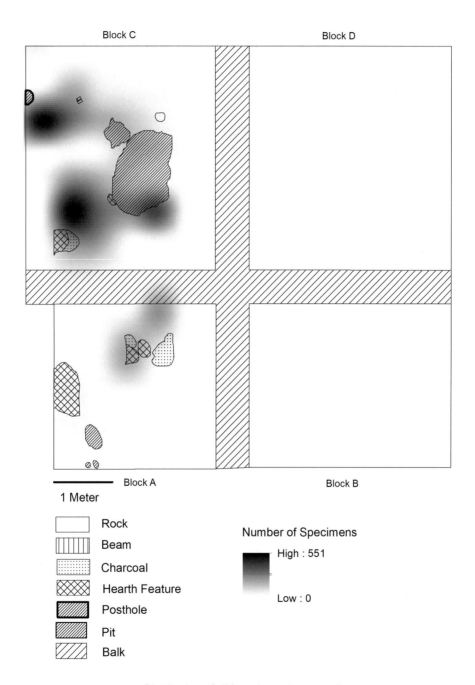

FIGURE 12.6. Distribution of all faunal specimens on Ilk.

Figure 12.5). The latter clusters may be some-what artificial given limited remaining floor in Block A due to impacts of deep features in the northeast, northwest, and southwest corners, plus the 2008 excavation trench. Thus, with those constraints in mind, we suggest that tool retouch was likely practiced throughout the IIk floor. This assessment brings IIk substantially in line with most other Housepit 54 floors where we recognize the ubiquitous presence of tool re-touch and more clustered distributions of tech-nologically specific flake types.

Lithic Tools and House
Floor Activity Organization

Knapping items (cores and hammerstones) cluster around the north-central Block A and southern Block C hearths (Supplemental Fig-ure 12.6). Heavy-duty tools (flake scrapers, pièces esquillé, and notches/denticulates) are scattered throughout the excavated portion of Block C, and only one is found around the hearths of north-central Block A (Supplemental Figure 12.7). Hunting/butchering tools (bifaces and projectile points) are not common and are scattered around Block C (Supplemental Figure 12.8). Hide-working/sewing tools (hide scrapers and piercers) occur exclusively in association with the hearths of south Block C (Supplemen-tal Figure 12.9). Groundstone (abraders) are clustered around the hearths of north-central Block A and southern Block C (Supplemental Figure 12.10). Given these results, activities re-quiring lithic tool applications appear to have been most frequently conducted in Block C around the hearths and cache pit. Significant overlap is observed between distinct activity classes including heavy-duty applications, hide hide-working and sewing, and use/disposal of hunting and butchery tools. This finding possi-bly suggests functional differentiation between features as preferred workspaces.

Faunal Remains and Spatial Organization

Fish remains are common on IIk (Supplemen-tal Figure 12.11) and cluster around features in north-central Block A, and southwest and southeast Block C. An additional cluster is found in northwest Block C. Mammal remains are distributed at low densities throughout IIk with the exception of a high-density area in northwest Block C (Supplemental Figure 12.12). Identifiable ungulate remains cluster adjacent to features in southwest and southeast Block C (Supplemental Figure 12.13). A low-density cluster is recognizable in northeastern Block A. High, medium, and low utility mammalian ele-ments are distributed in nearly the same fashion at highest densities in Block C and lower density in north-central Block A (Supplemental Figures 12.14, 12.15, and 12.16).

These data suggest a general relationship between accumulations of faunal remains and features in IIk. However, as with lithic items, these distributions are partially a byproduct of constrained analytical space resulting in many portions of IIk being lost to deep features from later dating floors and test trenches from the 2008 field season. Faunal remains also occur at much higher densities in Block C than Block A. Since similar pattern is noted in the lithic arti-facts, this distribution may have implications for how we understand the organization of work on floor IIk.

Summary: Site Structure on the IIk Floor

Spatial structure of activities on IIk is challeng-ing to reconstruct given impacts of later pits removing portions of the floor plus the effects of our 2008 test trenches. However, some gen-eral patterns are still ascertainable. First, small hearths with evidence for reuse are found in the central portion of the floor, while an additional much larger hearth is located on the west wall of Block A. The small hearths also are consistently associated with lithic debris and food remains, while the larger hearth in western Block A has few lithics or faunal remains in its vicinity.

This distribution suggests that these features likely had different functions. For example, the west Block A hearth may have functioned as a source of heated rock for stone boiling along with warmth for sleeping. It might also have served a unique social role compared to the other features. In contrast, the small hearths to the north and northeast were centers of multiple activities spanning tool maintenance to food processing. Second, the density of all cultural materials is far higher in Block C than Block A, suggesting that this area was more frequently used for toolmaking and maintenance, various tool applications, and food preparation. Given these distributions, one possible scenario could be that the central hearths and cache pit area were communal workspaces, while family groups slept and socialized in space provided by central and south Block A and north Block C. The house entrance is not clear from current data.

Sociality

Prentiss and colleagues (2018b) concluded that the IIk floor was a socially cooperative and egalitarian context. Spatial data from IIk confirm this finding. Only one canid specimen was found on IIk (Supplemental Figure 12.17). Nonlocal raw materials are patchily distributed around northern Block A and Block C, generally associated with features. Prestige raw materials and items are very rare and thus do not reflect social distinctions (Supplemental Figures 12.18 and 12.19).

Conclusions

Floor IIk contains a relatively high density of lithic artifacts and faunal remains. Little evidence is found for sweeping and cleaning of these spaces. Thus, these distributions are adequate for exploring the spatial configuration of house activities. One major constraint on interpretation is the limited remaining IIk space given impacts from later pits and the effects of test trenches in 2008. Artifact types suggest that while initiation, exploitation, and abandonment phases likely occurred, the exploitation phase may have been shorter than those on IIh and later. Also the exploitation phase may have been short with relatively little gearing-up for post-abandonment activities.

Spatially, the floor seems to be organized in three distinct spaces. The northern portion (north Block C) is empty of features but does show evidence for lithic reduction. The central portion of the floor is very dense with features, associated artifacts, and faunal remains. Other findings include a large cache pit and a series of small hearths with evidence for reuse. Each of these hearths has an associated cluster of faunal remains and discarded lithic tools and debitage. To the southwest, one large hearth is present on its western margin, but otherwise only a shallow depression and two small postholes. The southern portion of the floor (south Block A) appears to lack features or significant quantities of other cultural material.

Collectively, these data suggest empty spaces at the north and south ends with an extensive multitask workspace in the center of the floor. Small postholes hint at the presence of a small raised wooden structure at the south end of Block A. Given this scenario, we suggest that IIk may have held two domestic groups who worked together and stored food in a communal fashion. This assessment supports earlier conclusions that this house group was socially egalitarian and highly cooperative.

The First Rectangular House

Stratum IIl

Stratum IIl is the first of the seven-floor sequence associated with the rectangular manifestation of Housepit 54 (Figure 13.1). This floor appears to represent a substantial expansion of the house over the likely smaller Stratum IIm floor. As was the case with IIk, the Stratum IIl sediments are strongly dominated by clay in the 50–90% range, while silt and sand collectively appear in the 10–20% range and other clast sizes occur in lower percentages.

Only one hearth was found on IIl, located in north-central Block A (Figure 13.2). This feature is very small and shallow and located between a large cobble and a cobble-sized grinding slab/abrader. The lack of IIl hearths elsewhere on this floor may be in part due to impacts of previously excavated cache pits (from IIk, IIi, and IIj) or limitations to our excavation sampling. The overlapping shallow pits in north-central Block C also might have been the location of a hearth or boiling pit that was cleaned out in anticipation of later use. However, the pits were filled with clay prior to abandonment, and thus suggesting no intention to reuse these features as a hearth.

One cache pit was found in the northwest corner of Block A. One moderately large but shallow pit was recovered at the north-central portion of Block C. The size and position of this feature suggests that it could have held a roof post, though this function is not clear. Stratum IIl was fully buried by Stratum IIk sediments. Next, we discuss evidence for variation in occu-

pation and abandonment cycles, site structure, and sociality.

Occupation and Abandonment Cycle

This section provides a review of evidence for variation in occupation and abandonment cycles making use of frames of reference developed in Chapter 2 (Stratum IIa).

Occupation Cycle

Here, lithic artifacts are used to assess occupation cycles as reflected by expectations for initiation, exploitation, and abandonment phases in Chapter 2 (Stratum IIa).

The lithic assemblage from Stratum IIl is in many ways similar to those from later floors in having relatively consistent numbers of nearly all tool classes (Table 13.1). Heavy-duty woodworking is not well represented given the lack of adzes. However, manufacture of wood/bone/antler implements is represented by flake and key-shaped scrapers, drills/perforators, one pièce esquillées, and notches and denticulates. Activities associated with hunting are represented by bifaces, projectile points, and hide scrapers. Bipolar cores reflect the need to extend raw material use-life. Debitage are dominated by late stage retouch flakes and substantially fewer biface and core reduction flakes (Table 13.2). Thus, substantial attention is unlikely to have focused on production of bifacial tools or major reduction of cores for flake tools. This finding could either reflect a shorter winter

Stratum III

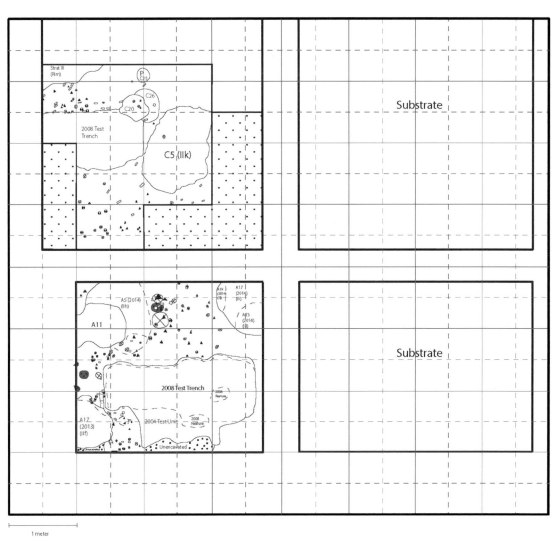

1 meter

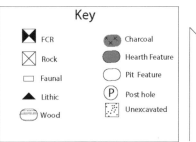

FIGURE 13.1. Comprehensive map of III showing point-provenienced artifacts, faunal remains, fire-cracked rock, prior excavations, and features.

Stratum III

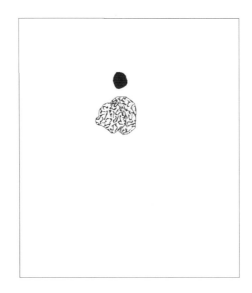

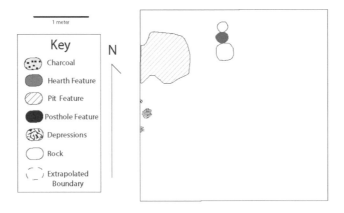

FIGURE 13.2. Features on III.

TABLE 13.1. Lithic Tools from III, Organized by Tool Class and Block.

	Tool Class																
	A	B	C	D	E	F	G	H	I	J	K	L	M	N	O	P	Q
Block A	3	1	1	4	4	2	0	0	1	0	6	5	4	0	4	5	5
Block C	2	3	1	1	12	3	0	1	1	0	3	1	2	0	0	14	2
Total	5	4	2	5	16	5	0	1	2	0	9	6	6	0	4	19	7

Note: A = flake and slate knives; B = bifaces; C = projectile points; D = flake and key-shaped scrapers; E = hide scrapers; F = drills and perforators; G = small piercers; H = pièces esquillées; I = notches and denticulates; J = adzes; K = abraders/groundstone; L = freehand cores; M = bipolar cores; N = slate objects; O = hammerstones; P = used flakes; Q = ritual/social items.

TABLE 13.2. Lithic Flake Types for Stratum IIl by Toolstone Category.

	Ext	Chal	Cher	Dac	Obs	Intr	Slates	Met.	Total
Biface	0	0	1	4	0	0	0	0	5
Core	0	0	1	4	0	2	2	0	9
Retouch	5	5	56	56	0	0	4	1	127

Note: Ext = extrusives (excluding dacite and obsidian); Dac = dacite; Cher = cherts; Chal = chalcedony; Obs = obsidian; Intr = intrusives plus gneiss; Slates = slate and silicified shale; Met = metamorphic rock inclusive of quartzites, nephrite, and steatite.

occupation cycle or a practice of transporting nearly finished tools from localities elsewhere for finishing touches and maintenance on IIl. Beyond this concern, all data considered, occupants of the IIl floor still appear likely to have pursued a fairly standard exploitation and abandonment phase.

Abandonment Process

Stratum IIl was fully buried by stratum IIk sediments, and no architectural elements were recovered from postholes or other contexts. These data suggest that abandonment at the end of the IIl generation was planned with the expectation of returning to add a new floor and most likely a new roof. No evidence suggests floor cleaning as indicated by a strong correlation between extra-small and larger debitage ($r = 0.779$, $p = 0.000$) and a similar correlation between extra-small and larger faunal items ($r = 0.965$, $p = 0.000$). These patterns are evident on plan maps illustrating extra-small and larger lithic artifacts and faunal remains (Figures 13.3 to 13.6). Variability in positioning items (Binford 1979), caches (Binford 1979; Hayden and Deal 1983), site furniture (Binford 1979), and de facto refuse (Schiffer 1972; Stevenson 1982) reveals some attention to organization of space and the abandonment process.

Cores and hammerstones are present and may have been moved frequently depending upon needs before permanent discard and abandonment. Two large cobbles flank the hearth in Block A and could reasonably be interpreted as site furniture but clearly not valuable enough to be salvaged and reused postabandonment. Function of one of these items is not clear as it does not show evidence for use as an anvil or

a grinding stone. The other is indeed a grinding stone and was likely an important tool for kitchen-related activities in this space. A cache pit is located in northwestern Block A, but it appears to have been filled with refuse before abandonment. Thus, all measures suggest that the IIl floor received a planned orderly abandonment with the intent of returning to establish the IIk floor.

Site Structure

We provide expectations for variability in spatial organization associated with rectangular houses in Chapter 7 (Stratum IIf). We now examine spatial variation in reference to lithic reduction, lithic tool use and discard, and subsistence activities as marked by faunal remains. These results are then analyzed to assess activity zonation, the nature of activity areas, and spatial contingencies.

Debitage and Spatial Structure of Lithic Reduction

Stone tool knapping was clearly practiced throughout the IIl floor but particularly in four concentrations: north-central Block C, southwest Block C, north-central Block A, and south-southwest Block A (Supplemental Figure 13.1). Early stage reduction flakes occur in limited frequencies but concentrate in the southwest of Block C (Supplemental Figure 13.2). Biface thinning and R-billet flakes are rare and present exclusively in Block C (Supplemental Figures 13.3 and 13.4). Retouch flakes are common and found throughout the IIl floor with particularly high densities in the areas of higher lithic concentration (Supplemental Figure 13.5). Similar to other floors, they are not obviously

III Extra-Small Sized Debitage Distribution

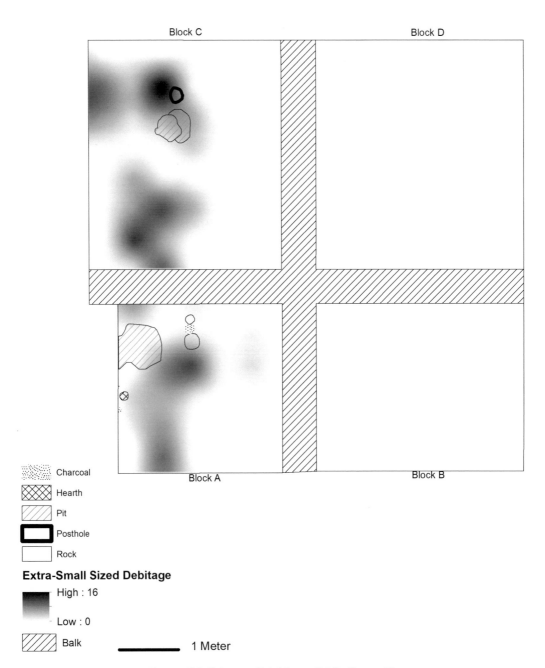

FIGURE 13.3. Extra-small debitage distribution on III.

N

lll Total Lithic Artifact Distribution

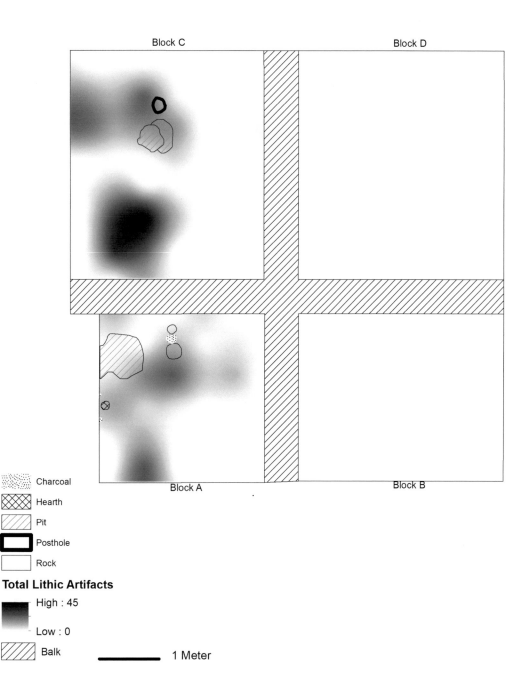

Block C

Block D

Block A

Block B

Charcoal

Hearth

Pit

Posthole

Rock

Total Lithic Artifacts

High : 45

Low : 0

Balk

1 Meter

FIGURE 13.4. Total artifact distribution on lll.

Ill Faunal Specimens Sized 1-9mm

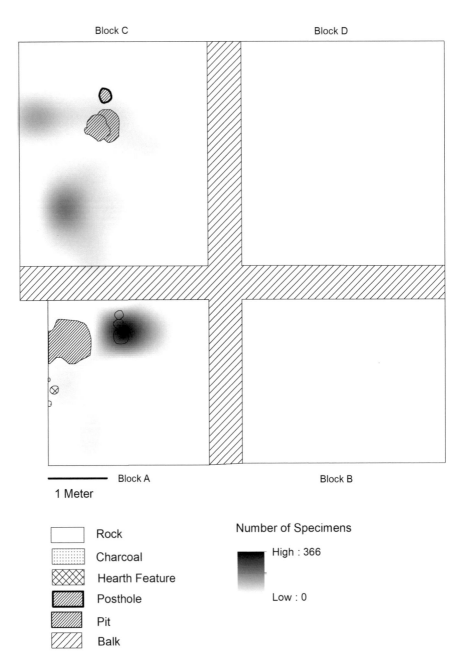

FIGURE 13.5. Distribution of extra-small faunal specimens on Ill.

Ill All Faunal Specimens

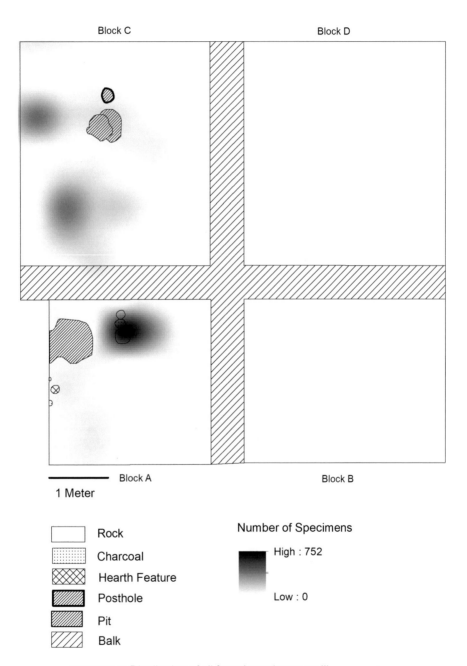

FIGURE 13.6. Distribution of all faunal specimens on Ill.

associated with features. However, features are not found in Block C, and they likely were either removed by later occupants (e.g., the IIk cache pit in Block C), or our excavation did not focus on the right space to find them. Also possibly the pit in north-central Block C may have been a hearth that was entirely cleaned out in anticipation of reuse.

Lithic Tools and House Floor Activity Organization

Knapping items (cores and hammerstones) were nearly always discarded in Block A (Supplemental Figure 13.6), while early stage reduction flakes cluster in southern Block C. This distribution suggests that the former items were kept or discarded in different spaces from locales of normal use. Heavy-duty tools (wood/bone/antler working: flake scrapers, key-shaped scrapers, pièces esquillées, notches/denticulates, and drills/perforators) are scattered relatively evenly throughout IIl with a slight concentration adjacent to the Block A hearth (Supplemental Figure 13.7). Hunting-butchering (bifaces and projectile points), hide-working/sewing (hide scrapers and small piercers), and groundstone (abraders) are also evenly scattered throughout much of the IIl floor, though few tools are found in south Block A (Supplemental Figures 13.8 to 13.10). Hide-working/sewing tools are most common in south to central Block C.

On the surface, these patterns are somewhat at odds from signatures recognized on many later rectangular house floors where tools generally concentrate around hearth features. As such, one possibility is that life on IIl was simply different from that of later floors. However, these tools are concentrated around the hearth in Block A and in places where we think that hearths or boiling pits may have existed (pit in north-central Block C) or were missed by our excavation (southern Block C). Thus, the spatial organization of activities involving lithic tools is entirely likely to be much the same as some later floors. Thus, a reasonable conclusion is that the Block A and C activity areas reflect the diverse activities of two to three domestic groups.

Faunal Remains and Spatial Organization

Fish remains are found in three concentrations, one directly over the Block A hearth and the other two in southwest and northwest Block C (Supplemental Figure 13.11). Mammal remains are distributed in a similar manner to that of fish with the addition of one other cluster in Southwest Block A (Supplemental Figure 13.12). Ungulate elements cluster around the shallow pits of north Block C, in southwest Block C, overlapping the cache pit in northwest Block A, and in southwest Block A (Supplemental Figure 13.13). High, medium, and low utility mammalian elements concentrate in a dense cluster in southwest Block C and in lower density areas of northwest Block C (Supplemental Figures 13.14, 13.15, and 13.16). High and medium utility elements are scattered in low numbers throughout Block A, while low utility elements cluster somewhat around the hearth in north-central Block A.

As with lithic debris, the clusters of faunal remains form a linear north to south trend, raising the possibility of at least three distinct activity areas equally distributed across the length of the house floor. However, we recognize that the visibility of IIl floor distributions is constrained by excavation limits, test trenches, and impacts of deep features excavated by later occupants.

Summary: Site Structure on the IIl Floor

The IIl floor is characterized by a very small hearth-like charcoal concentration located between two large cobbles in Block A and also a cache pit in northwest Block A. Two overlapping shallow pits are found in northern Block C, which could represent fully cleaned-out hearth features or remnants of boiling pits, though clearly their use as functional features ended when occupants filled the pits with clay before abandonment. Consequently, the presence of hearths in Block C is unclear. However, distributions of lithic artifacts and faunal remains raise that possibility.

Lithics and faunal remains implicate four activity areas located, respectively, in the northwest and southwest of Block C, as well as north-central and southwest Block A. Artifact and faunal distributions suggest diverse activities within each, consisting of lithic tool maintenance, multiple lithic tool applications (wood/bone/antler working, hide-working, manufacture and use of hunting/butchering tools, and use of groundstone), and preparation of food including mammals and fish. Processing and discard of mammalian remains appears to have been most intense in Block C, whereas fish processing occurred most intensely around the small hearth in northern Block A. Lithic reduction occurred in southern Block A, but little evidence for food processing was noted in that area of the house except for a limited degree in the southwest corner. This finding leaves the possibility that this portion of Il1 was primarily reserved for tool maintenance, sleep, socializing, and other activities. Limited cultural materials in north-central (above the pit features) and northeast Block C may imply a similar occupational pattern.

Data suggest two possibilities as to how families organized their space on Il1. First, two groups possibly resided on Il1, based in the north and south ends of the house and sharing the central portion (southern Block C). This scenario assumes that the north Block C activity area associated with the clay-filled pit represents what had been a domestic area centered around a hearth or boiling pit. A second scenario could be that the central zone could represent a third family. Without evidence for hearth features or storage facilities, this possibility cannot be confirmed. Thus, for now we suggest that the former scenario is most likely. This conclusion, in turn, implies a communal social strategy in the house given shared space and possible shared use of the single storage feature in northwest Block A. The position of the entrance to the house is not clear from these data.

Sociality

Prentiss and colleagues (2018b) concluded that Il1 was occupied by a cooperative egalitarian group. This assessment appears to be accurate given the spatial data considered here. Canid remains are limited and occur in both blocks (Supplemental Figure 13.17). Nonlocal raw materials are evenly distributed along the long-axis of Il1 (Supplemental Figure 13.18). The three items classified as prestige objects made from prestige materials are also evenly distributed between activity areas (Supplemental Figures 13.19 and 13.20).

Conclusions

Stratum Il1 represents the first generation to create and occupy the rectangular variant of Housepit 54. Lithic artifacts suggest that the initiation, exploitation, and abandonment phases are represented. Assessment of spatial positions of smallest and larger items suggests that little sweeping or other forms of cleaning occurred prior to abandonment, thus leaving artifact and faunal element distributions intact and thereby facilitating spatial analysis. The abandonment process appears to have been planned and associated with relinquishment of some large items such as the grinding stone adjacent to the hearth in Block A.

Spatial distributions of features and associated artifacts clearly indicate a domestic group occupying the Block A portion of the house. Similar activity areas with clusters of faunal remains and lithics implicate activity areas in Block C. However, no hearths or cache pits were uncovered in this area. In north Block C, concentrations of lithic and faunal items co-associate with overlapping clay-filled pits. We have raised the possibility that these are remnants of cooking features used by a domestic group. If that is the case or if we simply have not yet found the north end cooking/heating features, then we can conclude that another domestic unit occupied the north end of Il1.

The central activity areas (south Block C) is even more challenging given a similar profile of artifacts and faunal remains but no features. Thus, pending future discovery of a cooking/heating feature we conclude that this area was most likely a communal workspace. A common workspace and likely a single shared cache pit suggest a communal social strategy. Even distribution of nonlocal lithic raw materials and prestige items implicates egalitarian relationships between house members.

The Last Small House

Stratum IIm

Stratum IIm is the final floor for the three-floor sequence associated with the early oval-shaped manifestation of Housepit 54 (Figure 14.1). We do not know for sure the actual shape of the IIm version of Housepit 54 as its margins are not visible within Block A. The floor is not present in Blocks B or C, and we thus presume that its north and east walls are respectively within the north and east balks of Block A. This structure suggests an oval to square shape to the house at least on those sides. The west and south sides are challenging to reconstruct.

However, possibly the house was not much larger than the Block A area for two reasons. First, features line the perimeter of Block A, raising the possibility that the empty center represents public space for household occupants. If so, then we can imagine that the ring of features mark the kitchen zone adjacent to a bench/storage/sleeping zone just outside of our excavated area. Second, Housepit 32 lies just to the west of Housepit 54 and was occupied immediately before and possibly during the earliest portion of the Housepit 54 sequence (Prentiss et al. 2008). If that were the case, then the position of the floor and rim of this very large house would have severely constrained the western margin of early Housepit 54.

Stratum IIm sediments are clay-dominated in the 60–75% range, followed by silt and sand (when combined falling in the 5–15% range). Gravels are comparatively high with percentages spanning 8–20%, and pebbles are present in lower percentages. One large bowl-shaped hearth (A15 [2016]) was found on the north-central side of Block A (Figure 14.2). A smaller shallow hearth (A13 [2016]) overlaps A15(2016) on its west side. Three cache pits are also present, two in the northwest corner and one large and very deep pit in the south-central area. One shallow posthole-like pit was found on IIm. Next, we discuss evidence for variation in occupation and abandonment cycles, site structure, and sociality.

Occupation and Abandonment Cycle

This section permits us to assess evidence for the impacts of occupation and abandonment cycles using frames of reference outlined in Chapter 2 (Stratum IIa).

Occupation Cycle

Occupation cycles are defined in three phases termed initiation, exploitation, and abandonment. Archaeological expectations of these are outlined in Chapter 2 (Stratum IIa).

For a relatively small house, IIm offers a somewhat substantial lithic assemblage (Table 14.1). Heavy-duty woodworking is represented by one adze, and manufacture of tools from wood/bone/antler is also indicated by a substantial set of flake and key-shaped scrapers along with a drill/perforator, and one notch/denticulate. Hunting activities are represented by two projectile points and relatively large number of hide scrapers. The large collection

Block A Stratum IIm Level 1 (2016 excavations)

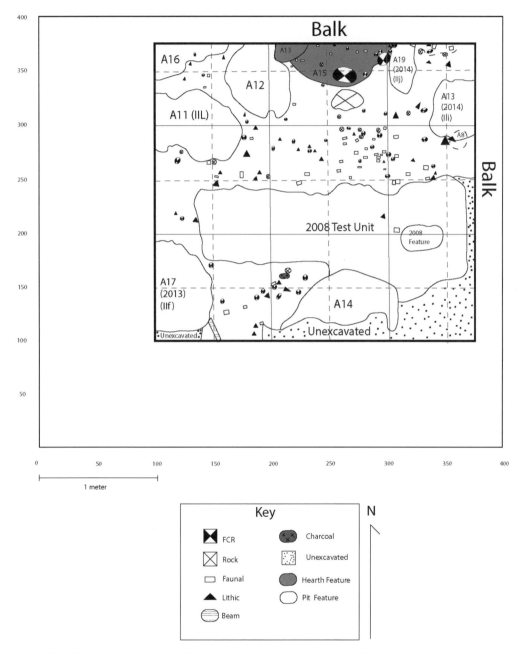

FIGURE 14.1. Comprehensive map of IIm showing point-provenienced artifacts, faunal remains, fire-cracked rock, prior excavations, and features.

Stratum IIm

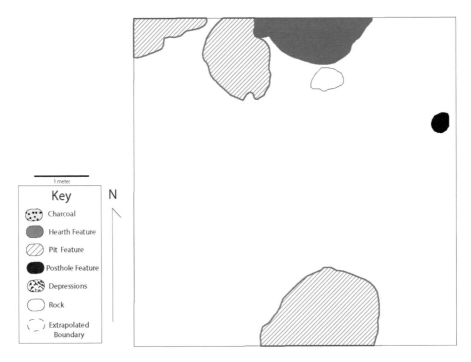

FIGURE 14.2. Features on IIm.

TABLE 14.1. Lithic Tools from IIm, Organized by Tool Class and Block.

	Tool Class																
	A	B	C	D	E	F	G	H	I	J	K	L	M	N	O	P	Q
Block A	4	0	2	16	12	1	0	0	1	1	24	2	5	1	1	11	0

Note: A = flake and slate knives; B = bifaces; C = projectile points; D = flake and key-shaped scrapers; E = hide scrapers; F = drills and perforators; G = small piercers; H = pièces esquillées; I = notches and denticulates; J = adzes; K = abraders/groundstone; L = freehand cores; M = bipolar cores; N = slate objects; O = hammerstones; P = used flakes; Q = ritual/social items.

TABLE 14.2. Lithic Flake Types for Stratum IIm by Toolstone Category.

	Ext	Chal	Cher	Dac	Obs	Intr	Slates	Met.	Total
Biface	0	0	0	4	0	0	0	0	4
Core	0	0	1	4	0	1	1	0	7
Retouch	2	3	40	49	1	1	2	2	109

Note: Ext = extrusives (excluding dacite and obsidian); Dac = dacite; Cher = cherts; Chal = chalcedony; Obs = obsidian; Intr = intrusives plus gneiss; Slates = slate and silicified shale; Met = metamorphic rock inclusive of quartzites, nephrite, and steatite.

of abraders is in part due to recycling these tools as cooking/heating stones. Bipolar cores are present, likely reflecting the application of tactics for extending the use-life of raw materials. Debitage are heavily dominated by late stage retouch flakes, followed by far fewer biface and core reduction flakes (Table 14.2).

The limited number of biface thinning and core reduction flakes implies that little attention was placed on intensive reduction to prepare lithic tools for transport elsewhere unless those efforts are reflected in the retouch assemblage. If the latter is the case, then tools entered IIm in nearly completed form, only requiring marginal retouch via pressure-flaking, for example. Also perhaps IIm was not occupied across a series of long winters. Regardless, this assemblage still suggests that the occupants of IIm pursued a well-planned exploitation and abandonment phase.

Abandonment Process

The close of the house associated with IIm included a major expansion of the house to the north, thus creating the first rectangular house occupied as the IIl floor. Stratum IIm was thus entirely covered by IIl sediments with no evidence for architectural elements. We can conclude from this information that the abandonment process of IIm was planned with the intent to return, expand, refloor, and reroof the house. Clearly, the IIm to IIL transition was a critical point in the long-term history of Housepit 54. Prior to abandonment, little evidence suggests cleaning of cultural debris from the IIm floor. Extra-small and large debitage are highly correlated ($r = 0.936$, $p = 0.000$), and extra-small and larger faunal remains are similar ($r = 0.722$, $p = 0.028$). These patterns are highly evident on plan maps of IIm (Figures 14.3–14.6).

Management of positioning items (Binford 1979), caches (Binford 1979; Hayden and Deal 1983), site furniture (Binford 1979), and de facto refuse (Schiffer 1972; Stevenson 1982) provides additional insight. Groundstone was very common on IIm, partially resulting from the reuse of abraders as heating and/or boiling stones for cooking. None of these items are very large and thus do not appear, by the abandonment of IIm, to have played such a significant role that they could be termed positioning items. Likewise, no obvious examples of site furniture or de facto refuse are present. While three substantial cache pits were found, all were used for deposition of refuse before the floor was abandoned. Thus, although IIm was not formally cleaned, useful items appear to have been removed and the house prepared to abandonment and reoccupation with significant expansion.

Site Structure

We have argued that IIm likely represents a much smaller house structure than any of the later floors. More specifically, we raised the possibility that this floor was used by single domestic group and was unlikely to have been more than 4–5 m in maximum diameter. Such a living arrangement would necessitate solving a somewhat different set of challenges compared to that of the rectangular or the full-size versions of Housepit 54. A hypothetical group would need to segregate space for sleeping, storage of gear, food storage, cooking, and messy activities like butchery, hide preparation, wood/bone/antler working, and stone tool manufacture.

Drawing from Teit's (1900 and 1906) descriptions of pithouses and aboveground long houses, a scenario is possible to imagine whereby these challenges could be solved with limited space. First, the roof of the house would extend well outside the perimeter of the formal floor, thus creating sheltered space for sleeping and gear storage. Second, the perimeter of the floor could be used for pit storage and cooking features, leaving the central portion of the house for public space. Alternatively, the central portion of the floor could be set aside for a communal cooking feature and perimeter areas used for pit storage and other activity zones. Smith (2017) documents both scenarios on successive floors dated ca. 300–350 cal BP at Housepit 1 of the S7istken site, a small housepit village located 2 km from the Bridge River site.

Thus, from an archaeological standpoint, we would expect a clear pattern of inner and outer zones as indicated by features and associated artifact and faunal debris. We might also

Ilm Extra-Small Debitage Distribution

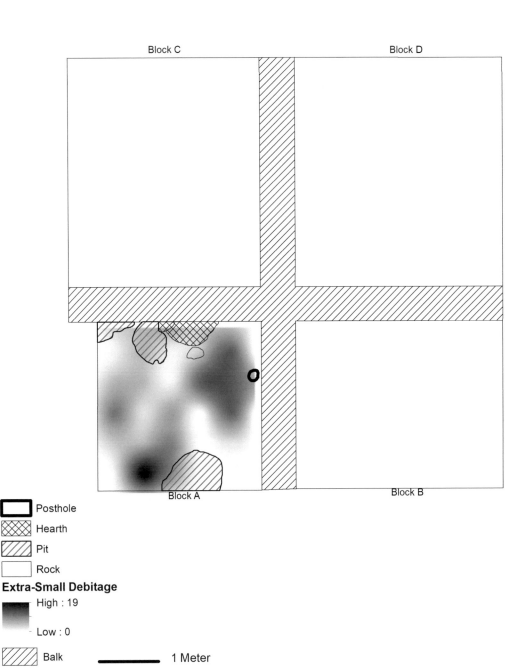

FIGURE 14.3. Extra-small debitage distribution on Ilm.

N

IIm Total Lithic Artifact Distribution

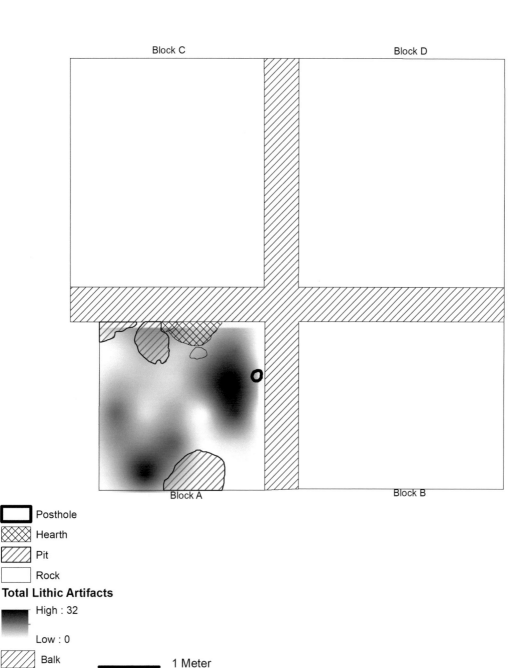

FIGURE 14.4. Total artifact distribution on IIm.

IIm Faunal Specimens Sized 1-9mm

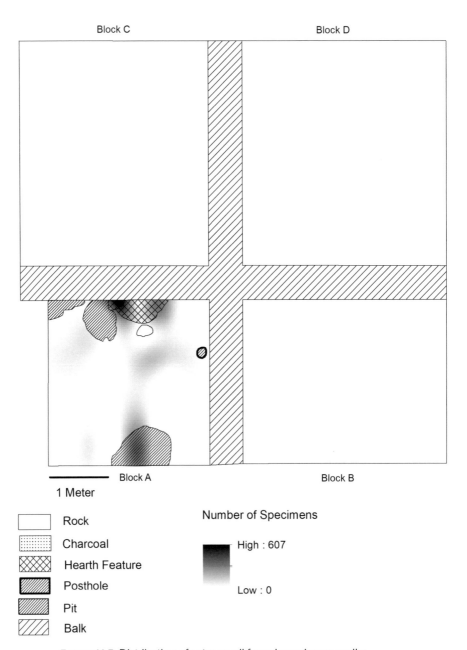

FIGURE 14.5. Distribution of extra-small faunal specimens on IIm.

Ilm All Faunal Specimens

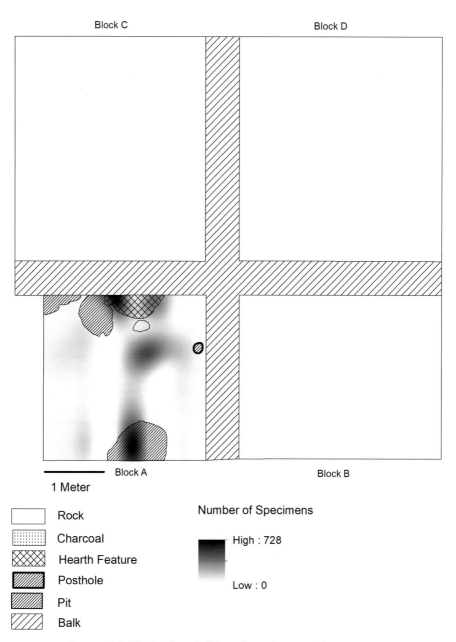

FIGURE 14.6. Distribution of all faunal specimens on Ilm.

expect to see either particular activity areas around the perimeter or mixed activities in the center of the floor. Finally, additional spatial contingencies could be associated with working around a likely side entrance and only very limited light from outside the house. In the following section, we examine distributions of lithic debitage, tools, and faunal remains to assess these possibilities.

Debitage and Spatial Structure of Lithic Reduction

Debitage cluster in several areas around the perimeter of IIm adjacent to features with greatest densities on the east and south sides (Supplemental Figure 14.1). Early stage reduction flakes are found in very limited numbers on the northeast perimeter (Supplemental Figure 14.2). No biface thinning flakes and only two R-billet flakes are present, the latter located on the southwest perimeter (Supplemental Figure 14.3). Tool retouch flakes are found around the perimeter of IIm (Supplemental Figure 14.4). This placement is in part a byproduct of the test trench in the south-central portion of Block A. However, retouch flakes are also very rare in the north-central portion of IIm, supporting a contention that retouch activities were more frequently practiced around the perimeter than the central portion of the floor. These data suggest that, like later floors, tool retouch was the most common knapping activity and that this work was generally accomplished in spaces around the perimeter of the floor.

Lithic Tools and House Floor Activity Organization

Knapping tools are uncommon and located on the north and western edges of IIm (Supplemental Figure 14.5). Heavy-duty tools (wood/bone/antler working: flake scrapers, key-shaped scrapers, pièces esquillées, notches/denticulates, and drills/perforators) cluster on the northeast corner of IIm (Supplemental Figure 14.6). Hunting/butchery tools (projectile points) are rare with one found on the west perimeter of IIm (Supplemental Figure 14.7). Hide-working and sewing tools (hide scrapers) also occur in a concentration in the northeast corner of the floor (Supplemental Figure 14.8). Groundstone tools are found throughout the floor, though they appear to concentrate in perimeter areas (Supplemental Figure 14.9). An activity area for apparent wood/bone/antler and hide-working is located in northeast IIm, while cores and hammerstones are discarded slightly to the west. Groundstone are scattered throughout. The central floor appears to have been kept relatively clean while work was done at the margins of the floor. In many ways, given the focus on a relatively clean central space surrounded by messy activity areas, this small house may reflect the same workspace ethos as the much larger house generations later.

Faunal Remains and Spatial Organization

Fish remains are found in two high-density clusters around the hearth on the north side and in an additional cluster adjacent to the cache pit on the south side. They are more sparsely scattered elsewhere (Supplemental Figure 14.10). Mammal remains cluster near the south-side cache pit and are distributed at low frequencies across the floor (Supplemental Figure 14.11). Ungulate remains have the same distribution as ungulates dominate the identified mammal group (Supplemental Figure 14.12). High, medium, and low utility elements are found at greatest density slightly north of the southern cache pit and at slightly lesser density to the south of the north hearth (Supplemental Figures 14.13–14.15). While these distributions are partially impacted by the test trench in the center of the block, the clusters of materials are spatially constrained to such a degree that they still highly suggest distinct discard locations and likely activity areas, especially around the north hearth. Food preparation around features clearly was a major activity on IIm.

Summary: Site Structure on the IIm Floor

We now have multiple lines of evidence to suggest that workspace on IIm was organized in a pattern resembling a concentric ring model. Features are distributed around the periphery of Block A. Then lithic reduction activities concentrate on the northeast and southwest portions. Most lithic tools are found around features. Groundstone is an exception, perhaps because many groundstone items were recycled as cooking rocks and maintained or discarded away from activity areas. Faunal remains also cluster around features on the north and south sides. Consequently, the central space appears to have been more of an open zone surrounded by kitchen-related areas. A third zone for sleeping and storage is highly likely to have existed under the eaves of the roof above the floor. Identification of any contingent spaces is not possible. Thus, where the side entrance was placed is unclear, as well as if any spaces were better lighted than others.

Sociality

Our current evidence from IIm suggests space for a single family. However, depending upon the actual size of the house, more than one family could have lived in this space. Given the small size of the group (in either scenario), strong signs of social status distinctions are unlikely to be evident on the floor. Canid remains are present and concentrated around the cache pit on the south side (Supplemental Figure 14.16). Nonlocal raw material is distributed around the periphery of the floor and appears in greatest concentration on the south side (Supplemental Figure 14.17). Prestige raw materials are rare and are found on the north side of the floor (Supplemental Figure 14.18).

Conclusions

Floor IIm represents a small winter house occupied by one to two families. Activities on the floor are diverse and represent all occupation phases including preparation for abandonment. Thus, we recognize tools associated with food preparation, hide-working and clothing manufacture, heavy-duty tool production, and maintenance of hunting gear. These activities are also reflected in the faunal assemblage where we find abundant fish and ungulates, all heavily processed, as well as a small collection of canid remains. While we do not have complete access to all of the IIm floor, current data suggest that activities were undertaken most intensely around the perimeter of the floor with most food-related work on the north and south sides and lithic reduction on the east and southwest areas. Given evidence for only one domestic group, no data suggests interfamily differentiation in access to wealth items. Following the close of IIm, the house was expanded to the north, thus creating the rectangular house form occupied across floors IIl to IIf.

15

The Second Small House

Stratum IIn

Stratum IIn is the second of three floors associated with the small ovoid-shaped variant of Housepit 54 (Figure 15.1). The eastern edge of the IIn house is visible within Block A illustrating a curving line connecting the north and south walls of the block. We know that the north margin of the house is within the north wall balk of Block A, while the south wall is likely just within the west side of the Block A south wall. The location of the IIn west wall is a greater challenge to reconstruct, though Housepit 32 is a significant constraint on space. Further, like IIm, the Stratum IIn floor is characterized by a ring of features around its visible margins leaving open space in its central zone. Sediments from IIn are clay-dominated (60–80%). All other sediment size classes occur at percentages in the 1–15% range.

Stratum IIn contains three hearth features, located on the northeastern, western, and southern margins of the exposed house floor (Figure 15.2). All are shallow bowl-shaped features. Southern and northeastern hearths clearly are on the floor periphery. However, the western hearth could be on the periphery if the west wall of the excavation is close to the western edge of the floor. If the floor extends substantially farther to the west, this hearth could be positioned closer to the center of the floor. Given the configuration of the east margin of the floor, the latter scenario seems most likely. Stratum IIn also contained one large cache pit on the north side

and a shallow bowl-shaped depression on the east side of the floor. Stratum IIn was fully buried by Stratum IIm deposits. Next, we discuss evidence for variation in occupation and abandonment cycles, site structure, and sociality.

Occupation and Abandonment Cycle

This section provides a review of evidence for occupation and abandonment cycles on IIn using frames of reference outlined in Chapter 2 (Stratum IIa).

Occupation Cycle

This section provides an assessment of occupation cycles focusing on evidence for initiation, exploitation, and abandonment phases. Archaeological expectations of these are outlined in Chapter 2 (Stratum IIa).

Compared to Stratum IIm, the IIn lithic tool assemblage is relatively sparse (Table 15.1). This phenomenon may have two possible explanations. First, our excavation simply missed the portion of the house where the majority of tools were discarded. However, we have argued that the spatial position of the floor and the arrangement of the features implicate the possibility that we did sample the majority of the house deposits. Second, given the probable small size of the house, it may have been occupied by a small group, perhaps for a seasonally limited period of time. A small collection of bifaces, projectile points, and hide scrapers suggests

Block A Stratum IIn Level 1 (2016 excavations)

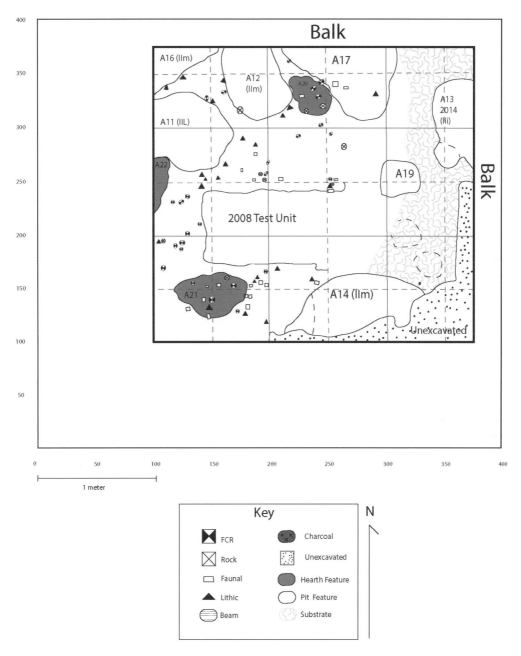

FIGURE 15.1. Comprehensive map of IIn showing point-provenienced artifacts, faunal remains, fire-cracked rock, prior excavations, and features.

Stratum IIn

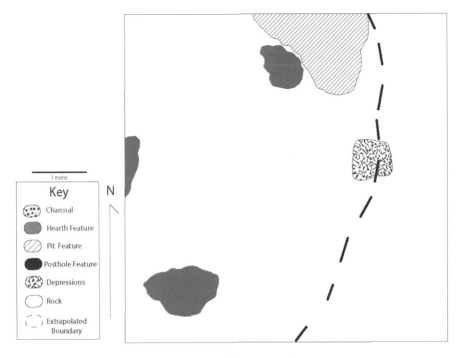

FIGURE 15.2. Features on IIn.

TABLE 15.1. Lithic Tools from IIn, Organized by Tool Class and Block.

	Tool Class																
	A	B	C	D	E	F	G	H	I	J	K	L	M	N	O	P	Q
Block A	1	1	1	0	2	0	0	0	0	0	2	0	0	1	1	2	0

Note: A = flake and slate knives; B = bifaces; C = projectile points; D = flake and key-shaped scrapers; E = hide scrapers; F = drills and perforators; G = small piercers; H = pièces esquillées; I = notches and denticulates; J = adzes; K = abraders/groundstone; L = freehand cores; M = bipolar cores; N = slate objects; O = hammerstones; P = used flakes; Q = ritual/social items.

TABLE 15.2. Lithic Flake Types for Stratum IIn by Toolstone Category.

	Ext	Chal	Cher	Dac	Obs	Intr	Slates	Met.	Total
Biface	0	0	0	1	0	0	1	0	2
Core	0	0	0	1	0	0	0	0	1
Retouch	0	2	11	5	0	0	2	0	20

Note: Ext = extrusives (excluding dacite and obsidian); Dac = dacite; Cher = cherts; Chal = chalcedony; Obs = obsidian; Intr = intrusives plus gneiss; Slates = slate and silicified shale; Met = metamorphic rock inclusive of quartzites, nephrite, and steatite.

some engagement with hunting activities. However, a lack of flake scrapers, key-shaped scrapers, pièces esquillées, notches/denticulates, and drills/perforators suggests little engagement with production of other wood/bone/antler based tools. The absence of bipolar cores, along with almost no retouched flake tools, likely means that raw material conservation and recycling was of little importance. Debitage are limited in number and focus on late stage retouch with nearly no biface and core reduction (Table 15.2). Sampling concerns aside, we suggest that exploitation phase was likely short with virtually no planned abandonment phase.

Abandonment Process

Stratum IIn was completely buried by IIm sediments after an expansion of the house by at least a meter to the east. No architectural elements were recovered, though IIn did not have any postholes. These data suggest that abandonment was planned with the intent to return and expand, refloor, and reroof the house. The IIn floor is distinct, however, from most other floors in that we could not establish a highly significant correlation between smallest and all other debitage ($r = 0.635$, $p = 0.176$). However, a visual examination of the distributions of extra-small debitage (Figure 15.3) versus all lithics (Figure 15.4) demonstrates substantial overlap between larger and smaller items. Faunal remains (Figures 15.5 and 15.6) also confirm the same pattern ($r = 0.964$, $p = 0.002$).

Caches (Binford 1979; Hayden and Deal 1983), positioning items (Binford 1979), and de facto refuse (Schiffer 1972; Stevenson 1982) can be examined for insight into abandonment process. One substantial cache pit, located on the northeast side of the floor, is filled with household refuse, but no other signs of caching behavior are present. Neither is there substantial evidence for positioning items nor de facto refuse. Only one small piece of groundstone was found on the floor, and it was likely discarded in that context. Overall, despite the weak correlation coefficient, we still argue that the IIn floor was not formally swept prior to abandonment.

However, given the sparse array of tools, useable items likely were collected and utilized in later occupations or transported elsewhere.

Site Structure

In Chapter 14 (Stratum IIm), we outlined two spatial scenarios by which the small floors might have been organized. Briefly, we imagined a first scenario where activities were primarily conducted around the perimeter of the floor, thus leaving the central space open. Our second scenario suggested that the central space was co-opted for cooking and other activities, while the margins were used for storage and social space. The position of the west hearth on IIn makes a central hearth scenario the most likely. We also raised the possibility that use of space could be constrained by a side entrance to the house. We now assess these possibilities by examining distributions of lithic debitage, tools, and faunal remains.

Debitage and Spatial Structure of Lithic Reduction

The spatial signatures for all items recovered from IIn are partially constrained by the centrally positioned 2008 excavation trench. However, specific positioning of concentrations of items still provides insights. Debitage are distributed in six concentrations, three on each side of the house (north and south) with highest densities around a hearth on the south side (Supplemental Figure 15.1). All concentrations of flakes are associated with hearths. One early stage reduction flake is found adjacent to the southern hearth (Supplemental Figure 15.2). The one thinning flake is found near the hearth to the northeast (Supplemental Figure 15.3), while the two R-billet flakes cluster around the southern hearth (Supplemental Figure 15.4). Tool retouch flakes are found throughout the floor but concentrate in particular around the west and south hearths (Supplemental Figure 15.5). Overall, it appears that lithic reduction focused on tool retouch that was accomplished around hearth features. Thus the central space between the features was likely somewhat clear.

IIn Extra-Small Debitage Distribution

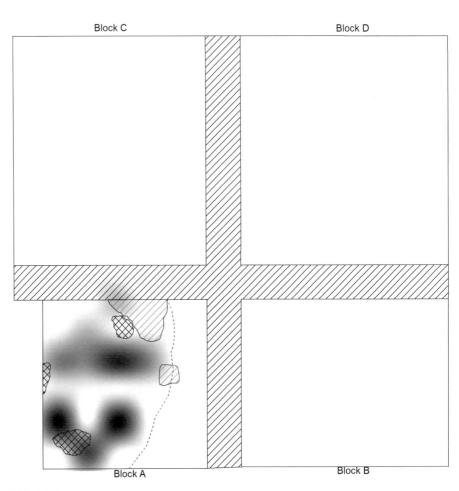

FIGURE 15.3. Extra-small debitage distribution on IIn.

IIn Total Lithic Artifact Distribution

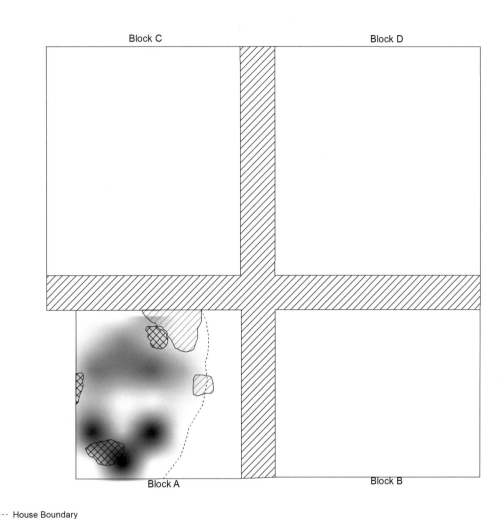

FIGURE 15.4. Total artifact distribution on IIn.

IIn Faunal Specimens Sized 1-9mm

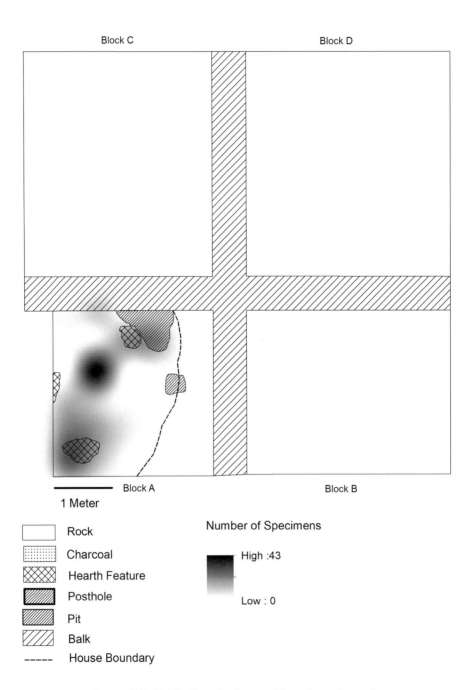

FIGURE 15.5. Distribution of extra-small faunal remains on IIn.

IIn All Faunal Specimens

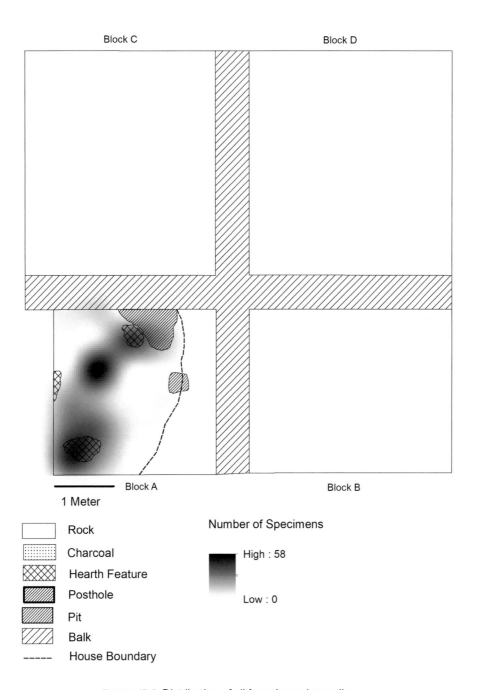

FIGURE 15.6. Distribution of all faunal remains on IIn.

Lithic Tools and House
Floor Activity Organization

Tools are rare on the IIn floor. Consequently, knapping-related or heavy-duty tools are present. Hunting tools (2) are found adjacent to the northeast and south hearths (Supplemental Figure 15.6). Hide-working/sewing tools cluster in the open space between the northeast and west hearths, along with one other adjacent to the southern hearth (Supplemental Figure 15.7). The one piece of groundstone is found adjacent to the west hearth (Supplemental Figure 15.8).

Faunal Remains and Spatial Organization

The count of faunal remains is substantially higher than that of lithic tools, and thus we are able to gain better insight into the use of space from these items. Fish remains are widely distributed but concentrate on and around the south hearth and toward the northeast hearth (Supplemental Figure 15.9). Mammal remains cluster around the southern and northeastern hearths (Supplemental Figure 15.10). Identifiable ungulate remains are rare and found next to the southern hearth and near the small pit on the east side (Supplemental Figure 15.11). Recognizing that the highly fragmentary mammal remains are mostly ungulate in origin, these data suggest the faunal processing for consumption purposes was largely conducted around the hearth features closer to the walls of the house. High utility mammalian elements and fragments also cluster near the south and northeast hearths (Supplemental Figure 15.12). Medium utility elements and fragments cluster in a manner that is similar to that of the fish remains, associated with the south hearth and approximately centrally positioned between the west and northeast hearths (Supplemental Figure 15.13). Low utility elements are distributed in approximately the same configuration as the high utility elements (Supplemental Figure 15.14).

Given that high utility parts are meaty upper limbs and low utility are the corresponding lower limbs, substantially intact limbs appear to have been processed in the same places, while nonlimb (axial) medium utility parts were processed and or dumped in a spatially disjunctive area of the floor. Notably the hearth on the west side does not have a strong association for animal processing. This absence may be because we have not sampled the area to the west of the feature but also could reflect a different use history, perhaps associated with other activities not involving preparation of food. This possibility is partially indicated by debitage, hide scrapers, and groundstone in this portion of the floor.

Summary: Site Structure on the IIn Floor

The spatial distribution of lithic artifacts and faunal remains suggests that neither of our expected scenarios is a perfect fit. We recognize tool maintenance and potentially hide-work near the western hearth. Most mammalian faunal remains are located around the margins. Fish remains are on the house floor margins but also concentrated toward the center, to the east of the west hearth. Thus we have hearth-centered activity areas clearly around the perimeter (south and northeast hearths), but possibly also additional activities conducted near the western hearth.

If the western hearth is really in the center of the floor, which seems most likely, and food preparation was mostly associated with the hearths on the house margins, then we suggest that the marginal areas likely were spaces for domestic groups, while the central portion was communal space for multiple activities. If so, IIn might have had three concentric occupation zones: an outer periphery surrounding the floor but still under the eaves of a roof, a domestic activity zone just inside the floor perimeter, and a central floor space for other activities. Not enough evidence is available to comment on entrances or other contingencies, though given its small size, the house likely had a side entrance.

Sociality

Since we recognize hearths on the northern and southern sides of IIn with similar kitchen-related materials, at least two domestic groups possibly occupied the house. The greatest quantity of nonlocal raw materials is distributed in an arc shape around the western hearth, thus suggesting that these materials were primarily used communally (Supplemental Figure 15.15). One abraded piece of nephrite is found near the southern hearth (Supplemental Figure 15.16). Overall these data are not adequate to point to wealth-related status distinctions within IIn. Rather, the household strategy appears to have been highly cooperative and thus communalistic.

Conclusions

Artifact distributions on IIn suggest a short exploitation phase and limited attention to gearing up for postabandonment activities, though clearly abandonment was still a planned process. Floor IIn included three hearths and one large cache pit, along with a much smaller pit feature. We infer that the hearths to the northeast and south likely represented activity loci for household domestic groups as primarily related to food preparation. Evidence seems to suggest that the western hearth was a more communal activity locus where lithic reduction, hide preparation, and likely other activities occurred. If true, we estimate that we have sampled about half the house, and thus, space for one or more domestic groups possibly remains unexcavated. Overall we conclude that the IIn floor represents households working together in a communalistic strategy and likely the founding approach to life in Housepit 54.

16

Housepit 54 Begins

Stratum IIo

Stratum IIo is the first floor of the small ovoid house sequence and, thus, was the first floor created in what would become the long occupation sequence of Housepit 54 (Figure 16.1). Stratum IIo is recognizable on the western half of Block A. Put differently, the curvilinear eastern edge of IIo is clearly visible across the center of Block A. Assuming that the IIo house was approximately the same size as those of IIn and IIm, we estimate that we sampled no more than about 40% of this house floor. The bulk of the remaining materials are still buried to the west and northwest of Block A. Stratum IIo sediments are virtually identical to those of IIn and IIm, clay-dominated at 60–80% with much lower percentages of silt, sand, gravel, and pebbles. Only one hearth was found, and it is very shallow and located on the eastern margin of the house floor (Figure 16.2). No cache pits or postholes were found. Stratum IIo is entirely buried by IIn deposits. The following sections provide data concerning variation in occupation and abandonment cycles, site structure, and sociality.

Occupation and Abandonment Cycle

As with the previous chapters, we first review evidence for occupation and abandonment cycles. We draw inferences based upon frames of reference outlined in Chapter 2 (Stratum IIa).

Occupation Cycle

We use lithic assemblage data to recognize the effects of variation in occupation cycle using the frames of reference provided in Chapter 2 (Stratum IIa).

Sampling of Stratum IIo is very limited, and thus, the tool assemblage is of reduced value in detecting indicators for occupation cycle (Table 16.1). This stratum reveals very little evidence for hunting or preparation of gear and only limited evidence for conservation and recycling of raw material. Debitage data are equally sparse and resemble those of IIn with a primary focus on late stage reduction and maintenance flakes (Table 16.2). IIo occupants likely operated under similar constraints to those of IIn. However, this hypothesis cannot be fully assessed with these data.

Abandonment Process

Stratum IIo was buried by IIn sediments, and no architectural elements were uncovered. After completion of its final occupation, the house clearly was expanded or repositioned to the east to create the IIn floor. Undoubtedly, a new roof was then constructed. Thus, IIo was finished with an abandonment focused on house expansion or repositioning, reflooring, and reroofing. Extra-small debitage correlate significantly with larger debitage ($r = 0.962$, $p = 0.009$), and that relationship is easily recognized on plan views showing distributions of smallest flakes (Figure 16.3) and the total lithic assemblage (Figure 16.4). This relationship is also evident ($r = 0.979$, $p = 0.004$) in comparisons between smallest and larger faunal items (Figures 16.5 and 16.6).

As with all other floors, we can further assess abandonment process by examining caches (Binford 1979; Hayden and Deal 1983),

Block A Stratum IIo Level 1 (2016 excavations)

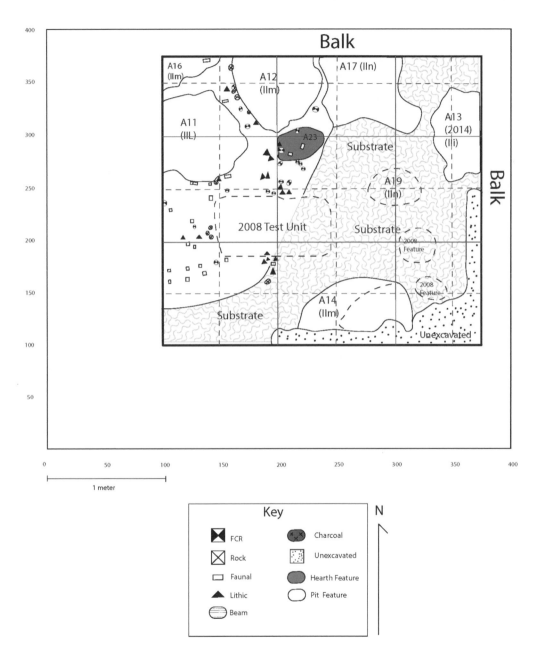

FIGURE 16.1. Comprehensive map of IIo showing point-provenienced artifacts, faunal remains, fire-cracked rock, prior excavations, and features.

Stratum Ilo

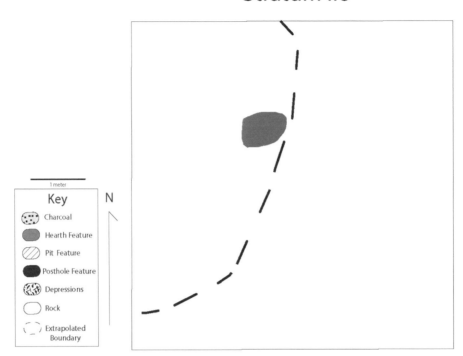

FIGURE 16.2. Features on Ilo.

TABLE 16.1. Lithic Tools from Ilo, Organized by Tool Class and Block.

	Tool Class																
	A	B	C	D	E	F	G	H	I	J	K	L	M	N	O	P	Q
Block A	0	0	0	0	1	1	0	1	0	0	2	0	1	1	1	3	0

Note: A = flake and slate knives; B = bifaces; C = projectile points; D = flake and key-shaped scrapers; E = hide scrapers; F = drills and perforators; G = small piercers; H = pièces esquillées; I = notches and denticulates; J = adzes; K = abraders/groundstone; L = freehand cores; M = bipolar cores; N = slate objects; O = hammerstones; P = used flakes; Q = ritual/social items.

TABLE 16.2. Lithic Flake Types for Stratum Ilo by Toolstone Category.

	Ext	Chal	Cher	Dac	Obs	Intr	Slates	Met.	Total
Biface	0	0	0	1	0	0	0	0	1
Core	0	0	0	2	0	0	0	0	2
Retouch	1	2	10	7	0	0	0	0	20

Note: Ext = extrusives (excluding dacite and obsidian); Dac = dacite; Cher = cherts; Chal = chalcedony; Obs = obsidian; Intr = intrusives plus gneiss; Slates = slate and silicified shale; Met = metamorphic rock inclusive of quartzites, nephrite, and steatite.

positioning items (Binford 1979), and de facto refuse (Schiffer 1972; Stevenson 1982). No evidence for caching is present on the portion of IIo exposed by these excavations. Neither do we see positioning items or de facto refuse. Thus, while the discarded materials on the IIo floor were probably not swept, larger items with some remaining utility were probably removed before IIn sediments buried IIo.

Site Structure

We did not excavate enough of Stratum IIo to permit an assessment of overall floor organization. We can ask, however, if the one hearth on the east side was a household activity area, and if so, what were the range of activities. To accomplish this analysis, we assess lithic debitage, tool forms, and faunal remains. Spatial distributions are constrained by intrusive features associated with later occupations and the bottom of the original test trench.

Debitage and Spatial Structure of Lithic Reduction

Debitage are concentrated immediately to the west of the hearth (Supplemental Figure 16.1). Two early stage reduction flakes are distributed along the east side of IIo (Supplemental Figure 16.2). One thinning flake was found in the northwest corner of Block A and is thus not associated with the one hearth feature (Supplemental Figure 16.3). Tool retouch flakes occur throughout IIo but concentrate to the west and northwest of the hearth feature (Supplemental Figure 16.4). These data suggest that the hearth on the east side of IIo was indeed the locus of lithic reduction activities.

Lithic Tools and House Floor Activity Organization

As with IIn, tools are somewhat rare on IIo. One core was located to the west of the hearth, near the Block A west wall (Supplemental Figure 16.5). One heavy-duty tool was located immediately adjacent to the hearth (Supplemental Figure 16.6). Hide-working/sewing tools are distributed across the south side of IIo, but only one of these tools is directly associated with the hearth (Supplemental Figure 16.7). Only two pieces of groundstone were found, located on the north and south sides of IIo (Supplemental Figure 16.8). Given the scattered nature of these items, no particular task was clearly focused directly around the hearth, though that usage is still possible as mediated by tool discard away from the hearth.

Faunal Remains and Spatial Organization

As with lithic artifacts, faunal remains are not highly abundant on IIo. However, they are frequent enough to recognize some degree of patterning. Fish remains are scattered west and southwest of the small hearth feature (Supplemental Figure 16.9). Mammal remains cluster in one spot just west of the hearth (Supplemental Figure 16.10). Only two definitively identifiable ungulate remains were found in the central and north-central portion of IIo (Supplemental Figure 16.11). Medium and high utility mammalian remains are distributed broadly to the west and southwest of the hearth feature (Supplemental Figures 16.12 and 16.13). Low utility items are found in a tighter cluster southwest of the feature (Supplemental Figure 16.14). Clearly faunal remains are found in and around the small hearth, thus raising the possibility of a hearth-centered activity area on the east side of the IIo floor.

Summary: Site Structure on the IIo Floor

Given that only portions of the small floor remain, the small size of the house overall, and impacts to the floor of later features, we are limited in our ability to draw extensive conclusions about the use of space on IIo. We do recognize overlapping distributions of debitage, several tool classes, and faunal remains inclusive of fish and mammals. Thus, the small hearth likely served as a focal point for multiple activities and thus represents the space used by a domestic group. Not enough evidence is available to define an entrance or to examine organization of space as related to other practical contingencies.

Ilo Extra-Small Debitage Distribution

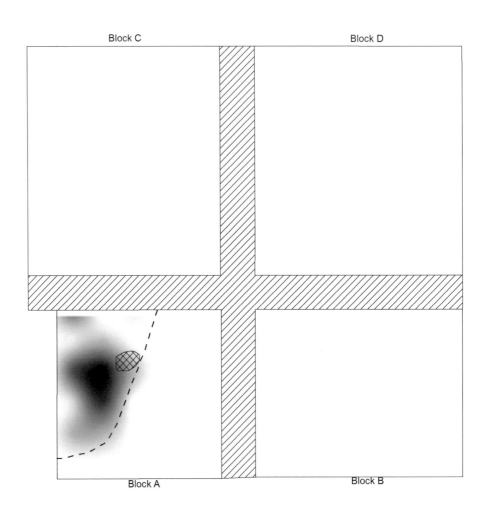

FIGURE 16.3. Extra-small debitage distribution on Ilo.

N

Ilo Total Lithic Artifact Distribution

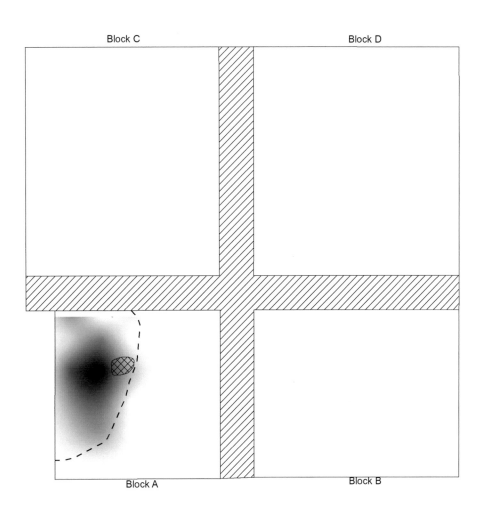

Block C

Block D

Block A

Block B

- - - House Boundary

Hearth

Total Lithic Artifacts

High : 30

Low : 0

Balk   1 Meter

FIGURE 16.4. Total artifact distribution on Ilo.

Ilo Faunal Specimens Sized 1-9mm

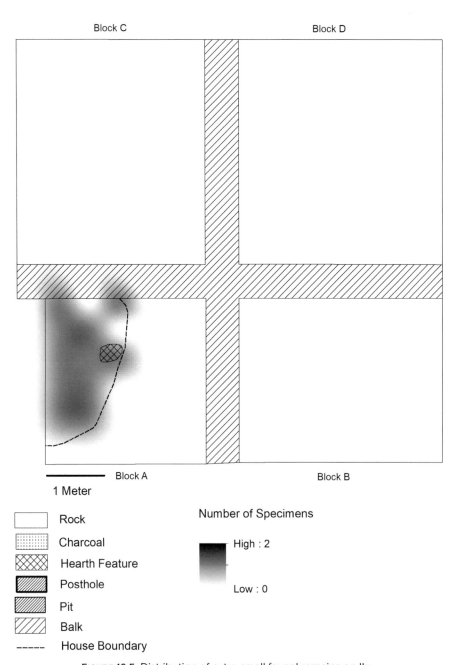

FIGURE 16.5. Distribution of extra-small faunal remains on Ilo.

Ilo All Faunal Specimens

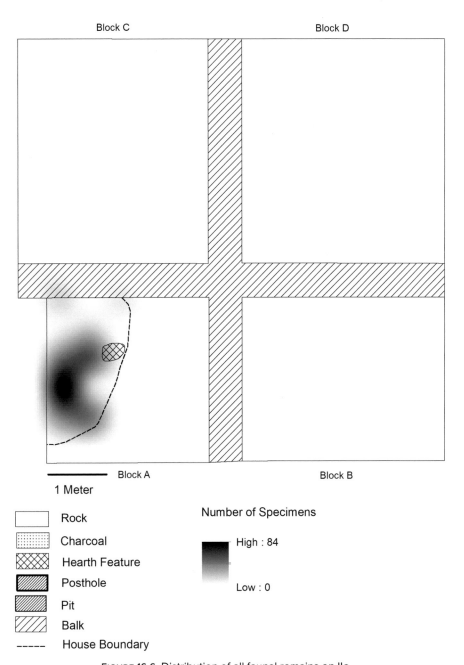

FIGURE 16.6. Distribution of all faunal remains on Ilo.

Sociality

We have identified the likely residential activities of a single domestic group. Thus we are not in a position to examine intergroup relations as related to access to or accumulation of wealth-related items. We can say that the IIo group did discard a dog bone, raising the possibility that they had consumed a dog (Supplemental Figure 16.5). Further, this group also maintained access to nonlocal lithic sources (Supplemental Figure 16.6). Thus, this small group was clearly connected socially within and likely beyond the village.

Conclusions

The IIo floor represents the founding of Housepit 54. From limited data, this house appears to have been small with at least one family activity space on its east side. In that context, group members maintained lithic tools, engaged in some heavy-duty tool applications, did sewing and hide-working, and processed mammalian and fish resources for food. They also traded and/or traveled far enough away from the village to obtain a set of distinct nonlocal lithic raw materials. Given limitations to the exposure of this floor, the remaining area to the west of the Block A excavation could contain enough space to have held another domestic unit. However, this possibility will remain unknown without further work. Regardless, the IIo people clearly flourished to enough of a degree to favor establishment of what we identify as the initiation of Housepit 54. More proximately, they persisted long enough to complete the IIo occupation and to establish the subsequent house floor and roof (IIn).

17

Conclusions

The overarching goal of this book is to test alternative hypotheses regarding the nature of Middle Fraser Canyon house groups during the period of peak village size at ca. 1,000–1,500 years ago using data from our excavations of Housepit 54 at the Bridge River site. In doing so, it offers us the chance to present the record of spatial relationships on 15 floors from Housepit 54. The Housepit 54 project has been and continues to be a cooperative effort between our archaeological team and the membership of the descendant community, the St'át'imc Nation and Xwísten, the Bridge River Band. Many of our interpretations regarding the meaning of distributions of cultural materials across the Housepit 54 floors derive in part from insights provided by our First Nations friends and collaborators (summarized on Table 1.1). This collaborative arrangement is increasingly common in the greater Pacific Northwest. We hope that this project provides a good example of the benefits of such partnerships.

We recognize two distinctly different interpretations of traditional Plateau social strategies. The standard Plateau model recognizes autonomous villages characterized by variable occupation patterns given extremely unstable group membership marked by a lack of clans or phratries, variable inheritance traditions, and temporary elected leaders who have no coercive powers (Ackerman 1994; Furniss 2004; Goldman 1941; Grossman 1965; Ray 1939; Teit 1900, 1909; Wickwire 1991). Ethnographers describe a high degree of residential flexibility to take advantage of seasonally variable resources. Consequently, settlement patterns reflect shifting cycles of aggregation and dispersal such that individual houses could not be expected to have been occupied for more than a few seasons. Egalitarian relations persist as a consequence of tension between self-interested goals of families with wider group ethics of shared goods (Furniss 2004).

In contrast, ethnography of the Middle Fraser Canyon area depicts networks of permanent villages with stable group membership and formal territories (Kennedy and Bouchard 1998; Teit 1906). Villages are organized by house groups and clans. The strongest clans could extend membership and influence across multiple villages. Aggregation and dispersal formed a stable annual cycle with families engaging in warm season mobility to access various mammals (especially deer), salmon, berries, geophytes, and a range of other resources of lesser importance, followed by winter sedentism in pithouse villages (Alexander 1992, 2000; Prentiss and Kuijt 2012). Nonegalitarian relations existed on the basis of inheritance of chiefly status or by achievement as associated with hunting and war prowess, along with recognition from developing social events such as potlatches (Romanoff 1992b; Teit 1906).

Scholars have argued that the Mid-Fraser pattern is different from the rest of the Plateau due to the spread of cultural ideas from the

Northwest Coast during the latest pre-Colonial and Colonial periods (Ackerman 1994; Grossman 1965; Harris 2012; Ray 1939; Teit 1906). However, we have suggested that much of this work is influenced by the speculations of James Teit who was certainly unaware of the full extent and time depth of the large villages on the Mid-Fraser. Thus, an alternative scenario is that the cultural process in the Mid-Fraser was qualitatively different from that elsewhere on the Plateau in that permanent villages, house-groups, clans, and social ranking developed in this area many centuries before the coming of Europeans. Put differently, the Mid-Fraser ethnographic cultural pattern is the historic manifestation of a more ancient tradition.

Archaeological research in the Mid-Fraser has suggested that the latter hypotheses may have validity. Hayden's (1997, 2000) excavations at the Keatley Creek site demonstrated the presence of large houses with histories spanning hundreds of years as, for example, at Housepit 7 (Prentiss et al. 2003). Hayden (1997) argues that material cultural inequality can be recognized on an intra- and inter-house basis at Keatley Creek. However, despite deep middens surrounding houses, the Keatley Creek housepits generally lack sequences of buried floors from which archaeologists could evaluate occupation patterns over time with any degree of precision. The Bridge River site offers this opportunity given multiple houses with stratified floor sequences.

Prentiss and colleagues (2008, 2012, 2014) demonstrated that the village was initiated nearly 2,000 years ago. We know relatively little about the earliest occupations termed BR1. However, during the second period (BR2), the village was organized on the landscape in the form of two concentric rings of housepits. The transition from BR2 to BR3 was coupled with a near-demographic collapse such that only three houses (from current data) crossed the transition. Demographic growth during early BR3 was rapid and led to the establishment of two neighborhood-like rings of houses. Evidence suggests inter- and intra-house inequality during this time (Prentiss et al. 2014; Prentiss et al. 2018b).

Combining the records from Keatley Creek and Bridge River, large villages with large houses and aspects of social complexity appear to have been established over a millennium ago. However, prior to the excavations of Housepit 54 at Bridge River, we had yet to fully evaluate the predictions of either model regarding occupational stability of individual houses. The accumulated archaeological record at individual housepits still possibly could be a byproduct of reoccupations across long time spans in different seasons and economic conditions by groups of diverse demographics and social configurations. The Housepit 54 record of 15 stratigraphically superimposed floors provides an ideal opportunity to test predictions of the two hypotheses.

In brief, standard Plateau model predicts short occupations by different groups under diverse economic and social conditions. Thus, the Housepit 54 floors should feature significant stochastic diversity in occupation patterns, floor structure, and interpersonal social relationships. The Mid-Fraser model suggests that houses were social entities, indeed reflective of group membership similar to the House groups described by Lévi-Strauss (1979). Thus, we would expect either long-term stability or patterned change in occupation patterns, floor structure, and social relations perhaps paralleling wider patterns of change across the village. If the latter is the case, then Housepit 54 would shift from an egalitarian residence to a somewhat non-egalitarian residence, at least as measured by variation in material goods between the BR2 and BR3 periods in line with wider developments at the site and across the local region (Prentiss et al. 2007, 2012; Prentiss et al. 2018c).

In this chapter, we review the results of our studies focused on the Housepit 54 floors. We review evidence for variation in occupation pattern with a focus on occupation phases: initiation, exploitation, and abandonment (Stevenson 1982, 1985). Under the standard Plateau model and given differing situation conditions, little consistency should be found in details of occupation and abandonment planning and execution. In contrast, we expect a high degree of consistency in the Mid-Fraser model.

We review evidence for variation in floor organization under the wider rubric of site structure. Under the standard Plateau model, floor organization should vary between occupations with no inherent inter-floor pattern or logic, under the assumption that different groups at different times brought their own approaches to life on the floors. The Mid-Fraser model predicts the likelihood of intergenerational transmission of traditions and thus a high degree of consistency even within a broader pattern of change as might be associated with growth in house size. Finally, under the Plateau model, we would not expect indicators of material wealth-based inequality, whereas this possibility may occur under the Mid-Fraser model. We already know that inequality developed late in the history of Housepit 54 (Prentiss et al. 2018b).

Occupation Patterns

Drawing from Stevenson (1982, 1985), we assessed each floor for the likelihood that each was occupied through initiation, exploitation, and abandonment phases. Briefly, initiation phase concerns activities happening during and immediately after the establishment of an occupation. In Mid-Fraser ethnography, these tasks would include refurbishing house architecture and furniture, preparing storage and cooking areas, and overall establishment of family living space. Primary lithic tools used in this context would be related to woodworking, thus including adzes, abraders, heavy-duty flake scrapers, and pièces esquillées. Exploitation phase would represent the majority of an occupation cycle during which a wide variety of activities would be conducted including food preparation, hide-working and clothing manufacture, basket-making and weaving, manufacture of nonlithic implements, and creation and maintenance of lithic tools. Consequently, lithic tool assemblages would be diverse, spanning a wide range of flake knives, scrapers, piercers, and drills, along with more formalized knives and scrapers. Abandonment of winter houses usually occurred in late winter, and according to ethnography, a critical activity was obtaining food, primarily deer and other game (Alexander 1992). Thus, abandonment phase should be particularly reflected in production of bifaces and projectile points. Bipolar core technology would have been essential for extending use-life of lithic raw material across complete winter cycles and thus would reflect activities of late exploitation and abandonment phases (French 2017).

We recognize abundant evidence in the lithic assemblages of IIa–IIh and IIk–IIm for the three occupation phases (Table 17.1). Each floor provided evidence for production and use of woodworking, kitchen-related, sewing and hide-working, and hunting/butchering tools, along with bipolar cores. Floors IIi and IIj showed few signs of biface production debitage, bifaces and projectile points, or bipolar cores. Given an overall low investment in storage (Prentiss et al. 2018a) and comparatively limited quantities of lithic items in general, these floors appear to have been occupied for shorter periods and may not have accumulated debris from typical abandonment phases. A pattern of shorter winter occupation and limited evidence for typical abandonment phase would be expected on these floors as other evidence suggests that this was a period of subsistence stress village-wide. Indeed, at this time most of the houses at Bridge River were abandoned.

Floors IIn and IIo also offer limited evidence for the abandonment phase. It is possible that this is a byproduct of limited sampling given that we encountered probably no more than 50% of each floor. Evidence from IIm and IIl suggests that household subsistence economies may have been quite strong during this period, thus raising the expectation of a full initiation-exploitation-abandonment cycle. All told, these data suggest a high degree of continuity in occupation cycles. The only exceptions are understandable in light of village history (IIi and IIj) and sampling limitations (IIn and IIo).

Abandonment Process

We postulated four possible scenarios regarding abandonment process. Sudden abandonment without return would be associated with a catastrophic situation in which people left their home with no plan to return. The archaeological consequence would consist of abandonment of

TABLE 17.1. Variation in Occupation Dates, Occupation Periods (BR2 and BR3), and Occupation Cycles across Housepit 54 Floors.

Floor	Estimated Date (BP)	BR Period	I	E	A
IIa	1123	3	X	X	X
IIb	1147	3	X	X	X
IIc	1171	3	X	X	X
IId	1195	3	X	X	X
IIe	1219	3	X	X	X
IIf	1243	3	X	X	X
IIg	1267	3	X	X	X
IIh	1292	3	X	X	X
IIi	1316	2	X	X	x
IIj	1340	2	X	X	x
IIk	1364	2	X	X	X
IIl	1388	2	X	X	X
IIm	1412	2	X	X	X
IIn	1436	2	X	X	x
IIo	1460	2	X	X	x

Note: The estimated dates draw on results of Bayesian analysis of calibrated radiocarbon dates in Prentiss et al. (2018a). I = initiation; E = exploitation; A = abandonment; X = full expression; x = limited expression.

TABLE 17.2. Variation in Abandonment Processes across Housepit 54 Floors.

	Sudden No Return	Planned No Return No Closing	Planned No Return Closing	Planned Return
IIa			X	
IIb				X
IIc				X
IId				X
IIe				X
IIf				X
IIg				X
IIh				X
IIi				X
IIj				X
IIk				X
IIl				X
IIm				X
IIn				X
IIo				X

Note: X = full expression.

tools and furniture and no treatment of architectural elements. Thus, we would expect wooden posts and beams to have decayed in place and the roof superstructure to collapse as a natural process. We recognize three forms of planned abandonment. Planned abandonment without reoccupation could also include scenarios with no formal closing of the house or in which the house is formally ended or closed. In the case of no formal closing, we could expect clearing of still-usable tools and furniture, and depending upon how long after abandonment the house is open, it could accumulate dumped material from neighboring houses. Where formal closing occurred, we expect similar removal of still usable items, followed by a sealing of the house floor by purposefully collapsing and/or burning of the roof. We would expect inconsistency in abandonment process under the standard Plateau scenario, whereas consistency in abandonments and reoccupations would be likely under the Mid-Fraser model.

Abandonment of the Housepit 54 floors appears to have been a highly consistent practice. Floors IIb through IIo exhibit evidence for abandonment with planned return (Table 17.2). All demonstrate abandonment with discard of generally broken and exhausted tools and consequent replacement with sediments to constitute a new floor layer. Typically, old roofs were removed without burning to make way for the new floor and roof. However, several exceptions point to the possibility of roof-burning rituals. Floors IIb, IId, IIe, and IIh are capped by burned roof materials but only within portions of one excavation block each. Analysis of sediment oxidation in the roof sediments and color variation in associated faunal remains implicates extremely high heat (Prentiss et al. 2020a). The fact that roof sediments only occur in limited spaces suggests that most roof materials were removed manually, leaving a portion to be burned. In line with contemporary St'át'imc ash-related cultural traditions, we suggest that sections of select roofs were burned as renewal rituals (Prentiss et al. 2020a). Of particular interest, this practice began at IIh, which marks the beginning of the BR3 period, and persisted in earnest (IIb–IIe) during the time in which

Housepit 54 had achieved its maximum size, highest demographics, and greatest indicators of social inequality. Clearly the practice of reoccupation and renewal ended with the close of the IIa floor, given that it was fully capped by an extensive (all blocks) burned roof. Consequently, we conclude that the history of Housepit 54 was characterized by regular cycles of occupation and reoccupation that included reflooring and reroofing approximately once every 20- to 25-year generation. At the end of its full occupational history, the house was formally closed with a large-scale roof-burning ritual.

Social Strategies

We conducted an analysis of the use of space to determine the major organizing principle guiding interpersonal and interfamily relationships on each floor. To accomplish this assessment, we sought evidence to confirm communalist versus collectivist social strategies (Coupland et al. 2009; Williams-Larson et al. 2017). Communalist strategies are reflected by house floors organized into task-related activity areas shared by all. Thus, a fully communalist house would have a common cooking area (central hearth for example), toolmaking and hide-working/sewing zones, and sleeping and socializing space. Communalist households could be made up of one to many family groups. However, the use of space would largely preclude identification of individual groups. In contrast, the collectivist strategy would be evident in the establishment of family-specific activity spaces. Thus, we would expect to recognize two or more distinct hearth-centered activity areas with evidence for the full range of cooking, toolmaking, and other domestic activities spaced at even intervals along or around the house floor.

In the Plateau context, communalist living arrangements were the norm in socioeconomically egalitarian houses and communities (Teit 1900, 1909). In contrast, many Mid-Fraser and nearby Northwest Coast groups historically relied upon collectivist house strategies in which success of the house depended upon successes of the individual families who were free to cooperate to varying degrees with others within

the same structure (Coupland et al. 2009; Teit 1906; Williams-Larson et al. 2017). Consequently, one common byproduct of these living arrangements was some degree of material wealth-based inequality. Under the standard Plateau model, we would therefore not expect inequality to develop or persist on the Housepit 54 floors. Inequality could develop within the Mid-Fraser ethnographic scenario perhaps in line with wider changes within the village as a whole.

Housepit 54 grew from a small oval to rectangular shape (IIm–IIo), to a larger rectangular form (IIf–IIl), and finally to its large oval form (IIa–IIe). The primary cause for change in house form appears to have been growth in house population (Prentiss et al. 2018a). However, social conditions possibly changed as well. Evidence from distributions of features, faunal remains, and lithic artifacts suggests that social strategies evolved over time (Table 17.3). Early floors (IIm–IIo) most likely reflect a specialized activity area based organization and thus a communalist strategy. As noted in those respective chapters, our sampling is less complete for these floors and thus conclusions are tentative.

The IIl floor marks an abrupt shift with the establishment of the rectangular house. The distribution of materials appears to implicate two domestic activity areas with a common shared space in between. While this conclusion is tentative given challenges to monitoring the organization of materials on this floor, for now the social strategy on this floor appears to have been most likely communalist. Floors IIk through IIh provide a consistent pattern whereby hearths, cache pits, and extensive associated distributions of faunal remains and lithic materials cluster in north Block A and south Block C. Above and below this area, not only scattered concentrations of cultural materials occur but also significant open space. We suggest that this pattern of organization could reflect a more dominant communalistic strategy with elements of collectivism. The central features and discarded cultural materials could reflect common workspaces used by domestic groups residing at each end of the rectangular

TABLE 17.3. Variation in Social Strategies across Housepit 54 Floors.

	Collectivist	Communalist
IIa	X	
IIb	X	
IIc	X	
IId	X	
IIe	X	x
IIf	X	x
IIg	X	x
IIh	x	X
IIi	x	X
IIj	x	X
IIk	x	X
IIl	x	X
IIm		X
IIn		X
IIo		X

Note: X = full expression; x = limited expression.

house. In our experience, this spatial pattern is unique in the Plateau region.

Floors IIg and IIf feature a different pattern, consisting of three hearth-centered activity areas evenly spaced across the floors and in nearly the same positions. However, each floor includes only one large cache pit located in the southern portion of Block A. These floors appear to be collectivist in organization given the possibility of three distinct domestic groups on each. However, the single large cache pit on each floor implies some degree of shared facilities and thus a remnant of communalism.

Floors IIa–IIe are clearly collectivist in organization. Each includes spatially distinct hearth-centered activity areas with largely redundant artifact and faunal element contents (Prentiss et al. 2018b). However, some interesting variation is present. The early occupation of IIe included the doubling of house size from IIf and the establishment of an entire sector of the floor (Block B and south Block D) as a storage area that included six cache pits, some extremely large and developed in an arc-like arrangement with the possibility of at least some being capped by a wooden structure, perhaps a bench-like feature. Domestic activity areas on early IIe are found in the other blocks, and

by late IIe, the cache pits in Block B and south Block D were largely filled with either kitchen debris or layers of clay (presumed to be associated with annual reconditioning of those pits) and covered with floor material and in some cases hearths. Consequently, by late IIe times, Block B had also become a domestic activity area. We recognize four domestic activity areas evenly distributed around the IId through IIb floors. Clearly the largest hearths and densest accumulation of cultural material was in Block D. Block D also became the only area to develop cache pits. North Block C also accumulated significant quantities of materials during occupations of these floors.

A major change occurred on the final floor (IIa) in which floor sediments were established for all areas except Block D. In the place of floor materials, the area was filled with thin beds of rim-like material and was not occupied. Elsewhere on IIa, we find abundant evidence of domestic occupation and a continuation of the collectivist strategy.

Clearly, social relationships trended from a communalist to a collectivist strategy at Housepit 54. Simultaneously we recognize evidence for changes in the ability of individual family groups to establish social networks beyond the house and to develop differential degrees of material wealth. Statistical analysis of inter- and intra-floor variation suggests that material wealth-based inequality emerged and persisted across the IIb–IIe floors (Prentiss et al. 2018b). Our examinations of spatial distributions across the floors confirm these conclusions (Table 17.4). Even though floors IIh–IIk were substantially communalistic, each retained some evidence for the possibility of dedicated family spaces. Thus, even these floors offered the chance to assess the possibility of differential accumulated material wealth along with the clearly collectivist IIf through IIa sequence.

Examination of spatial distributions on each floor confirms the findings of Prentiss and colleagues (2018b). No evidence for measurable inequality is found on IIo through IIf or on IIa. Inequality is clearly present on IIe through IIb. Block D consistently accumulated the greatest

TABLE 17.4. Variation in Social Relations across Housepit 54 Floors.

	Inequality/Cooperation	
	Egalitarian/ Higher	Non-Egalitarian/ Lower
IIa	X	
IIb		X
IIc		X
IId		X
IIe		X
IIf		
IIg	X	
IIh	X	
IIi	X	
IIj	X	
IIk	X	
IIl	X	
IIm	X	
IIn	X	
IIo	X	

Note: X = full expression.

densities of nonlocal lithic materials, prestige raw materials, prestige objects, dog remains, and deer remains. These materials are accompanied by the presence of large hearths, ovens, and cache pits on IIe through IIc. Floor IIb lacks cache pits or hearths. However, given the similarly high density of cultural materials, we suggest that this seeming absence could result from sampling issues. Such features could easily have been removed by the large pit excavated during the IIa1 (brief postabandonment reoccupation) occupation on the west side of Block D. A charcoal dump in the center of the block implicates the likelihood of a nearby hearth.

We recognize a clear trend in social relationships across the history of Housepit 54. As the house grew in size, it also changed in terms of preferred social strategy, shifting from largely communalist to fully collectivist. The shift from communalist to collectivist was accompanied by a reduction in interfamily cooperation, which might be expected as families increasingly created and exclusively operated within their own spaces. This shift apparently opened the door to exclusive networks and the ability to amass goods at different rates. Once

this possibility was in place, evidently during the IIe occupation, rights to goods, collection of goods, and social networks were clearly passed down across generations. Thus, the Block D domestic group remained better connected, and thus wealthier, than other units on those floors. Apparently, however, some form of social crisis occurred between IIb and IIa such that the occupants of the house did not create a new living space in the Block D area but instead filled it with rim midden.

When we examine this history, clearly we are not recognizing stochastic variation in residential norms. Instead we see an apparent trend from entirely communalistic toward a gradual increase in collectivist attributes to full-on collectivist strategies. Simultaneously we recognize a reorganization of cooperation and the development of material wealth-based inequalities. The change in the norms of cooperation and the development of inequalities is in line with our understanding of similar developments across the Bridge River village (Prentiss et al. 2012, 2014) and elsewhere in the Mid-Fraser at this time (Prentiss et al. 2007). The wider pattern of change during the period of ca. 1200–1400 cal BP appears to be linked with fluctuations in the salmon fishery, variation in deer populations, and consequent effects on human livelihoods and demography (Prentiss et al. 2011, 2014; Prentiss et al. 2020b).

The communalist-collectivist model offers wider implications for general understanding of social change. At Bridge River, changes in the structure of work and sharing of goods came before persistent interfamily wealth distinctions. In essence, people had to get used to the idea of private goods before they could accept differential access to wealth-related resources (i.e., Eerkens 2013). Seen in this light, social inequality was the outcome of a historical process but never a foregone conclusion. If this social process was historically situational, then it is easy to imagine it being repeated in different ways in different places across the Pacific Northwest region and elsewhere. For example, inequality possibly emerged more than once on the Central Northwest Coast (e.g., Coupland et al. 2016;

Prentiss and Walsh 2016). Repeated emergences of complex hunting and gathering societies in the Bering Strait region (Mason and Friesen 2017) could provide another good example.

Discussion

Early in this project, we proposed two alternative scenarios for the history of Housepit 54 that had significant implications for our understanding of the development of Mid-Fraser cultural traditions. Either the strata accumulated via disparate reoccupations by diverse groups with varying economic, social, and political agendas, or the house was founded and consistently occupied by a long-lived group who passed on their traditions generation by generation while participating in wider community developments. The history of Housepit 54 as reflected in 15 floors is one of substantial stability coupled with periods of change. Alignment is clear between growth in house size, population, and change in social strategies, as a lengthy early period dominated by egalitarian communalism gave way to another lengthy period of collectivism within which we recognize four generations characterized by material wealth-based inequality. The house evidently survived the major economic downturn at the end of the BR2 that caused most of the village to be abandoned. The house subsequently grew in size and population during the period of rapid village growth in early BR3 and subsequently declined in population in line with the same process village-wide (Prentiss et al. 2018a). This history stretched over about 350 years and led to the accumulation of nearly three meters of cultural strata on the outer rim of the housepit. It is impossible not to conclude that this place was the residence of long-lived house group whose fortunes waxed and waned over the centuries. Thus, we conclude that a cultural scenario close to the Mid-Fraser ethnographic model operated at dates of ca. 1,100–1,460 years ago.

These results confirm findings elsewhere that houses were long-lived and representative of stable groups. Housepit 7 at Keatley Creek is probably the best known of this group (Hayden 1997). The fine-grained chronology of that house developed by Prentiss and colleagues (2003) can be reinterpreted in light of these results. Housepit 7 is stratigraphically defined by a sequence of three houses. The small Sub-housepit 3 dated ca. 1600–1700 cal BP is followed somewhat later by a larger Sub-housepit 1 dated ca. 1300–1400 cal BP. Capping these small floors are the more extensive floor and rims of Housepit 7, postdating the Sub-housepit 1 occupation. If this scenario is correct, then Housepit 7 was probably established in a similar date range to the early rectangular house floors at Housepit 54 and then persisted slightly longer, ending just shy of ca. 1000 cal BP. Thus, we conclude that this house was also occupied steadily for about 300 years.

Many housepits at Bridge River are known to have multi-floor sequences. The large Housepit 20, for example, closely reflects the Housepit 54 sequence with floors dating to the BR2, BR3, and BR4 periods. Overall, the accumulated cultural materials at Bridge River are so extensive that the site resembles a shallow Near Eastern tell in the sense of accumulated anthropogenic sediments in its core area. The same impression can be gained in the core portion of the Keatley Creek site. These sites are not the consequence of random reoccupations by small groups over long time spans. Rather, they are the result of centuries of sustained occupation that included select houses occupied for much of that time.

Clearly some houses at Bridge River were long-lived, housing social groups of likely considerable influence. We have yet to examine the degree of networking between houses. At this point, we think it likely that much larger multi-house social units, perhaps resembling clans, existed, as reflected by the semicircular arrangements of houses during BR2 and BR3 (Prentiss et al. 2018c). We do not understand details of the interrelationships between houses. Did each house act autonomously within these social groups? Were there more select sets of houses that formed lineage groups within the clans? Regardless of these future research directions, we can say that the Mid-Fraser ethnographic pattern had its origin not in the recent traditional societies of the Northwest Coast but in a much more ancient history unique to the Middle Fraser Canyon. Some coastal concepts regarding social structure and select belief systems still possibly could have been spread into the region during the past 2,000 years. However, the concepts are equally likely to have developed in the Mid-Fraser context and transmitted outward to the coast.

Archaeologists who study long-lived houses should pay attention to these outcomes. Archaeological manifestations of large houses so often poorly reflect their long-term histories. In some contexts, only the final floor remains, thus tempting archaeologists to interpret the history of that house in light of that single context (Hayden 1997). Our work at Housepit 54 clearly illustrates the perils of such an approach. The structure of activity areas and associated social implications on II was substantially different from nearly all of the early floors. Other long-lived houses may have thick floor strata but lack clear stratigraphic separations between floors,

thus often forcing archaeologists to combine materials from different depths for analytical purposes (Grier 2006; McMillan and St. Claire 2012). Repeated use of common activity spaces over time could lead to coherent spatial patterns in the archaeological record.

However, if activity areas shifted over time, the resulting palimpsest could be challenging to interpret. At Housepit 54, we recognized shifts in the use of space between specialized activities and general domestic spaces. For example, compare the use of southern Block C between the IIf–IIg floors versus the IIh–IIl sequence. An even starker example would be the center of the house, for example, southwestern Block D between Stratum II in the Fur Trade period (Williams-Larson et al. 2017) and the IIb–IId sequence. In this example, a largely empty central portion of the house was transformed to be the center of household activities with significant implications for our understanding of life on those floors.

References

Ackerman, Lillian A.
1994 Nonunilinear Descent Groups in the Plateau Culture Area. *American Ethnologist* 21(2): 286–309.

Adams, Ron L.
2007 Maintaining Cohesion in House Societies of West Sumba, Indonesia. In *The Durable House: House Society Models in Archaeology*, edited by Robin A. Beck Jr., pp. 344–364. Occasional Paper No. 35, Center for Archaeological Investigations, Southern Illinois University, Carbondale.

Alexander, Diana.
1992 Prehistoric Land Use in the Mid-Fraser Area Based on Ethnographic Data. In *A Complex Culture of the British Columbia Plateau*, edited by Brian Hayden, pp. 99–176. University of British Columbia Press, Vancouver.
2000 Pithouses on the Interior Plateau of British Columbia: Ethnographic Evidence and Interpretation of the Keatley Creek Site. In *The Ancient Past of Keatley Creek, Vol. II: Socioeconomy*, edited by Brian Hayden, pp. 29–66. Archaeology Press, Burnaby, British Columbia, Canada.

Ames, Kenneth M.
2006 Thinking about Household Archaeology on the Northwest Coast. In *Household Archaeology on the Northwest Coast*, edited by Elizabeth A. Sobel, D. Ann Trieu Gahr, and Kenneth M. Ames, pp. 16–36. International Monographs in Prehistory, International Series 16, Ann Arbor, Michigan.

Ames, Kenneth M., and Herbert D. G. Maschner
1999 *Peoples of the Northwest Coast: Their Archaeology and Prehistory*. Thames and Hudson, London.

Barnett, Kristen D., and Brenda Frank
2017 Indigenous Spatial Analysis. In *The Last House at Bridge River: The Archaeology of an Aboriginal Household in British Columbia during the Fur Trade Period*, edited by Anna Marie Prentiss, pp. 209–225. University of Utah Press, Salt Lake City.

Beck, Robin A., Jr.
2007a *The Durable House: House Society Models in Archaeology*. Occasional Paper No. 35, Center for Archaeological Investigations, Southern Illinois University, Carbondale.
2007b The Durable House: Material, Metaphor, and Structure. In *The Durable House: House Society Models in Archaeology*, edited by Robin A. Beck, Jr., pp. 464–486. Occasional Paper No. 35, Center for Archaeological Investigations, Southern Illinois University, Carbondale.

Bettinger, Robert L.
2015 *Orderly Anarchy: Sociopolitical Evolution in Aboriginal California*. University of California Press, Oakland.

Binford, Lewis R.
1978a Dimensional Analysis of Behavior and Site Structure: Learning from an Eskimo Hunting Stand. *American Antiquity* 43(3):330–361.
1978b *Nunamiut Ethnoarchaeology*. Academic Press, New York.
1979 Organization and Formation Processes: Looking at Curated Technologies. *Journal of Anthropological Research* 35(3):255–273.
1980 Willow Smoke and Dogs Tails: Hunter-Gatherer Settlement Systems and Archaeological Site Formation. *American Antiquity* 45(1):4–20.
1983 *In Pursuit of the Past*. Thames and Hudson, New York.
1991 When the Going Gets Tough, the Tough Get Going: Nunamiut Local Groups, Camping Patterns, and Economic Organization. In *Ethnoarchaeological Approaches to Mobile Campsites: Hunter-Gatherer and Pastoralist Case Studies*, edited by C. S. Gamble and W. A. Boismier, pp. 25–137. International Monographs in Prehistory, Ethnoarchaeological Series 1, Ann Arbor, Michigan.

Blanton, Richard E.

1994   *Houses and Households: A Comparative Study.* Plenum Press, New York.

Borgerhoff Mulder, Monique, Samuel Bowles, Tom Hertz, Adrian Bell, Jan Beise, Greg Clark, Ila Fazzio, Michael Gurven, Kim Hill, Paul L. Hooper, William Irons, Hillard Kaplan, Donna Leonetti, Bobbi Low, Frank Marlowe, Richard McElreath, Suresh Naidu, David Nolin, Patrizio Piraino, Rob Quinlan, Eric Schniter, Rebecca Sear, Mary Schenk, Eric A. Smith, Christopher von Rueden, and Polly Weissner

2009   Intergenerational Wealth Transmission and the Dynamics of Inequality in Small-Scale Societies. *Science* 326(5953):682–687.

Bronk Ramsey, C.

2009   Bayesian Analysis of Radiocarbon Dates. *Radiocarbon* 51(1):337–360.

Brooks, Robert L.

1993   Household Abandonment among Sedentary Plains Societies: Behavioral Sequences and Consequences in the Interpretation of the Archaeological Record. In *The Abandonment of Settlements and Regions: Ethnoarchaeological and Archaeological Approaches*, edited by Catherine M. Cameron and Steve Tomka, pp. 178–190. Cambridge University Press, Cambridge, England.

Brown, James

2007   The Social House in Southeastern Archaeology. In *The Durable House: House Society Models in Archaeology*, edited by Robin A. Beck, Jr., pp. 227–247. Occasional Paper No. 35, Center for Archaeological Investigations, Southern Illinois University, Carbondale.

Cail, Hanna S.

2011   Feasting on Fido: Cultural Implications of Eating Dogs at Bridge River. Master's thesis, Department of Anthropology, University of Montana, Missoula.

Chatters, James C.

1987   Hunter-Gatherer Adaptations and Assemblage Structure. *Journal of Anthropological Archaeology* 6(4):336–375.

1989   The Antiquity of Economic Differentiation within Households in the Puget Sound Region, Northwest Coast. In *Households and Communities*, edited by Scott MacEachern, David J. W. Archer, and Richard D. Garvin, pp. 168–178. University of Calgary Archaeological Association, Calgary, Canada.

Chesson, Meredith S.

2007   House, Town, and Wadi: Landscapes of the Early Bronze Age Southern Levant. In *The Durable House: House Society Models in Archaeology*, edited by Robin A. Beck, Jr., pp. 317–343. Occasional Paper No. 35, Center for Archaeological Investigations, Southern Illinois University, Carbondale.

Coupland, Gary

2006   A Chief's House Speaks: Communicating Power on the Northern Northwest Coast. In *Household Archaeology on the Northwest Coast*, edited by Elizabeth A. Sobel, D. Ann Trieu Gahr, and Kenneth M. Ames, pp. 80–96. International Monographs in Prehistory, Archaeological Series 16, Ann Arbor, Michigan.

Coupland, Gary, David Bilton, Terence Clark, Jerome S. Cybulski, Gay Frederick, Alyson Holland, Bryn Letham, and Gretchen Williams

2016   A Wealth of Beads: Evidence for Material Wealth-Based Inequality in the Salish Sea Region, 4000–3500 Cal BP. *American Antiquity* 81(2):294–315.

Coupland, Gary, Terence Clark, and Amanda Palmer

2009   Hierarchy, Communalism, and the Spatial Order of Northwest Coast Plank Houses. *American Antiquity* 74(1): 77–106.

Craig, Douglas B.

2007   Courtyard Groups and the Emergence of House Estates in Early Hohokam Society. In *The Durable House: House Society Models in Archaeology*, edited by Robin A. Beck, Jr., pp. 446–463. Occasional Paper No. 35, Center for Archaeological Investigations, Southern Illinois University Carbondale.

Crellin, David F.

1994   Is There a Dog in the House: The Cultural Significance of Prehistoric Domesticated Dogs in the Mid-Fraser River Region of British Columbia. Master's thesis, Department of Archaeology, Simon Fraser University, Burnaby, British Columbia, Canada.

Deal, Michael

1985   Household Pottery Disposal in the Maya Highlands: An Ethnoarchaeological Interpretation. *Journal of Anthropological Archaeology* 4(4):243–291.

Diehl, Michael W.

1998   The Interpretation of Archaeological Floor Assemblages: A Case Study from the American Southwest. *American Antiquity* 63(4): 617–634.

Dietz, Catherine A.
2005 Structure, Function, and Dating of External Cooking Features at the Bridge River Site. Master's Thesis, Department of Anthropology, University of Montana, Missoula.

Douglass, John G., and Nancy Gonlin
2012 *Ancient Households of the Americas: Conceptualizing what Households Do.* University Press of Colorado, Boulder.

Drucker, Philip
1955 *Indians of the Northwest Coast.* Anthropological Handbook No. 10, American Museum of Natural History, McGraw Hill, New York.

Dyson-Hudson, R., and Eric A. Smith
1978 Human Territoriality: An Ecological Reassessment. *American Anthropologist* 80(1):21–41.

Eerkens, Jelmer W.
2013 Free-Riding, Cooperation, and Population Growth: The Evolution of Privatization and Leaders in Owens Valley, California. In *Cooperation and Collective Action: Archaeological Perspectives*, edited by David M. Carballo, pp. 151–174. University Press of Colorado, Boulder.

Environmental Systems Research Institute (ESRI)
2017 *How Spline Works.* Electronic document, http://pro.arcgis.com/en/pro-app/tool-reference/3d-analyst/how-spline-works.htm, accessed January 29, 2020.

Flannery, Kent V., and Marcus C. Winter
1976 Analyzing Household Activities. In *The Early Mesoamerican Village*, edited by Kent V. Flannery, pp. 34–48. Academic Press, Orlando, Florida.

Fleisher, Jeffrey B., and Adria LaViolette
2007 The Changing Power of Swahili Houses, Fourteenth to Nineteenth Centuries AD. In *The Durable House: House Society Models in Archaeology*, edited by Robin A. Beck Jr., pp. 175–197. Occasional Paper No. 35, Center for Archaeological Investigations, Southern Illinois University, Carbondale.

French, Kelly
2017 Lithic Technology and Risk: A Winter Household at the Bridge River Village Site during the Fur Trade Period. In *The Last House at Bridge River: The Archaeology of an Aboriginal Household in British Columbia during the Fur Trade Period*, edited by Anna

Marie Prentiss, pp. 90–106. University of Utah Press, Salt Lake City.

Furniss, Elizabeth
2004 Cycles of History in Plateau Sociopolitical Organization: Reflections on the Nature of Indigenous Band Societies. *Ethnohistory* 51(1):137–170.

Galm, Jerry R.
1994 Prehistoric Trade and Exchange in the Interior Plateau of Northwestern North America. In *Prehistoric Exchange Systems in North America*, edited by Timothy G. Baugh and Jonathon E. Ericson, pp. 279–305. Plenum, New York.

Galm, Jerry R., and Ruth A. Masten
1985 *Avey's Orchard: Archaeological Investigation of a Late Prehistoric Columbia River Community.* Eastern Washington University Reports in Archaeology and History 100-61. Archaeological and Historical Services, Eastern Washington University, Cheney.

Gillespie, Susan D.
2000 *Lévi-Strauss: Maison and Societé á Maisons.* In *Beyond Kinship: Social and Material Reproduction in House Societies*, edited by Rosemary A. Joyce and Susan D. Gillespie, pp. 22–52. University of Pennsylvania Press, Philadelphia.
2007 When is a House? In *The Durable House: House Society Models in Archaeology*, edited by Robin A. Beck, Jr., pp. 25–52. Occasional Paper No. 35, Center for Archaeological Investigations, Southern Illinois University, Carbondale.

Goldberg, Paul
2010 Appendix D: Bridge River Micromorphology. In *Report of the 2009 University of Montana Investigations at the Bridge River Site (EeRl4)*, by Anna Marie Prentiss, Lisa Smith, Lee Reininghaus, Maggie Schirack, Michael Wanzenried, and Ogden Ward, pp. 301–343. Report on file, National Science Foundation and Bridge River Band Office, Lillooet, British Columbia, Canada.

Goldman, Irving
1941 The Alkatcho Carrier: Historical Background of Crest Prerogatives. *American Anthropologist* 43(3):396–418.

Gordillo, Inés, and Bruno Vindrola-Padrós
2017 Destruction and Abandonment Practices at La Rinconada, Ambata Valley (Catamarca, Argentina). *Antiquity* 91(355):155–172.

Gorecki, Pawel

1991   Horticulturalists as Hunter–Gatherers: Rock
        Shelter Usage in Papua, New Guinea. In
        *Ethnoarchaeological Approaches to Mobile
        Campsite: Hunter-Gatherer and Pastoralist
        Case Studies*, edited by C. S. Gamble and
        W. A. Boismier, pp. 237–262. International
        Monographs in Prehistory, Ethnoarchaeo-
        logical Series 1, Ann Arbor, Michigan.

Gougeon, Ramie A.

2012   Activity Areas and Households in the Late
        Mississippian Southeast United States: Who
        Did What Where? In *Ancient Households of
        the Americas: Conceptualizing What House-
        holds Do*, edited by John G. Douglass and
        Nancy Gonlin, pp. 141–162. University Press
        of Colorado, Boulder.

Graham, Martha

1993   Settlement Organization and Residential
        Variability among the Rarámuri. In *The
        Abandonment of Settlements and Regions:
        Ethnoarchaeological and Archaeological Ap-
        proaches*, edited by Catherine M. Cameron
        and Steve Tomka, pp. 25–42. Cambridge
        University Press, Cambridge, England.

Grier, Colin

2006   Temporality in Northwest Coast House-
        holds. In *Household Archaeology on the
        Northwest Coast*, edited by Elizabeth A.
        Sobel, D. Ann Trieu Gahr, and Kenneth M.
        Ames, pp. 97–119. International Monographs
        in Prehistory, Archaeological Series 16, Ann
        Arbor, Michigan.

Grossman, Daniel

1965   The Nature of Descent Groups of Some
        Tribes in the Interior of Northwestern North
        America. *Anthropologica* 7(2):249–262.

Harris, Lucille

2012   Heterarchy and Hierarchy in the Forma-
        tion and Dissolution of Complex Hunter-
        Gatherer Communities on the Northern
        Plateau of Northwestern North America,
        ca. 2000–300 BP. PhD thesis, Department of
        Anthropology, University of Toronto.

Hayden, Brian

1994   Competition, Labor, and Complex Hunter-
        Gatherers. In *Key Issues in Hunter-Gatherer
        Research*, edited by Ernest S. Burch, Jr., and
        Linda J. Ellana, pp. 223–239. Berg Press,
        Oxford, England.

1997   *The Pithouses of Keatley Creek*. Harcourt
        Brace College Publishers, Fort Worth, Texas.

1998   Practical and Prestige Technologies: The
        Evolution of Material Systems. *Journal of
        Archaeological Method and Theory* 5:1–55.

Hayden, Brian (editor)

2000   *The Ancient Past of Keatley Creek, Volume I,
        Taphonomy*. Archaeology Press, Simon Fra-
        ser University, Burnaby, British Columbia,
        Canada.

Hayden, Brian, and Ron Adams

2004   Ritual Structures in Transegalitarian Com-
        munities. In *Complex Hunter-Gatherers:
        Evolution and Organization of Prehistoric
        Communities on the Plateau of Northwestern
        North America*, edited by William C. Prentiss
        and Ian Kuijt, pp. 84–102. University of Utah
        Press, Salt Lake City.

Hayden, Brian, Edward Bakewell, and Robert
Gargett

1996a   World's Longest-Lived Corporate Group:
        Lithic Analysis Reveals Prehistoric Social
        Organization Near Lillooet, British Colum-
        bia. *American Antiquity* 61(2): 341–356.

Hayden, Brian, and Aubrey Cannon

1982   The Corporate Group as an Archaeological
        Unit. *Journal of Anthropological Archaeology*
        1(2):132–158.

Hayden, Brian, and Michael Deal

1983   Where the Garbage Goes: Refuse Disposal
        in the Maya Highlands. *Journal of Anthropo-
        logical Archaeology* 2(2):117–163.

Hayden, Brian, and W. Karl Hutchings

1989   Whither the Billet Flake? In *Experiments in
        Lithic Technology*, edited by Daniel S. Amick
        and Raymond P. Mauldin, pp. 235–258. BAR
        International Series 528, Oxford, England.

Hayden, Brian, Reinhardt, G.A., MacDonald, R.,
Homberg, D., Crellin, D.

1996b   Space Per Capita and the Optimal Size
        of Housepits. In *People Who Lived in Big
        Houses: Archaeological Perspectives on Large
        Domestic Structures*, edited by Gary Coup-
        land and E. Banning, pp. 151–164. Prehistory
        Press, Madison, Wisconsin.

Hayden, Brian, and Rick Schulting

1997   The Plateau Interaction Sphere and Late
        Prehistoric Cultural Complexity. *American
        Antiquity* 62(1):51–85.

Hayden, Brian, and James Spafford

1993   The Keatley Creek Site and Corporate
        Group Archaeology. *BC Studies* 99:10–139.

Hendon, Julia A.

2010   *Houses in a Landscape: Memory and Every-*

day Life in Mesoamerica. Duke University Press, Durham, North Carolina.

Hill-Tout, Charles
1905   Report on the Ethnology of the Stlatlumh (Lillooet) of British Columbia. *Journal of the Royal Anthropological Institute* 35: 126–218.

Hofmann, Daniela, and Jessica Smyth
2013   *Tracking the Neolithic House in Europe: Sedentism, Architecture, and Practice*. Springer, New York.

Joyce, Rosemary A., and Susan D. Gillespie (editors)
2000   *Beyond Kinship: Social and Material Reproduction in House Societies*. University of Pennsylvania Press, Philadelphia.

Kahn, Jennifer G.
2007   Power and Precedence in Ancient House Societies: A Case Study from the Society Island Chiefdoms. In *The Durable House: House Society Models in Archaeology*, edited by Robin A. Beck Jr., pp. 198–226. Occasional Paper No. 35, Center for Archaeological Investigations, Southern Illinois University, Carbondale.

Keeley, Lawrence H.
1988   Hunter-Gatherer Economic Complexity and "Population Pressure": A Cross-Cultural Analysis. *Journal of Anthropological Archaeology* 7(4):373–411.

Kennedy, Dorothy I. D., and Randy Bouchard
1978   Fraser River Lillooet: An Ethnographic Summary. In *Reports of the Lillooet Archaeological Project, Number 1: Introduction and Setting*, edited by Arnoud H. Stryd and Stephen Lawhead, pp. 22–55. Archaeological Survey of Canada Paper No. 73, National Museum of Man, Mercury Series, Ottawa.
1998   Lillooet. In *Handbook of North American Indians, Vol. 12, Plateau*, edited by Deward E. Walker Jr., pp. 174–190. Smithsonian Institution, Washington, DC.

Kew, Michael
1992   Salmon Availability, Technology, and Cultural Adaptation in the Fraser River Watershed. In *A Complex Culture of the British Columbia Plateau*, edited by Brian Hayden, pp. 177–221. University of British Columbia Press, Vancouver, Canada.

Kuhn, Steven L.
1994   A Formal Approach to the Design and Assembly of Mobile Toolkits. *American Antiquity* 59(3):426–442.

LaForet, Andrea, and Annie York
1981   Notes on the Thompson Winter Dwelling. In *The World Is as Sharp as a Knife: An Anthology in Honour of Wilson Duff*, edited by Donald A. Abbott, pp. 95–104. British Columbia Provincial Museum, Victoria, Canada.

Lamb, W. Kaye (editor)
1960   *Simon Fraser: Letters and Journals, 1806–1808*. MacMillan, Toronto.

LaMotta, Vincent M., and Michael B. Schiffer
1999   Formation Processes and House Floor Assemblages. In *The Archaeology of Household Activities*, edited by Penelope M. Allison, pp. 19–29. Routledge, London.

Leroi-Gourhan, André, and Michel Brézillon
1966   *L'Habitation Magdalénienne No. 1 de Pincevent près Montereau (Seine-et-Marne)*. Gallia Prehistoire, Fouilles et Monuments Archéologiques en France Metropolitain Tome 9, Fascicule 2, Paris.

Lévi-Strauss, Claude
1979   Nobles Sauvages. In *Culture, Science et Développement: Contribution á une Histoire d'l'Homme*, Mélanges en l'honneur de Charles Morazé, pp. 41–55. Privat, Toulouse, France.

Lepofsky, Dana, Karla Kusmer, Brian Hayden, and Ken Lertzman
1996   Reconstructing Prehistoric Socioeconomies from Paleoethnobotanical and Zooarchaeological Data: An Example from the British Columbia Plateau. *Journal of Ethnobiology* 16(1):31–62.

Lepofsky, Dana, and Sandra L. Peacock
2004   A Question of Intensity: Exploring the Role of Plant Foods in Northern Plateau Prehistory. In *Complex Hunter-Gatherers: Evolution and Organization of Prehistoric Communities on the Plateau of Northwestern North America*, edited by William C. Prentiss and Ian Kuijt, pp. 115–139. University of Utah Press, Salt Lake City.

Lyons, Natasha, Anna Marie Prentiss, Naoko Endo, Dana Lepofsky, and Kristen D. Barnett
2017   Plant Use Practices of an Historic St'át'imc Household, Bridge River, British Columbia. In *The Last House at Bridge River: The Archaeology of an Aboriginal Household in British Columbia during the Fur Trade Period*, edited by Anna Marie Prentiss, pp. 150–164. University of Utah Press, Salt Lake City.

Lyons, Natasha, Anna Marie Prentiss, Sandra Peacock, and Bill Angelbeck

2018   Some Like It Hot: Exploring the Archaeobotany of Roasting Features in Southern British Columbia. *Inlet: Contributions to Archaeology* 1:1–13.

Lyons, Natasha, and Morgan Ritchie

2017   The Archaeology of Camas Production and Exchange on the Northwest Coast: With Evidence from a Sts'ailes (Chehalis) Village on the Harrison River, British Columbia. *Journal of Ethnobiology* 37(2): 346–367.

Madrigal, T. Cregg, and Julie Zimmermann Holt

2002   White-tailed Deer Meat and Marrow Return Rates and their Application to Eastern Woodlands Archaeology. *American Antiquity* 67(4):745–759.

Marshall, Yvonne

2000   Transformations of Nuu-chah-nulth Houses. In *Beyond Kinship: Social and Material Reproduction in House Societies*, edited by Rosemary Joyce and Susan Gillespie, pp. 73–102. University of Pennsylvania Press, Philadelphia.

2006   Houses and Domestication on the Northwest Coast. In *Household Archaeology on the Northwest Coast*, edited by Elizabeth A. Sobel, D. Ann Trieu Gahr, and Kenneth M. Ames, pp. 37–56. International Monographs in Prehistory, Archaeological Series 16.

Mason, Owen K., and T. Max Friesen

2017   *Out of the Cold: Archaeology on the Arctic Rim of North America*. The SAA Press, Washington DC.

Matson, R. G., and Gary Coupland

1995   *The Prehistory of the Northwest Coast*. Academic Press, San Diego, California.

Mattison, Siobhan M., Eric A. Smith, Mary Shenk, and Ethan E. Cochrane

2016   The Evolution of Inequality. *Evolutionary Anthropology* 25(4):184–199.

McMillan, Alan D., and Denis E. St. Claire

2012   *Huu7ii: Household Archaeology at a Nuu-chah-nulth Village Site in Barkeley Sound*. Archaeology Press, Simon Fraser University, Burnaby, British Columbia, Canada.

Metcalf, Duncan, and Kathleen M. Heath

1990   Microrefuse and Site Structure: The Hearth and Floors of the Heartbreak Hotel. *American Antiquity* 55(4):781–796.

Morin, Jesse

2015   Near-Infrared Spectroscopy of Stone Celts

in Precontact British Columbia, Canada. *American Antiquity* 80(3):530–547.

Nastich, Milena

1954   The Lillooet: An Account of the Basis of Individual Status. Master's Thesis, Department of Economic, Political Science, and Sociology, University of British Columbia, Vancouver, Canada.

Nicholson, Annie, and Scott Cane

1991   Desert Camps: Analysis of Australian Aboriginal Protohistoric Campsites. In *Ethnoarchaeological Approaches to Mobile Campsite: Hunter-Gatherer and Pastoralist Case Studies*, edited by C. S. Gamble and W. A. Boismier, pp. 263–354. International Monographs in Prehistory, Ethnoarchaeological Series 1, Ann Arbor, Michigan.

O'Connell, James F.

1987   Alyawara Site Structure and Its Archaeological Implications. *American Antiquity* 52(1):74–108.

Prentiss, Anna Marie

2017a   Introduction. In *The Last House at Bridge River: The Archaeology of an Aboriginal Household in British Columbia during the Fur Trade Period*, edited by Anna Marie Prentiss, pp. 1–18. University of Utah Press, Salt Lake City.

2017b   The Archaeology of the Fur Trade Occupation at Housepit 54. In *The Last House at Bridge River: The Archaeology of an Aboriginal Household in British Columbia during the Fur Trade Period*, edited by Anna Marie Prentiss, pp.42–66. University of Utah Press, Salt Lake City.

Prentiss, Anna Marie (editor)

2017   *The Last House at Bridge River: The Archaeology of an Aboriginal Household in British Columbia during the Fur Trade Period*. University of Utah Press, Salt Lake City.

Prentiss, Anna Marie, Hannah S. Cail, and Lisa M. Smith

2014   At the Malthusian Ceiling: Subsistence and Inequality at Bridge River, British Columbia. *Journal of Anthropological Archaeology* 33:34–48.

Prentiss, Anna Marie, James C. Chatters, Natasha Lyons, and Lucille E. Harris

2011   Archaeology in the Middle Fraser Canyon, British Columbia: Changing Perspectives on Paleoecology and Emergent Cultural Complexity. *Canadian Journal of Archaeology* 35(1):143–174.

Prentiss, Anna Marie, Guy Cross, Thomas A. Foor, Dirk Markle, Mathew Hogan, and David S. Clarke
2008 Evolution of a Late Prehistoric Winter Village on the Interior Plateau of British Columbia: Geophysical Investigations, Radiocarbon Dating, and Spatial Analysis of the Bridge River Site. *American Antiquity* 73(1):59–82.

Prentiss, Anna Marie, Alysha Edwards, Ashley Hampton, Ethan Ryan, Kathryn Bobolinski, and Emma Vance
2020a Burned Roofs and Cultural Traditions: Renewing and Closing Houses in the Ancient Villages of the Middle Fraser Canyon, British Columbia. In *Agent of Change: The Deposition and Manipulation of Ash in the Past*, edited by Barbara Roth and E. Charles Adams, pp. 94–112. Berghahn Books, New York.

Prentiss, Anna Marie, Thomas A. Foor, Guy Cross, Lucille E. Harris, and Michael Wanzenried
2012 The Cultural Evolution of Material Wealth Based Inequality at Bridge River, British Columbia. *American Antiquity* 77(3): 542–564.

Prentiss, Anna Marie, Thomas A. Foor, and Ashley Hampton
2018a Testing the Malthusian Model: Population and Storage at Housepit 54, Bridge River, British Columbia. *Journal of Archaeological Science: Reports* 18: 535–550.

Prentiss, Anna Marie, Thomas A. Foor, Ashley Hampton, Ethan Ryan, and Matthew J. Walsh
2018b The Evolution of Material Wealth-Based Inequality: The Evidence from Housepit 54, Bridge River, British Columbia. *American Antiquity* 83(4):598–618.

Prentiss, Anna Marie, Thomas A. Foor, and Mary-Margaret Murphy
2018c Testing Hypotheses about Emergent Inequality (using Gini Coefficients) in a Complex Fisher-Forager Society at the Bridge River Site, British Columbia. In *Ten Thousand Years of Inequality: The Archaeology of Wealth Differences*, edited by Timothy A. Kohler and Michael E. Smith, pp. 96–129. University of Arizona Press, Tucson.

Prentiss, Anna Marie, Kelly French, Sara Hocking, Matthew Mattes, Matthew Walsh, Mary Bobbitt, and Kristen D. Barnett
2017 Lithic Technology during the Fur Trade Period at Housepit 54. In *The Last House at Bridge River: The Archaeology of an Aborig-inal Household in British Columbia during the Fur Trade Period*, edited by Anna Marie Prentiss, pp. 67–89. University of Utah Press, Salt Lake City.

Prentiss, Anna Marie, Nathan B. Goodale, Lucille E. Harris, and Nicole Crossland
2015 The Evolution of the Ground Slate Tool Industry at the Bridge River Site, British Columbia. In *Lithic Technological Systems: Stone, Evolution, and Behavior*, edited by Nathan B. Goodale and William Andrefsky Jr., pp. 267–292. Cambridge University Press, Cambridge, England.

Prentiss, Anna Marie, and Ian Kuijt
2012 *People of the Middle Fraser Canyon: An Archaeological History of the St'át'imc.* University of British Columbia Press, Vancouver.

Prentiss, Anna Marie, Natasha Lyons, Lucille E. Harris, Melisse R. P. Burns, and Terrence M. Godin
2007 The Emergence of Status Inequality in Intermediate Scale Societies: A Demographic and Socio-Economic History of the Keatley Creek Site, British Columbia. *Journal of Anthropological Archaeology* 26(2):299–327.

Prentiss, Anna Marie, and Matthew J. Walsh
2016 Was There a Neolithic "(R)evolution" in North America's Pacific Northwest Region? Exploring Alternative Models of Socio-Economic and Political Change. In *The Origins of Food Production*, edited by Nuria Sans, pp. 276–291. World Heritage Papers (HEADS 6), UNESCO, Paris.

Prentiss, Anna Marie, Matthew J. Walsh, Thomas A. Foor, Kathryn Bobolinski, Ashley Hampton, Ethan Ryan, and Haley O'Brien
2020b Malthusian Cycles among Semi-Sedentary Fisher-Hunter-Gatherers: The Socioeconomic and Demographic History of Housepit 54, Bridge River Site, British Columbia. *Journal of Anthropological Archaeology* 59:101181. DOI:10.1016/j.jaa.2020.101181, accessed October 18, 2021.

Prentiss, Anna Marie, Matthew J. Walsh, Randall R. Skelton, and Matt Mattes
2016 Mosaic Evolution in Cultural Frameworks: Skateboard Decks and Projectile Points. In *Cultural Phylogenetics: Concepts and Applications in Archaeology*, edited by Larissa Mendoza Straffon, pp. 113–130. Interdisciplinary Evolution Research, Springer International Publishing, Cham, Switzerland.

Prentiss, William C.
2000   The Formation of Lithic Debitage and Flake
       Tool Assemblages in a Canadian Plateau
       Winter Housepit Village: Ethnographic and
       Archaeological Perspectives. In *The Ancient
       Past of Keatley Creek, Volume I: Taphonomy*,
       pp. 213–230, edited by Brian Hayden. Ar-
       chaeology Press, Burnaby, British Columbia,
       Canada.

Prentiss, William C., James C. Chatters, Michael
Lenert, David S. Clarke, and Robert C. O'Boyle
2005   The Archaeology of the Plateau of North-
       western North America During the Late
       Prehistoric Period (3500–200 BP): Evolution
       of Hunter and Gathering Societies. *Journal
       of World Prehistory* 19(1):47–118.

Prentiss, William C., Michael Lenert, Thomas A.
Foor, Nathan B. Goodale, and Trinity Schlegel
2003   Calibrated Radiocarbon Dating at Keatley
       Creek: The Chronology of Occupation at
       a Complex Hunter-Gatherer Community.
       American Antiquity 68(4):719–735.

Ray, Verne
1939   *Cultural Relations in the Plateau of North-
       western North America*. Southwest Museum,
       Los Angeles.

Rodning, Christopher B.
2007   Building and Rebuilding Cherokee Houses
       and Townhouses in Southwestern North
       Carolina. In *The Durable House: House
       Society Models in Archaeology*, edited by
       Robin A. Beck, Jr., pp. 464–486. Occasional
       Paper No. 35, Center for Archaeological
       Investigations, Southern Illinois University,
       Carbondale.

Romanoff, Steven
1992a Fraser Lillooet Salmon Fishing. In *A Com-
       plex Culture of the British Columbia Plateau*,
       edited by Brian Hayden, pp. 222–265. Uni-
       versity of British Columbia Press, Vancouver.
1992b The Cultural Ecology of Hunting and
       Potlatches among the Lillooet Indians. In
       *A Complex Culture of the British Columbia
       Plateau*, edited by Brian Hayden, pp. 470–
       505. University of British Columbia Press,
       Vancouver.

Rousseau, Mike K.
2004   A Culture Historic Synthesis and Changes
       in Human Mobility, Sedentism, Subsistence,
       Settlement, and Population on the Canadian
       Plateau. In *Complex Hunter-Gatherers:
       Evolution and Organization of Prehistoric*
       *Communities on the Plateau of Northwestern
       North America*, edited by William C. Prentiss
       and Ian Kuijt, pp. 3–22. University of Utah
       Press, Salt Lake City.

Samuels, Stephan R.
1983   Spatial Patterns and Cultural Processes in
       Three Northwest Coast Longhouse Floor
       Middens from Ozette. PhD dissertation,
       Washington State University, Pullman.
2006   Households at Ozette. In *Household Ar-
       chaeology on the Northwest Coast*, edited by
       Elizabeth A. Sobel, D. Ann Trieu Gahr, and
       Kenneth M. Ames, pp. 200–232. Interna-
       tional Monographs in Prehistory, Archaeo-
       logical Series 16, Ann Arbor, Michigan.

Scarborough, Vernon L.
1989   Site Structure of a Village of the Late
       Pithouse–Early Pueblo Period in New
       Mexico. *Journal of Field Archaeology* 16(4):
       405–425.

Schiffer, Michael B.
1972   Archaeological Context and Systemic Con-
       text. *American Antiquity* 37(2):156–165.

Schlanger, Sarah H.
1991   On Manos, Metates, and the History of Site
       Occupations. *American Antiquity* 56(3):
       460–473.

Schmader, Matthew F., and Martha Graham
2015   Ethnoarchaeological Observation and
       Archaeological Patterning: A Processual
       Approach to Studying Sedentism and Space
       Use in Pitstructures from Central New Mex-
       ico. *Journal of Anthropological Archaeology*
       38:25–34.

Smith, Cameron McPherson
2006   Formation Processes of a Lower Columbia
       River Plankhouse Site. In *Household Ar-
       chaeology on the Northwest Coast*, edited by
       Elizabeth A. Sobel, D. Ann Trieu Gahr, and
       Kenneth M. Ames, pp. 233–269. Interna-
       tional Monographs in Prehistory, Archaeo-
       logical Series 16, Ann Arbor, Michigan.

Smith, Lisa M.
2014   The Effects of the Fur Trade on Aboriginal
       Households in the Middle Fraser Region
       of British Columbia. PhD dissertation,
       Department of Anthropology, University of
       Montana, Missoula.
2017   Cultural Change and Continuity across
       the Late Pre-Colonial and Early Colonial
       Periods in the Bridge River Valley: Archae-
       ology of the S7istken Site. In *The Last House*

at Bridge River: The Archaeology of an Aboriginal Household in British Columbia during the Fur Trade Period, edited by Anna Marie Prentiss, pp. 226–246. University of Utah Press, Salt Lake City.

Snow, Dean R.
2012   Iroquoian Households: A Mohawk Longhouse at Otstungo, New York. In *Ancient Households of the Americas: Conceptualizing What Households Do*, edited by John G. Douglass and Nancy Gonlin, pp. 117–140. University Press of Colorado, Boulder.

Sobel, Elizabeth A., Gahr, D. Ann Trieu, and Kenneth M. Ames
2006   *Household Archaeology on the Northwest Coast*. International Monographs in Prehistory Archaeological Series 16, Ann Arbor, Michigan.

Sobel, Elizabeth A.
2006   Household Prestige and Exchange in Northwest Coast Societies: A Case Study from the Lower Columbia River Valley. In *Household Archaeology on the Northwest Coast*, edited by Elizabeth A. Sobel, D. Ann Trieu Gahr, and Kenneth M. Ames, pp. 159–199. International Monographs in Prehistory Archaeological Series 16, Ann Arbor, Michigan.

Spafford, Jim
2000   Socioeconomic Inferences from Floor Distributions of Lithics at Keatley Creek. In *The Ancient Past of Keatley Creek Volume II: Socioeconomy*, edited by Brian Hayden, pp. 167–178. Archaeology Press, Simon Fraser University, Burnaby, British Columbia, Canada.

Spencer, Charles S., and Kent V. Flannery
1984   Spatial Variation of Debris at Guilá Naquitz: A Descriptive Approach. In *Guilá Naquitz: Archaic Foraging and Early Agriculture in Oaxaca, Mexico*, edited by Kent V. Flannery, pp. 331–368. Academic Press, Orlando, Florida.

Steere, Benjamin A.
2017   *The Archaeology of Houses and Households in the Native Southeast*. University of Alabama Press, Tuscaloosa.

Stevanović, Mirjana
1997   The Age of Clay: The Social Dynamics of House Construction. *Journal of Anthropological Archaeology* 16(4):334–395.

Stevenson, Mark G.
1982   Toward an Understanding of Site Abandonment Behavior: Evidence from Historic Mining Camps in the Southwest Yukon. *Journal of Anthropological Archaeology* 1(3): 237–265.

1985   The Formation of Artifact Assemblages at Workshop/Habitation Sites: Models from Peace Point in Northern Alberta. *American Antiquity* 50(1):63–81.

1991   Beyond the Formation of Hearth-Associated Artifact Assemblages. In *The Interpretation of Archaeological Spatial Patterning*, edited by Ellen M. Kroll and T. Douglas Price, pp. 269–300. Plenum Press, New York.

Stryd, Anoud H.
1973   The Later Prehistory of the Lillooet Area, British Columbia. PhD Dissertation, Department of Archaeology, University of Calgary, Canada.

Teit, James
1900   The Thompson Indians of British Columbia. In *Memoirs of the American Museum of Natural History, Jesup North Pacific Expedition*, Vol I, Part 4, edited by Franz Boas, pp. 163–392. New York.

1906   The Lillooet Indians. In *Memoirs of the American Museum of Natural History, Jesup North Pacific Expedition*, Vol. II, Part 5, edited by Franz Boas, pp. 193–300. New York.

1909   The Shuswap. In *Memoirs of the American Museum of Natural History, Jesup North Pacific Expedition*, Vol. II, Part 7, edited by Franz Boas, pp. 443–789. New York.

1930   *The Salishan Tribes of the Western Plateaus*. Annual Report Bureau of American Ethnology 45:23–396.

Walsh, Mathew J.
2017   Historical Ecology of the Middle Fraser Canyon, British Columbia, during the Nineteenth Century. In *The Last House at Bridge River: The Archaeology of an Aboriginal Household in British Columbia during the Fur Trade Period*, edited by Anna Marie Prentiss, pp. 19–41. University of Utah Press, Salt Lake City.

Wickwire, Wendy
1991   On Evaluating Ethnographic Representations: The Case of the Okanagan of South-Central British Columbia. *The Canadian Journal of Native Education* 18(2):233–244.

Wiessner, Polly
2002   The Vines of Complexity: Egalitarian Structures and the Institutionalization of Inequality. *Current Anthropology* 43(2):233–271.

Williams-Larson, Alexandra
2017   Faunal Remains and Artifacts from the Fur
        Trade Period Occupation at Housepit 54. In
        *The Last House at Bridge River: The Archae-
        ology of an Aboriginal Household in British
        Columbia during the Fur Trade Period*,
        edited by Anna Marie Prentiss, pp. 125–149.
        University of Utah Press, Salt Lake City.
Williams-Larson, Alexandra, Kristen D. Barnett,
Pei-Lin Yu, Matthew Schmader, and Anna Marie
Prentiss
2017   Spatial Analysis of the Fur Trade Floor and
        Roof at Housepit 54. In *The Last House at
        Bridge River: The Archaeology of an Aborig-
        inal Household in British Columbia during
        the Fur Trade Period*, edited by Anna Marie
        Prentiss, pp. 182–208. University of Utah
        Press, Salt Lake City.
Yellen, John
1977   *Archaeological Approaches to the Present.*
        Academic Press, New York.

Index

Page locators in *italics* refer to figures and tables.